KYOTO CSEAS SERIES ON ASIAN STUDIES 16
Center for Southeast Asian Studies, Kyoto University

MARRIAGE MIGRATION IN ASIA

KYOTO CSEAS SERIES ON ASIAN STUDIES 16
Center for Southeast Asian Studies, Kyoto University

MARRIAGE MIGRATION IN ASIA
Emerging Minorities at the Frontiers of Nation-States

Edited by
Sari K. Ishii

NUS PRESS
Singapore

in association with

KYOTO UNIVERSITY PRESS
Japan

The publication of this book is funded by the Japan Society for the Promotion of Science (JSPS) as Grant-in-Aid for Publication of Scientific Research Results.

© Sari K. Ishii

All rights reserved. This book, or parts thereof, may not be reproduced in any form or by any means, electronic or mechanical, including photocopying, recording or any information storage and retrieval system now known or to be invented, without written permission from the Publisher.

NUS Press
National University of Singapore
AS3-01-02, 3 Arts Link
Singapore 117569
http://nuspress.nus.edu.sg

ISBN 978-981-4722-10-0 (Paper)

First edition 2016
Reprint 2017

Kyoto University Press
Yoshida-South Campus, Kyoto University
69 Yoshida-Konoe-Cho, Sakyo-ku
Kyoto 606-8315
Japan
www.kyoto-up.or.jp

ISBN 978-4-87698-892-1

National Library Board, Singapore Cataloguing-in-Publication Data

Names: Ishii, Sari K., editor.
Title: Marriage migration in Asia: emerging minorities at the frontiers of nation-states/edited by Sari K. Ishii.
Other titles: Kyoto CSEAS series on Asian studies.
Description: Singapore: NUS Press; Japan: in association with Kyoto University Press, [2016] | Includes index.
Identifiers: OCN 931000889 | ISBN 978-981-4722-10-0 (paper)
Subjects: LCSH: Intercountry marriage—Asia. | Women immigrants—Asia—Social conditions. | Children of immigrants—Asia—Social conditions.
Classification: LCC HQ1032 | DDC 306.845095—dc23

Printed by: Markono Print Media Pte Ltd

CONTENTS

List of Figures   vii

List of Tables   viii

Foreword   ix

Acknowledgements   xi

Introduction: Marriage Migrants as Multi-marginalized Transnational Diaspora   1
Sari K. Ishii

PART I   MIGRATION FLOWS BEYOND THE MARRIAGE-SCAPES

Chapter 1: Forging Intimate Ties in Transnational Spaces: The Life Trajectories of Japanese Women Married to Pakistani Migrants   27
Masako Kudo

Chapter 2: Unintentional Cross-cultural Families: The Diverse Community of Japanese Wives in Shanghai   43
Chie Sakai

Chapter 3: Marriage "During" Work Migration: Lived Experiences of Filipino Marriage Migrants in Malaysia   73
Linda A. Lumayag

PART II   REVERSED GEOGRAPHIES OF POWER

Chapter 4: "Centre/Periphery" Flow Reversed?: Twenty Years of Cross-border Marriages between Philippine Women and Japanese Men   105
Ikuya Tokoro

Chapter 5:	Child Return Migration from Japan to Thailand *Sari K. Ishii*	118
Chapter 6:	Assimilation of the Descendants of Caucasian Muslims in Sarawak, Malaysia *Caesar Dealwis*	135

PART III MARRIAGE MIGRANTS AS MULTI-MARGINALIZED DIASPORA

Chapter 7:	Lives in Limbo: Unsuccessful Marriages in Sino-Vietnamese Borderlands *Caroline Grillot*	153
Chapter 8:	Lives of Mixed Vietnamese-Korean Children in Vietnam *Hien Anh Le*	175
Chapter 9:	Born to Be Stateless, Being Stateless: Transnational Marriage, Migration and the Registration of Stateless People in Japan *Lara, Chen Tien-shi*	187
Chapter 10:	Legal Problems of Marriage between Irregular Workers from Myanmar and Thai Nationals in Thailand *Chatchai Chetsumon*	202

Contributors	212
Index	214

LIST OF FIGURES

Figure 0.1	Migration flows analyzed in each chapter	5
Figure 1.1	Number of registered Pakistani residents in Japan, 1984–2012	29
Figure 1.2	Various trajectories of relocation observed among the Japanese wives and their children	36
Figure 2.1	Number of Japanese nationals living abroad	47
Figure 2.2	Number of Japanese nationals living in Asian countries, excluding Japan	48
Figure 2.3	Number of female Japanese nationals living in foreign countries	48
Figure 2.4	International marriages registered in Japan in 2012	49
Figure 2.5	Marriages between Japanese and Chinese citizens	50
Figure 7.1	The Sino-Vietnamese border and research sites	154
Figure 8.1	Number of Vietnamese-Korean marriages	178
Figure 9.1	Number of registered stateless people from 1992 to 2013	189
Figure 9.2	Number of registered stateless people in Japan by age	196

LIST OF TABLES

Table 0.1	Migration type and theme in each chapter	4
Table 1.1	Educational levels of Japanese wives interviewed	30
Appendix	Summary of informants' characteristics	69
Table 3.1	Summary of the characteristics of interviewed Filipino women married to Malaysian men	77
Table 3.2	Top 10 countries of destinations of Filipinos	78
Table 3.3	Number of registered marriages between foreigner and Malaysian citizen, 2004–14	79
Table 3.4	Filipino marriages in Malaysia, 2012–15	80
Table 3.5	Number of overseas Filipino workers (new hires and rehires), 2009–13	82
Table 4.1	Number of Filipina-Japanese marriages (and divorces) registered in selected years between 1995 and 2013	106
Table 5.1	Marriages, divorces and children born between Japanese men and Thai women registered in Japan	120
Table 5.2	Background characteristics of interviewed return migrant children	124
Table 10.1	Legal status of migrant workers in Thailand	203

FOREWORD

Hsiao-Chuan Hsia

Based on field research conducted in urban and rural communities of various Asian countries, *Marriage Migration in Asia* provides us with three key insights that will enrich marriage migration discussions. The first insight pertains to the complexity of the multidirectional trajectories followed by marriage migrants from a long-term perspective. Previous studies on marriage migration have tended to analyze these movements using a global south to global north geographical framework. In contrast, *Marriage Migration in Asia* calls attention to the repetitive, extended and cyclical nature of migration trajectories followed by marriage-related migrants and their long-term outcomes. The chapters in Section One highlight cases of marriage-related migrations from the global north to the global south and marriage migrations within the north or within the south.

The second insight expands the scope of our understanding of marriage migrants to include children and others who have become migrants as a consequence of marriage migration. While current discussions of marriage migration tend to focus on female migrants as "brides", the authors in Section Two present the circumstances of child migrants who have adopted their parents' marriage migration patterns, spousal migrants who moved from the north to the south and husbands who follow their wives after several decades of marriage. The status of these migrants has been examined several decades after their initial marriage-related journeys to develop an analytical framework for discussing the notion of "geographies of power" and to consider whether it could be possible to reverse these traditional south-to-north frameworks to explore marriage-related migrations that occur after marriage.

The third insight is that some of these migrants, many of whom are child migrants, become either formally or virtually stateless because of international divorces or unregistered trans-border marriages. The increase of marriage migrants has undoubtedly led to an increase of trans-border divorces. However, earlier discussions have scarcely addressed the topic of international divorce. The chapters in Section Three illustrate the intricate difficulties that arise following a divorce in terms of personal emotions, family ties, and issues of legitimacy and endorsement that migrants sometimes face when they enter or return to local cultures. These difficulties are further complicated by economic and political power imbalances between countries.

As the keynote speaker at the international conferences in 2011 and 2012 that led to this edited volume, I believe that the very rich empirical research included in *Marriage Migration in Asia* will contribute to broadening marriage migration studies. Our analyses do not focus merely on the geographically oriented south-north framework; we also focus on developing a more complex and extended framework that can account for not only initial "bride" migrations but also for migrations that happen decades later as the result of a first marriage migration.

ACKNOWLEDGEMENTS

We would like to offer our sincere thanks to all our interlocutors—marriage migrants, their families and their friends—and we dedicate this volume to them. We also wish to thank the various institutes who have supported our research: the Research Institute for Languages and Cultures of Asia and Africa (ILCAA) at the Tokyo University of Foreign Studies, the Center for Southeast Asian Studies (CSEAS) at Kyoto University and the Japan Society for the Promotion of Science (JSPS).

This book developed from the International Conference on Dynamics of Marriage/Divorce-related Migration in Asia (Tokyo, 15 December 2012) that was organized as part of an ILCAA joint research project (2010–12). The conference and the joint research project received administrative support from the ILCAA and financial support from JSPS (2011–13, Grant no. 23251006). This support made possible the eight workshops and two international conferences held over four years that advanced the goal of our joint research project—to deepen the discourse on the topic of marriage migration. The details of the joint research project and the conference are on our official website: http://marriage.aa-ken.jp. We welcome interactive comments. Likewise we would like to thank CSEAS and JSPS for publishing our manuscript. We deeply thank the professors, editorial staff and anonymous reviewers of Kyoto University and NUS Press for their thoughtful comments. We thank JSPS for the financial support for the publication (2015, Grant no. 15HP5148).

Earlier versions of the chapters in this volume were selected papers originally presented at the 2012 conference. The only exception is Chapter 7, which is part of the author's dissertation.

The editor hopes, like a respectful daughter, that this volume will reward Mae Alema from the Lisu hill tribal group in Northern Thailand who, like a caring mother, inspired me to study and give voice to the multi-marginalized marriage migrants who have emigrated from her village.

INTRODUCTION

Marriage Migrants as Multi-marginalized Transnational Diaspora

Sari K. Ishii

Toward New Horizons in Marriage Migration Studies

Although decades have passed since transnational Asian marriages increased in the 1990s (Amrith 2011: 176; Jones and Shen 2008: 9; Tseng 2010: 31) most, but not all[1] researchers see marriage migration as a female migration flow from the global south to the global north[2] which has been variously described as "hypergamy" (Schans 2012: 366; Lavely 1991: 305) or "global marriage-scapes" (Constable 2005: 3). According to Constable (2005: 4), a key commentator on marriage migration, "a majority of international marriage migrants are women, and most of these women move from poorer countries to wealthier ones, from the less developed global 'south' to the more industrialized 'north'". Similar arguments regarding marriage migration as female migration flow from the south to the north are also propounded by such authors as Jones (2012: 287), Kim (2009: 82–3), Nguyen and Tran (2010: 157), Piper and Roces (2003: 55) and Wang and Chang (2002: 101). The reason is simple: the body of research has thus far focused on only the initial migration of the brides. However, "[o]ne migration experience is often only part of a shifting pattern of mobility and engagement across national borders" (Willis, Yeoh and Fakhri 2004: 4).

The main aim of this volume is to expand the discussion on marriage migration by examining more complex and diversified migratory trajectories that include the family members of marriage migrants such as children and elderly parents (Kofman 2004: 244). The authors in the following chapters provide empirical data based on long-term field research in East and Southeast Asia that sheds new light on two points.

1

First, the female migration of the "bride" is only a part of the life-course events embedded in complex migration trajectories due to "interactions between family dynamics, life course events and migration decisions" (Cooke 2008: 260). Cooke (2008) utilizes the notion of "family migration" as a wider scope of analysis. Charsley, Benson and Van Hear (2012: 864) present the terms "marriage-related migration" and "spousal migration" as umbrella terms encompassing all situations where marriage plays a substantial role in an individual's migration. In this volume, the authors use the terms, "marriage migration" and "marriage migrants", with the intent of presenting research that broadens the scope of these terms.

Second, the direction and actors of marriage migration are diverse and include male migrants from less industrialized countries who marry women in more developed countries (for example, Kudo 2008; Schans 2012) and female migrants who move from an economically more affluent society to a less affluent society (for example, Toyota and Thang 2012: 347). Also to be considered are children who return-migrate from more industrialized countries to less industrialized areas after their parents' cross-border divorces, and children who undertake repeat migrations as their life circumstances change.

The goal of this book is to bring issues involving marriage migration to the foreground of migration research (Charsley, Benson and Hear 2012: 880; Cooke 2008: 262), especially regarding marriage migrants as part of a global diaspora.[3] While many marriage migration studies "pay due attention to gendered aspects of transnationalism" (Kofman 2004: 244), the studies in this book investigate the hypothesis that some marriage migrants are part of a multi-marginalized diaspora, that is, these marriage migrants are marginalized by the "entangled relationship between the nation-state and diaspora" (Parreñas and Siu 2007: 15) both in the communities that they leave and the ones that they go to. The results of these studies may provide a conceptual framework for supporting marriage migrants' access to full citizenship. According to Lie,

> …due to current globalization, migrants are no longer assumed to make a single journey from their homeland to the destination country[;] there have emerged complex trajectories, including return, circular, and multiple trajectories. Many of them live a life with ambiguous "home" and "destination" identities regardless of any imaginative or substantive link with them. As such, the theoretical theme among migration studies has been shifting from "international migration" to "transnational diaspora". (1995: 304)

The cases presented in this volume serve as testimonies that marriage migration is a migratory movement and not only a simple home-to-destination movement corresponding to Lie's conclusion about the nature of globalized migration. Terms that refer to diaspora migratory tendencies such as "repeat migration" (Kenny 2013: 87), "circular migration" (Amrith 2011: 159) and "complex and diversified migratory movement" (Kofman 2004: 244) are often observed in the long-term situations of marriage migrants.

Marriage migrants may not see themselves part of a diaspora because the relationship between self-identity and other factors that define being part of a diaspora are not self-evident.

> Not everyone is a diaspora because they say they are. Social structures, historical experiences, prior conceptual understandings, and the opinions of other social actors (among other factors) also influence whether we can legitimately label a particular group a diaspora. Understanding a social actor's viewpoint is important, but it is not the end of the argument. We would be on stronger ground, however, if we were to argue that diasporas can be formed and mobilized in certain circumstances. (Cohen 2008: 15–6)

Marriage migration can be considered one of the "certain circumstances" mentioned by Cohen. In the context of migrants seeking to claim "full citizenship", migrants who cross borders for marriage, their children, elderly parents and siblings may be regarded as members of a transnational diaspora even though they do not see themselves as such.

Although some marriage migrants described in this volume may not have experienced trans-border migration themselves, they are the children or descendants of cross-border married couples, and as such they share a defining characteristic of diaspora groups—"dual or hybrid identity" (Safran 2005: 39). Thus, their experiences are discussed herein. William Safran, a noted scholar in diaspora studies, observes: "For a number of scholars, diaspora has come to embrace not only immigrants, but ethnic and religious minorities and other categories of groups—and even individuals—who wish to be part of society on their own terms" (Safran 2005: 50). By broadening the scope of analysis, the chapters in this volume will provide cases to demonstrate that marriage migrants are a marginalized minority group in both their home and host countries despite their dual or hybrid identity.

Of course, not all marriage migrants are diasporic. Narrowing the marriage migration discussion to those who have been marginalized is equal to confining the discourse to south-to-north female migration. To broaden the discussion of marriage migration, this work considers the kinds of contradictions that marriage migrants' multi-affiliated identities and limited access to full citizenship in any country can lead them to.

Williams sees all types of intimate unions "in which one or both partner lacks formal status or citizenship, that is, when one or both partners, are classed as 'migrant' by the state" (2012: 24). Their children are included as migrants in this analysis regardless of their status as legitimate/non-legitimate, authorized/unauthorized or registered/unregistered citizens. Although "the very notion of the 'international marriage' is itself a product of the modern twentieth century state" (Toyota 2008: 2), the researchers in this volume have focused on analysing the daily experience of migrants rather than determining if marriage migrants are entitled to citizenship and the benefits associated with citizenship. The migration trajectories and theoretical themes discussed in subsequent chapters are summarized in Table 0.1 and Figure 0.1 below.

Table 0.1 Migration type and theme in each chapter

	Migration type	Theme	Trajectories	
Chapter 1	Diverse sojourn	Transnational households	Pakistan	Japan England ⇔ New Zealand UAE
Chapter 2	Intra-north	Female marriage migrants	Japan	⇔ Chiang Hai (China)
Chapter 3	Intra-south	Highly educated female migrants	Philippines	⇒ Malaysia
Chapter 4	north to south	Male marriage migrants	Philippines	⇔ Japan
Chapter 5	north to south	Child return migration	Thailand	⇔ Japan
Chapter 6	north to south	Assimilation to mainstream ethnicity	England	⇒ Sarawak (Malaysia)
Chapter 7	Border zone	Non-existing marriage/children	Vietnam	∼ China
Chapter 8	north to south	Child return migration	Vietnam	⇔ Korea

Introduction 5

Table 0.1 Continued

	Migration type	*Theme*	*Trajectories*
Chapter 9	Endless sojourn	Migration and marriage for stateless people	⇔ Japan ⇔
Chapter 10	Intra-south	Migration and marriage for stateless people	Myanmar ⇒ Thailand

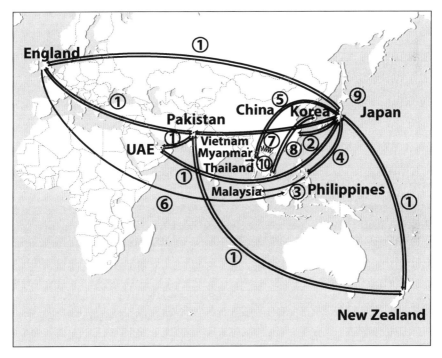

Figure 0.1 Migration flows analyzed in each chapter

First, the diverse, long-term, duplicated migration trajectories of marriage migrants will be demonstrated (especially by Chapter 1). Second, cases will be presented to illustrate the multi-marginalized situation of marriage migrants in their home and host societies (Barabantseva and Sutherland 2012: 4) economically (Chapters 3 and 4), socially (Chapters 2 and 5), ethnically (Chapter 6) and legally (Chapters 7, 8, 9 and 10).

Beyond Global Marriage-scapes

The first key point of this volume is that marriage migrants have complex, long-term, diversified migratory trajectories with a focus on the following: (1) the long-term trajectory is rarely simple and may involve return, circular or duplicated migration; (2) the direction of migratory movements is diverse including north-to-north, south-to-south and north-to-south trajectories; and (3) migrants are also diverse, including men, children and the elderly aside from women. The traditional analytical framework is driven by the notion of "marriage-scapes" which is common to many marriage migration studies.

> [M]arriages that cross the borders of nation-states…do not represent a global free-for-all in which all combinations—regardless of class, nationality, ethnicity, or gender, for example—are possible. Rather, they form marriage-scapes that are shaped and limited by existing and emerging cultural, social, historical and political-economic factors. …A majority of international marriage migrants are women, and most of these women move from poorer countries to wealthier ones, from the less developed global "south" to the more industrialized "north"…. (Constable 2005: 3–4)

This analytical framework is important, but it only analyses the first step of marriage migrants' sojourn—the bride's journey from her home to the groom's home. Researchers have developed two distinct lines of analysis from this framework.

The first line explains this south-to-north migration as a form of importing cheap female foreign labour from the south, the goal of which is maintaining the economic competitiveness of countries in the north by sustaining the social reproduction in middle-class families in these countries (Palriwala and Uberoi 2008: 27). In this context, the distinction between being a domestic worker and wife is blurred (Ito and Adachi 2008: 9–11; Lauser 2008: 101–2; Piper and Roces 2003: 4). As Lauser (2008: 102) explains the "only distinction between a foreign wife and a domestic worker is that one is regarded as providing domestic care work as an unpaid 'madam' while the other is a paid 'maid'." From this perspective marriage migration is described as commodified reproductive labour (Yang and Lu 2010: 16), the social dumping of reproductive labour (Truong 1996: 47). East Asian countries—Japan, Korea, Taiwan, Hong Kong and Singapore—are classified as receiving countries while Southeast Asian countries such as the Philippines, Thailand, Vietnam,

Indonesia and parts of China are classified as sending countries (Constable 2005: 4–7; Ito and Adahi 2008: 9).

The second line of analysis, however, explains south-to-north migration in terms of women's agency, that is, the ability to take advantage of opportunities that seem unavailable in their homelands (Constable 2003: 176). Women's agency refers to four sometimes intertwined expectations of women migrating south to north: (1) to improve their economic, legal, social and economic status to fulfil expected womanhood and daughterhood roles at home by remitting money to support their families (Constable 2005: 15; Lu 2012: 246; Suzuki 2005: 143); (2) to provide a good future for their children if they are impoverished, divorced or widowed women (Tosakul 2010: 185–96); (3) to acquire a secure legal status in order to gain access to the benefits of a migration destination such as citizenship (Lauser 2008: 103; Mix and Piper 2003: 54; Piper and Roces 2003: 15); and (4) to acquire the social status of a married woman or mother that women may not be capable of achieving at home when their home communities see them not marriageable due to being overaged, overly successful or divorced (Constable 2005: 12; Lauser 2008: 102; Piper and Roces 2003: 8–10; del Rosario 2008: 87). In addition, a number of women opt to migrate to escape local norms or experiences that they are unwilling to accept, such as traditional marriage, gender constraints or difficult personal and familial situations (Constable 2005: 7–15; Lu 2008: 129; Piper and Roces 2003: 4).

The cases discussed in Chapters 1, 2 and 3 highlight how marriage migrants travel many more diversified complicated migration pathways than the straightforward south-to-north migratory movement. These migration trajectories often emerge as diversified return, circular or multiple trajectories over the life course of marriage migrants. Many marriage migration studies pay close attention to the gendered aspects of transnationalism (Kofman 2004: 244). Although the authors of the chapters in this volume are not gender studies specialists, they have been involved as sociologists and anthropologists in East and Southeast Asian communities for more than a decade. They have similarly witnessed the astonishing growth of transnational migration related to cross-border intimacy and the expansion of transnational households in these regions that involve complex migration trajectories.

In Chapter 1 Masako Kudo presents cases of Pakistani husband–Japanese wife cross-marriage couples who develop transnational households. Their "life course events and migration are highly interdependent events and contingent upon each other" (Cooke 2008: 262). These migration trajectories appear to be complicated in that families' strategies reflect interrelated purposes: (1) to determine the best circumstances in which to raise their multi-ethnic Muslim children; (2) to determine the optimal life circumstances for Japanese wives who have converted to Islam; and (3) to enable Pakistani husbands to engage in transnational family businesses. According to Kudo, the migration trajectories chosen as survival strategies by these transnational households cannot be described as merely moving from the south to the north. As their families' life stages change, a number of Japanese wives migrate from Japan to Pakistan to provide a better Muslim educational environment for their children. Upon finding life in Pakistan to be difficult for them, some wives return to Japan or migrate to other Muslim communities in third countries such as England, New Zealand or the United Arab Emirates. A number of the Japanese wives repeat migrations between several countries to form transnational households that suit the needs of their families. Kudo's cases show that the migration trajectories of the marriage migrants in these trans-border households are far more complex than migration flows from the south to the north.

Chapters 2 and 3 show that even intra-area migration may degrade the legal, economic and social status of marriage migrants. Although researchers have emphasized the need for empirical studies of marriage migration from a comparative intra-Asian perspective (Palriwala and Uberoi 2008: 50), few studies have pursued empirical research on this point. Chapters 2 and 3 investigate the degradation of marriage migrants' status by providing studies of intra-East Asian marriage migrants and intra-Southeast Asian migrants, respectively. Chapter 2 introduces cases of marriage migrants moving from Japan to Shanghai. The author, Chie Sakai, shows that even when marriage migrants move between two countries with similar socio-economic profiles, the destination country may limit their legal rights and socio-economic opportunities as the spouse of a citizen, which in turn will "result in a loss of status and security as women lose their independence and their sense of place in society" (Williams 2010: 130). This finding is similar to the findings of other studies examining global south-to-north marriage migration (Wang and Bélanger 2008: 98). In Chapter 3, Linda A. Lumayag examines the detrimental effects on the careers of professional Philippine women married to Malaysian men. She provides examples of highly educated Filipino marriage migrants who encounter difficulties in pursuing professional occupations in Malaysia owing to their restricted status as marriage migrants. Lumayag argues that marriage migrants who do not match the global marriage-scapes scheme are often ignored in academic discussion and policymaking.

The cases discussed in Chapters 1, 2 and 3 indicate that the flow of marriage migration is not limited to a single global south-to-north migration path. The issues faced by marriage migrants who do not fall into the existing framework of global marriage-scapes have tended to be overlooked. Sociologists argue, "income inequality within nations became an increasingly salient component of inequality in the world distribution of income, while between-nation inequality declined in significance" (Goesling 2001: 756). Appadurai (1996: 32) notes that the new global cultural economy has to be seen as a complex overlapping disjunctive order. It can no longer be understood in terms of centre-periphery models or simple push-pull models. Appadurai's point also applies to marriage migration theory.

Reversed Geographies of Power

The second key point of this volume is that geographies of power (a type of post-colonial framework embedded in the north-south framework) may not be able to account for how the daily life experiences of transnational marriage migrants shape their long-term migration trajectories. The analytical framework of marriage-scapes is based on Massey's notion of geographies of power:

> [A b]undle of terms local/place/locality is bound in to sets of dualisms, in which a key term is the dualism between masculine and feminine, and in which, on these readings, the local/place/feminine side of the dichotomy is deprioritized and denigrated. (Massey 1994/2007: 10)

Existing studies of marriage migration discuss various dimensions of geographies of power from a post-colonial perspective. These dimensions include economic power (Davin 2008: 68; Nguyen and Tran 2010: 169); national power (Bélanger et al. 2010: 166; Horstmann 2009: 161) and ethnically based power (Kelsky 2006: 16–7; Tosakul 2010: 185; del Rosario 2008: 84). These studies provide insightful analyses of marriage migrants' first migrations from their homes to new destinations with their spouses. They represent the above dimensions of the geographies of power as motivating marriage migration, that is, marriage migrants form expectations based on hopes that someplace other than where they are will provide them a better life. In contrast, Chapters 4, 5 and 6 show that gendered geographies of power can weaken, fade or reverse by subsequent migrations regardless of a marriage migrant's economic, national or ethnic power.

Sökefeld (2006: 267) sees diasporas as *"imagined transnational communities,...* that unite segments of people that live in territorially separated locations". Parreñas and Siu (2007: 15) further describe "being diasporic" as imagining that there are places which are always changeable and changing to one's advantage. The discussions of cases in Chapters 4, 5 and 6 merge the above notions of "geographies of power" and "diaspora" to suggest that if marriage migrants conclude from their experience of daily life that they cannot attain their goals for a better life through marriage in the places where they have migrated to, they will feel powerless even when they have enjoyed the high status of being a citizen of a developed nation. This seems to be especially true for marriage migrants in diasporic situations that repeatedly migrate.

In Chapter 4, Ikuya Tokoro's case studies of reverse male marriage migrant flows show that economic geographies of power can be reversed in the long term. The geographies-of-power model assumes that people move from economically poor areas (peripheries) to more wealthy areas (centres) in order to change their life circumstances. He presents cases of Japanese men who do the opposite. These men follow their Filipino wives or girlfriends to the Philippines. They quickly fall into poverty and are soon abandoned by these women. Because these men have also been abandoned by their families and friends in Japan, they feel that they cannot return. Thus, they are socially and economically marginalized in both the Philippines and Japan. Tokoro calls this phenomenon a reverse flow of marriage migration. These cases suggest that the geographies-of-power model does not account for the seriously negative effects of failed relations that may occur between cross-border couples involved in initial south-north migrations and followed by north-south migrations.

In Chapter 5, Sari K. Ishii provides cases in which the expected geographies of power embedded in nationality may work in the reverse manner for second-generation marriage migrants. Although existing studies have discussed the vulnerability of marriage migrants when marriages end in widowhood or separation (Williams 2010: 94), there are only a few case studies that have examined children in such situations. Ishii examines the situations of Japanese-Thai children who migrate to their Thai mothers' home villages after their mothers separate from their Japanese fathers. The period from the mid-1980s to the early 1990s saw a flow of migrants from Northern Thailand to Japan which increased the number of Thai-Japanese cross-border marriages and Thai-Japanese births. It was a common narrative for women to marry foreign men to provide a better life for their children compared with life in a lower-class community in rural Thailand. However, these mothers decided not to raise their mixed-race children in Japan, often after several years of being separated from their Japanese partners. As a result, a number of these children were sent back to their mother's home village in Thailand without sufficient financial support from Japan. These children occasionally experienced strained relationships with the Thai immigration bureau because of their Japanese nationality. Although the mothers believed that having Japanese nationality would be advantageous for their children, it worked as a disadvantage for the children who "returned" to rural Thai villages without financial support.

In Chapter 6, Caesar Dealwis discusses how geographies of power in ethnicity can be reversed for the offspring of marriage migrants in the long term. Dealwis describes the assimilation of the descendants of Caucasian migrants married to local people into Malay ethnicity in Sarawak, Malaysia. Sarawak has a number of marriage migrants from Western countries and their descendants. During the Brooke administration (1841–1941) and the British colonial rule (1946–63) many Caucasian men—especially from Britain, Ireland and Australia—came to work in Sarawak as missionaries, soldiers and public officials. Many of these men married local Malay, Chinese and Dayak women. Later Caucasian migrants, who came to Sarawak to work in the oil and gas industry, also married local women. Children born from marriages between Caucasians and Sarawakians and the offspring of these children became acknowledged as Eurasians in Sarawak. However, these Eurasians have begun to identify themselves as Malays because they see that assuming Malay identity is the best way to secure their political, economic and social interests within the framework of the Malaysian nation-state. These cases show that geographies of power in ethnicity can also be reversed in the process of adopting pragmatic survival skills in the context of citizenship. In short, despite the image that "children born from mixed marriages with [a] Western (Caucasian) father or vice versa [are] successful movie actors, supermodels,... modern and cosmopolitan" (Tosakul 2010: 185), marriage migrants and their descendants may give up a "superior" image for a "more ordinary image" if doing so is likely to be advantageous in the long term.

Multi-marginalized Marriage Migrants

The last, and maybe the most important key point, demonstrated by the cases in this volume is the "multiply displaced" (Cohen 2008: 8) status of marriage migrants. Cases from Chapters 7 to 10 show how duplicated migration trajectories degrade the legal, linguistic, cultural, occupational and socio-economic status of marriage migrants (Cooke 2008: 256) on the fringes and in the gaps between nation-states. Marriage migration studies indicate that people choose to become marriage migrants to acquire a more secure legal status (Yang and Lu 2010: 18; Mix and Piper 2003: 54; Williams 2010: 85) and to avoid uncomfortable situations at home, such as being a member of a marginalized ethnic minority (Horstmann 2009: 161), a vulnerable migrant worker seeking a secure residential status (Liaw, Ochiai and Ishikawa 2010: 62; Mix and Piper 2003: 54), a poor divorced or widowed woman with children experiencing difficulty in gaining access to social security (Tosakul 2010: 196). However, marriage migrants without formal citizenship often find themselves in much more precarious situations after marriage (Piper and Roces 2003: 16).

Cases provided in Chapters 7 to 10 demonstrate situations of marriage migrants as being doubly marginalized, that is, unable to realize their goals in both sending or receiving nation-states (Yeoh, Leng and Dung 2013: 152). Willis, Yeoh and Fakhri (2004: 3) point out that the "transnational movement involved is not the death of the nation-state per se but rather a reconfiguration". In Chapter 7, Caroline Grillot concentrating on cases in the borderlands between Vietnam and China demonstrates how the position of subalterns or stigmatized individuals—on whom this research focuses—leads them to adopt non-conventional marriage patterns as a strategy to improve their lives. Daily life in the borderlands occurs in a cross-border space; therefore, many Chinese men and Vietnamese women marry and create families there. However, the Vietnamese wives and their children are left in a vulnerable state of virtual non-existence because their marriages and births are not formally registered in either China or Vietnam. As a result, when couples face marital problems (for example, they decide to separate) their mixed-race children are not recognized by either state. Grillot presents extreme cases showing that regardless of how "transnational" an individual's lifestyle may be it is only through the laws of a state that marriages will be recognized as legal and that marriage migrants and their children can be recognized as citizens (Toyota 2008: 2). The borderlands are dynamic and heterogeneous transnational spaces. Nevertheless, lives and activities carried out in these areas—border-crossing migrations marriages, trade and conflicts—are nonetheless bound by state laws (Askew 2009: 180–1; Horstmann 2009: 173).

In Chapter 8, Hien Anh Le documents the situation of children whose future is at risk in the "borderlands" between Vietnam and Korea. The children have mothers who are divorced from their Korean partners but the mothers hesitate to acquire Vietnamese nationality for their children. Several existing studies have discussed divorce among marriage migrants (Lee 2008: 113) and mentioned the increasing number of Vietnamese-Taiwanese and Vietnamese-Korean children left in Vietnam without any rights to education (Wang and Bélanger 2008: 100). However, few studies have examined this situation. In her chapter, Le investigates the conditions surrounding these children. Because children born in Korea do not possess Vietnamese birth certificates, they cannot claim Vietnamese nationality, which implies exclusion from public education and any form of social welfare in Vietnam. However, mothers hesitate to convert their children's nationality from Korean to Vietnamese because they still hope that their children will live in Korea someday. These mothers attempt to maintain their children's Korean nationality although the children suffer as a result. These children cannot obtain citizenship or rights as either Korean or Vietnamese citizens. Le analyses the long-term effects on such children who fall into the gap between the situation that they actually live in and an imagined better place (Constable 2005: 8) as a result of marriage migration.

In Chapter 9 Lara Chen Tien-shi's case studies make two points: (1) cross-border intimacy can lead to people becoming stateless; and (2) stateless people cannot easily enter into cross-border marriages or sustain them. Chen introduces a case that shows how Japanese-Filipino children born out of wedlock become stateless. Another case illustrates the difficulty of cross-border marriage for stateless people as exemplified in the difficulties encountered by a stateless woman from Thailand and a Japanese man trying to legally register their marriage. Chen also shows the vulnerability of stateless male marriage migrants through the case of a stateless Rohingya man from Myanmar. He married an Indonesian woman and established a family, and he operates a successful business. However, he remains vulnerable in many ways because he cannot change his stateless status.

In Chapter 10, Chatchai Chetsumon uses the case of marriage between irregular workers from Myanmar and Thailand nationals to show

how states absorb or reject undocumented workers who try to normalize their situations through legal means. Undocumented workers from Myanmar can marry Thai nationals by fulfilling the requirements for formal marriage under Thai law. However, a number of marriage applications are rejected by Thai authorities when it becomes clear that workers from Myanmar are not Myanmar citizens or citizens of other nations. Chetsumon illustrates this situation in two cases. The first case shows that a number of undocumented workers' marriage applications are rejected because the applicants were never issued any identification documents from Myanmar owing to their minority status there. The second case deals with undocumented workers from Myanmar who have lived in Thailand for decades and fear they will lose the lives that they have built for themselves and their families if they reveal their undocumented status to the authorities, which could nullify their marriages. The cases presented by Chetsumon demonstrate that stateless people are unable to attain more secure legal statuses through cross-border marriages because they are deprived of the fundamental right to marry. Cases of long-term marriage migrants' situations in the above chapters exemplify the "key features of diaspora" as "dispersal from a 'centre' to at least two 'peripheries'" (Tsolidis 2014: 5).

Marriage Migrants as Transnational Diaspora

The idea of marriage and family are social constructs that have evolved with the evolution of modern nation-states to control the vast populations within their boundaries (Toyota 2008: 3–4; Turner 2008: 49; Williams 2010: 172). Studies such as Hsia (2009), Toyota (2008) and Yeoh, Leng and Dung (2013) have discussed the marginalized status of marriage migrants from the standpoint of international marriage as an arena of contention over rights, privileges and access to citizenship.

When the gendered discourse embedded in citizenship laws are applied to marriages involving trans-national households and multi-identified children, these households and their children become transgressive forces that challenge the boundaries and sovereignty of nation-states and their notions of what constitutes citizenship (Hsia 2009: 19; Lee 2008: 112; Toyota 2008: 3; Turner 2008: 49; Yeoh, Leng and Dung 2013: 140; Williams 2010: 171). Legal status and rights of divorced men and women who are migrants and have children born in a nation-state also challenge the definition of nationhood and citizenship for the state (Jørgensen 2012: 76; Lee 2008: 113). Transnational practices are often viewed as threatening by national governments (Charsley 2012: 8). Nation-states see the repetitive nature of marriage migrants' border crossings as a challenge to the states' need to control access across their borders and the tendency of first-generation marriage migrants and their children to retain their transnational identity as a challenge to the states' definition of citizens (Wray 2012: 57).

The number of people with de-territorialized, multi-affiliated identity has increased, but systems to secure human rights of such people have not been developed yet. Researchers have argued that economic globalization-induced denationalizing of national territory—recontextualizations of "nationness" within the universalistic discourse of human rights—blurs the meanings and boundaries of nation and nation-state (Sassen 1996/2015: 33; Soysal 1994: 162). They also argue for "postnational rights or universalistic rights based on the inalienable right of personhood with 'cultural pluralist' or 'multiculturalist positions' and posit alternatives to a 'national' sense of identity" (Soysal 1994: 153–4; Sassen 2006: 288). However, these ideas have not been put to use, at least not in East and Southeast Asian countries, yet. Parreñas and Siu articulated on this point as follows:

> By now, a postnational world is hardly imaginable. In place of earlier predictions that suggest the blurring of national borders and the diminishing power of the state, we see instead the continuing, if not increasing, significance of nationalism and the vitality of the state in redefining its citizens and national borders. (Parreñas and Siu 2007: 17)

Regardless of how transnational an individual's lifestyle is (Toyota 2008: 2) or how de-territorialized or multi-affiliated their identities turn out to be (Colombo and Rebughini 2012: 32), citizenship for marriage migrants and their children can only be structured within the laws of a territorialized nation-state (Hsia 2009: 17–8; Toyota 2008: 2; Yeoh, Leng and Dung 2013: 140). That said, "the practice of transnational marriage has proved hard to dislodge and the expansion of the border has had little effect in that regard" (Wray 2012: 57). Whether before or after marriage, marriage migrants are often seen as bringing out the tension between the state's roles as a maintainer of the family institution and as the gatekeeper who decides who gets to be a citizen (Leng 2011: 185). States often build the ideology of family care into nation building discourses but define care of the family and children as women's domains (Ho 2008: 168). While this potentially enfolds marriage migrants into host nation-states, the laws of these states only allow partial incorporation as citizens (Yeoh, Leng and Dung 2013: 151–2). They "resid[e] within the state without full citizenship" (Williams 2010: 76).

The above analysis of marriage migrants is consistent with situations articulated in diaspora studies as mentioned above. Diaspora is described as being "multiply displaced" (Cohen 2008: 8) both in the host and home countries amid the increasing number of individuals with multi-affiliated identities (Aguilar 1996: 6; Saperstein and Penner 2012: 712). Arguments on diaspora point out that the "distinctive aspect of diasporic identity is that members of diaspora (or indeed individual migrants) are only marginally included in both their host society and their 'home'" (Barabantseva and Sutherland 2012: 4). This kind of exclusion is expressed as "*de facto* segregation" (Glenn 2011: 5), "second-class citizenship" (Conover, Searing and Crewe 2004: 1037), "a hierarchy within citizenship" (Barabantseva and Sutherland 2012: 7), "hierarchies of citizenship" (Shipper 2010: 14), "majoritarianisms…within the nation-state" (Appadurai 1996: 39–40), "more sociological versions of citizenship, not confined by formal political criteria for specifying citizenship" (Sassen 2006: 288) or being "a formal citizen who is fully authorized yet not fully recognized" (Sassen 2006: 294).

According to Safran, "[t]oday, 'diaspora' and, more specifically, 'diaspora community' seem increasingly to be used as metaphoric designations for several categories of people—expatriates, expellees, political refugees, alien residents, immigrants, and ethnic and racial minorities *tout court*" (1991: 83). Marriage migrants should be added as a category. Going beyond the simple polarity of homeland and host land, the idea of diaspora offers a powerful perspective on migration based on the three interrelated dimensions of movement connectivity and return (Kenny 2013: 105–8). The discussion in the following chapters is hoped to set the stage for the dialogue on the abovementioned situation of marriage migrants based on cases in Asia.

Cases provided in the following chapters of this volume will add a new axis to the abovementioned existing studies that examine the standards for certifying the "full-citizenship" of marriage migrants in relation to modern notions of citizenship, family and nation-state. This axis has two dimensions: (1) the diversified, complicated and duplicated migratory trajectories of marriage migration in the long term may work as a factor in creating a situation where the marriage migrants, like the ones noted above, become even more marginalized and more vulnerable; and (2) marriage migrants who do not match the south-to-north migration schema may also be marginalized for their status of being marriage migrants regardless of geographies of power or gender bias and regardless of whether they follow a horizontal trajectory (intra-north and intra-south migration) or a north-to-south trajectory.

Although we believe this volume presents a first step in locating marriage migrants as a transnational diaspora in migration studies, the chapters in this volume also raise difficult empirical and theoretical problems for future studies, such as issues related to male marriage migrants and child migrants. Half of the chapters herein mention male marriage migrants directly or indirectly (Chapters 1, 4, 6, 9 and 10); however, none of them involve interviews with male marriage migrants. Research on potential legal, economic and social issues faced by male marriage migrants will be an inevitable part of future studies on the relationship of citizenship to marriage migration.

Child migration is another theme left for further discussion. Chapters 1, 5 and 8 examine child migration. However, the authors acknowledge that child migration involves many more diverse problems than those discussed in this volume.[4] Children carry out repeat migrations in search of better circumstances (for example, for their education) or return migrate to their mother's home after their parents' divorce, as shown in this volume. However, a number of other factors result in child migration aside from parents divorcing or (re)marrying. For example, child migration may also be driven by laws that prevent children from becoming citizens because complicated migration trajectories have not equipped these children with the language proficiency and professional qualification needed to gain citizenship. Empirical studies on child migration will be an important part of the discussion of marriage migrants as an international diaspora.

Notes

1. Exceptions include Charsley, Benson and Hear (2012); Cooke (2008); Kudo (2008); Schans (2012); and Toyota and Thang (2012).
2. The term "global north and south" refers to a geographical concept that indicates a "European-dominated network of political, economic, and cultural exchange" that existed from the late eighteenth century up to the 1980s (Steger 2003/13: 31). Oluwafemi noted as follows:

   > The global North is made up of the industrial countries of North America, Western Europe, and Japan. Africa, South America and Asia constitute the South.... The situation in the global economy is such that the North, with 1/4th of world population controls 4/5th of world income, while the South's 3/4th of world population has access to only 1/5th of world income. (2012: 47)

3. For further details on diaspora studies, see Appadurai (2006); Barabantseva and Sutherland (2013); Bauböck and Faist (2010); Cohen (1997/2008); Dufoix (2008); Kenny (2013); Parreñas and Siu (2007); Safran (1991, 2005) and Tsolidis (2014).
4. Yeoh et al. (2012) also indicated the importance of further research on child migration in Asia.

References

Aguilar, V. Filomeno, Jr. 1996. "Guest Editor's Preface." *Philippine Sociological Review* 44: 4–11.
Amrith, S. Sunil. 2011. *Migration and Diaspora in Modern Asia*. Cambridge: Cambridge University Press.
Appadurai, Arjun. 1996. *Modernity at Large: Cultural Dimensions of Globalization*. Minneapolis: University of Minnesota Press.
———. 2006. *Fear of Small Numbers: An Essay on the Geography of Anger*. Durham, NC: Duke University Press.
Askew, Mark. 2009. "Sex and the Sacred: Sojourners and Visitors in the Making of the Southern Thai Borderland." In *Centering the Margin: Agency and Narrative in Southeast Asian Borderlands*, ed. Alexander Horstmann and Reed L. Wadley. New York: Berghahn Books, pp. 177–206.
Barabantseva, Elena and Claire Sutherland. 2012. *Diaspora and Citizenship*. London: Routledge.
Bauböck, Painer and Thomas Faist, eds. 2010. *Diaspora and Transnationalism: Concepts, Theories and Methods*. Amsterdam: Amsterdam University Press.
Bélanger, Danièle, Tran Giang Linh, Le Bach Duong and Khuat Thu Hong. 2010. "From Farmer's Daughters to Foreign Wives: Marriage Migration and Gender in Sending Communities of Vietnam." In *Asian Gender under Construction: Global Reconfiguration of Human Reproduction*, ed. Emiko Ochiai. Kyoto: International Research Center for Japanese Studies, pp. 157–80.
Charsley, Katharine. 2012. "Transnational Marriage." In *Transnational Marriage: New Perspectives from Europe and Beyond*, ed. Katharine Charsley. New York: Routledge, pp. 3–22.
Charsley, Katharine, Michaela Benson and Nicholas Van Hear. 2012. "Marriage-Related Migration to the UK." *International Migration Review* 46(4): 861–90.
Cohen, Robin. 2008. *Global Diasporas: An Introduction*. 2nd ed. London: Routledge.
Colombo, Enzo and Paola Rebughini. 2012. *Children of Immigrants in a Globalized World: A Generational Experience*. London: Palgrave Macmillan.
Conover, Pamela Johnson, Donald D. Searing and Ivor Crewe. 2004. "The Elusive Ideal of Equal Citizenship: Political Theory and Political Psychology in the United States and Great Britain." *The Journal of Politics* 66(4): 1036–68.

Constable, Nicole. 2003. "A Transnational Perspective on Divorce and Marriage: Filipina Wives and Workers' Identities." *Global Studies in Culture and Power* 10: 163–80.

———. 2005. "Introduction: Cross-Border Marriages, Gendered Mobility and Global Hypergamy." In *Cross-Border Marriages: Gender and Mobility in Transnational Asia*, ed. Nicole Constable. Philadelphia: University of Pennsylvania Press, pp. 1–16.

Cooke, Thomas J. 2008. "Migration in a Family Way." *Population, Space and Place* 14: 255–65.

Davin, Delia. 2008. "Marriage Migration in China: The Enlargement of Marriage Markets in the Era of Market Reforms." In *Marriage, Migration and Gender*, ed. Rajni Palriwala and Patricia Uberoi. Los Angeles: SAGE Publications, pp. 63–77.

del Rosario, Teresita C. 2008. "Bridal Diaspora: Migration and Marriage among Filipino Women." In *Marriage Migration and Gender*, ed. Rajni Palriwala and Patricia Uberoi. Los Angeles: SAGE Publications, pp. 78–97.

Dufoix, Stéphane. 2008. *Diasporas*. Trans. William Rodarmor. Berkeley: University of California Press. Originally published as *Les Diasporas* in 2003 by Presses Universitaires de France.

Glenn, Evelyn Nakano. 2011. "Constructing Citizenship: Exclusion Subordination and Resistance." *American Sociological Review* 76(1): 1–24.

Goesling, Brian 2001. "Changing Income Inequalities within and between Nations: New Evidence." *American Sociological Review* 66(5): 745–61.

Ho Lynn-Ee, Elaine. 2008. "'Flexible Citizenship' or Familial Ties that Bind? Singaporean Transmigrants in London." *International Migration* 46(4): 145–75.

Horstmann, Alexander. 2009. "Deconstructing Citizenship from the Border: Dual Ethnic Minorities and Local Reworking of Citizenship at the Thailand-Malaysian Frontier." In *Centering the Margin: Agency and Narrative in Southeast Asian Borderlands*, ed. Alexander Horstmann and Reed L. Wadley. New York: Berghahn Books, pp. 155–76.

Hsia, Hsiao-Chuan. 2009. "Foreign Brides, Multiple Citizenship and the Immigrant Movement in Taiwan." *Asian and Pacific Migration Journal* 18(1): 17–46.

Ito, Ruri and Mariko Adachi. 2008. "Jyobun" [Introduction]. In *Kokusaiido to <rensasuru jenda>: saiseisan ryouikino grobaruka* [Trans-border Migration and "Gender Chains": Globalization in Reproductive Domain], ed. Ruri Ito and Mariko Adachi. Tokyo: Sakuhinsha, pp. 5–15.

Jones, Gavin W. 2012. "Marriage Migration in Asia: An Introduction." *Asian and Pacific Migration Journal* 21(3): 287–316.

Jones, Gavin and Hsiu-hua Shen. 2008. "International Marriage in East and Southeast Asia: Trends and Research Emphases." *Citizenship Studies* 12(1): 9–25.

Jørgensen, Martin Bak. 2012. "Danish Regulations on Marriage Migration: Policy Understandings of Transnational Marriages." In *Transnational Marriage: New Perspectives from Europe and Beyond*, ed. Katharine Charsley. New York: Routledge, pp. 60–78.

Kelsky, Karen. 2006. *Women on the Verge: Japanese Women Western Dreams*. Durham, NC: Duke University Press.

Kenny, Kevin. 2013. *Diaspora: A Very Short Introduction*. Oxford: Oxford University Press.

Kim, Andrew Eungi. 2009. "Global Migration and South Korea: Foreign Workers, Foreign Brides and the Making of a Multicultural Society." *Ethnic and Racial Studies* 32(1): 70–92.

Kofman, Eleonore. 2004. "Family-Related Migration: A Critical Review of European Studies." *Journal of Ethnic and Migration Studies* 30(2): 243–62.

Kudo, Masako. 2008. *Ekkyo no jinruigaku: Zainichi pakisutanjin musurimu imin no tsuma tachi* [An Anthropology of Border-Crossing in Japan: Japanese Wives of Pakistani Muslim Migrants]. Tokyo: University of Tokyo Press.

Lauser, Andrea. 2008. "Philippine Women on the Move: Marriage across Borders." *International Migration* 46: 85–110.

Lavely, William. 1991. "Marriage and Mobility under Rural Collectivism." In *Marriage and Inequality in Chinese Society*, ed. Watson Rubie and Patricia B. Ebrey. Berkeley: University of California Press, pp. 286–312.

Lee, Hye-Kyung. 2008. "International Marriage and the State in South Korea: Focusing on Governmental Policy." *Citizenship Studies* 12: 107–23.

———. 2011. "International Marriages in Malaysia: Issues Arising from State Policies and Processes." In *Changing Marriage Patterns in Southeast Asia: Economic and Socio-cultural Dimensions*, ed. Gavin W. Jones, Terrence H. Hull and Maznah Mohamad. New York: Routledge, pp. 185–201.

Liaw Lao-Lee, Emiko Ochiai and Yoshitaka Ishikawa. 2010. "Feminization of Immigration in Japan: Marital and Job Opportunities." In *Asian Cross-border Marriage Migration*, ed. Wen-Shan Yang and Melody Chia-Wen Lu. Amsterdam: Amsterdam University Press, pp. 49–86.

Lie, John. 1995. "Review of Journals: From International Migration to Transnational Diaspora." *Contemporary Sociology* 24(4): 303–6.

Lu, Melody Chia-Wen. 2008. "Commercially Arranged Marriage Migration: Case Studies of Cross-border Marriages in Taiwan." In *Marriage, Migration and Gender*, ed. Rajni Palriwala and Patricia Uberoi. Los Angeles: SAGE, pp. 125–51.

———. 2012. "Transnational Marriages as a Strategy of Care Exchange: Veteran Soldiers and their Mainland Chinese Spouses in Taiwan." *Global Networks* 12(2): 233–51.

Massey, Doreen. 1994/2007. *Space, Place and Gender*. Cambridge: Polity Press.

Mix, Prapairat R. and Nicola Piper. 2003. "Does Marriage 'Liberate' Women from Sex Work? – Thai Women in Germany." In *Wife or Worker?: Asian*

Women and Migration, ed. Nicola Piper and Mina Roces. Lanham, MD: Rowman and Littlefield, pp. 53–71.
Nguyen, Xoan and Xuyen Tran. 2010. "Vietnamese-Taiwanese Marriages." In *Asian Cross-border Marriage Migration: Demographic Patterns and Social Issues*, ed. Yang Wen-Shan and Melody Chia-Wen Lu. Amsterdam: Amsterdam University Press, pp. 157–78.
Oluwafemi, N. Mimiko. 2012. *Globalization: The Politics of Global Economic Relations and International Business*. Durham, NC: Carolina Academic Press.
Palriwala, Rajni and Patricia Uberoi. 2008. "Exploring the Links: Gender Issues in Marriage and Migration." In *Marriage, Migration and Gender*, ed. Rajni Palriwala and Patricia Uberoi. Los Angeles: SAGE Publications, pp. 23–60.
Parreñas, Rhacel S. 2001. *Servants of Globalization: Women Migration and Domestic Work*. Redwood City, CA: Stanford University Press.
Parreñas, Rhacel S. and Lok C.D. Siu. 2007. "Introduction: Asian Diasporas—New Conceptions, New Frameworks." In *Asian Diasporas: New Formations, New Conceptions*, ed. Rhacel S. Parreñas and Lok C.D. Siu. Redwood City, CA: Stanford University Press, pp. 1–27.
Piper, Nicola and Mina Roces. 2003. "Introduction: Marriage and Migration in an Age of Globalization." In *Wife or Worker?: Asian Women and Migration*, ed. Nicola Piper and Mina Roces. Lanham, MD: Rowman and Littlefield, pp. 1–21.
Safran, William. 1991. "Diasporas in Modern Societies: Myths of Homeland and Return." *Diaspora* 1(1): 83–99.
———. 2005. "The Jewish Diaspora in a Comparative and Theoretical Perspective." *Israel Studies* 10(1): 36–60.
Saperstein, Aliya and Andrew M. Penner. 2012. "Racial Fluidity and Inequality in the United States." *American Journal of Sociology* 118(3): 676–727.
Sassen, Saskia. 2006. *Territory Authority Rights: From Medieval to Global Assemblages*. (Updated edition). Princeton, NJ: Princeton University Press.
———. 1996/2015. *Losing Control?: Sovereignty in an Age of Gobalization*. New York: Columbia University Press.
Schans, Djamila. 2012. "Against the Grain: International Marriages between African Men and Japanese Women." *Asian and Pacific Migration Journal* 21(3): 365–86.
Shipper, Apichai W. 2010. "Introduction: Politics of Citizenship and Transnational Gendered Migration in East and Southeast Asia." *Pacific Affairs* 83(1): 11–29.
Sökefeld, Martin. 2006. "Mobilizing in Transnational Space: A Social Movement Approach to the Formation of Diaspora." *Global Networks* 6(3): 265–84.
Soysal, Yasemin Nuhoglu. 1994. *Limits of Citizenship: Migrants and Postnational Membership in Europe*. Chicago: University of Chicago Press.
Steger, Manfred B. 2003/13. *Globalization: A Very Short Introduction*. Oxford: Oxford University Press.

Suzuki, Nobue. 2005. "Tripartite Desires: Filipina-Japanese Marriages and Fantasies of Transnational Traversal." In *Cross-Border Marriages: Gender and Mobility in Transnational Asia*, ed. Nicole Constable. Philadelphia: University of Pennsylvania Press, pp. 124–44.

Tosakul, Ratana. 2010. "Cross-border Marriages: Experiences of Village Women from northeastern Thailand with Western Men." In *Asian Cross-border Marriage Migration: Demographic Patterns and Social Issues*, ed. Wen-Shan Yang and Melody Chia-Wen Lu. Amsterdam: Amsterdam University Press, pp. 179–99.

Toyota, Mika. 2008. "Editorial Introduction: International Marriage Rights and the State in East and Southeast Asia." *Citizenship Studies* 12: 1–7.

Toyota, Mika and Lang Lang Thang. 2012. "'Reverse Marriage Migration': A Case Study of Japanese Brides in Bali." *Asian and Pacific Migration Journal* 21(3): 345–64.

Truong, Thanh-Dam. 1996. "Gender International Migration and Social Reproduction: Implications for Theory Policy Research and Networking." *Asian and Pacific Migration Journal* 5: 27–52.

Tseng Yen-Fen. 2010. "Marriage Migration to East Asia: Current Issues and Propositions in Making Comparisons." In *Asian Cross-border Marriage Migration: Demographic Patterns and Social Issues*, ed. Yang Wen-Shan and Melody Chia-Wen Lu. Amsterdam: Amsterdam University Press, pp. 31–45.

Tsolidis, Georgina. 2014. "Introduction: Does Diaspora Matter When Living Cultural Difference?" In *Migration Diaspora and Identity: Cross-National Experiences*, ed. Georgina Tsolidis. New York: Springer, pp. 1–15.

Turner, Bryan S. 2008. "Citizenship Reproduction and the State: International Marriage and Human Rights." *Citizenship Studies* 12: 45–54.

Wang Hong-zen and Shu-Ming Chang. 2002. "The Commodification of International Marriages: Cross-border Marriage Business in Taiwan and Viet Nam." *International Migration* 40: 93–114.

Wang Hong-zen and Danièle Bélanger. 2008. "Taiwanizing Female Immigrant Spouses and Materializing Differential Citizenship." *Citizenship Studies* 12: 91–106.

Williams, Lucy. 2010. *Global Marriage: Cross-Border Marriage Migration in Global Context*. Hampshire: Palgrave Macmillan.

———. 2012. "Transnational Marriage Migration and Marriage Migration: An Overview." In *Transnational Marriage: New Perspectives from Europe and Beyond*, ed. Katharine Charsley. New York: Routledge, pp. 23–37.

Willis, Katie, Brenda S.A. Yeoh and S.M. Abdul Khader Fakhri. 2004. "Introduction: Transnationalism as a Challenge to the Nation." In *State/Nation/Transnation: Perspectives on Transnationalism in the Asia-Pacific*, ed. Brenda S.A. Yeoh and Katie Willis. London and New York: Routledge, pp. 1–15.

Wray, Helena. 2012. "Any Time Any Place Anywhere: Entry Clearance Marriage Migration and the Border." In *Transnational Marriage: New Perspectives from Europe and Beyond*, ed. Charsley Katharine. New York: Routledge, pp. 41–59.

Yang Wen-Shan and Melody Chia-Wen Lu. 2010. "Introduction." In *Asian Cross-border Marriage Migration: Demographic Patterns and Social Issues*, ed. Wen-Shan Yang and Melody Chia-Wen Lu. Amsterdam: Amsterdam University Press, pp. 15–29.

Yeoh Brenda S.A., Chee Heng Leng and Vu Thi Kieu Dung. 2013. "Commercially Arranged Marriage and the Negotiation of Citizenship Rights among Vietnamese Marriage Migrants in Multiracial Singapore." *Asian Ethnicity* 14(2): 139–56.

PART I

Migration Flows Beyond the Marriage-scapes

CHAPTER 1

Forging Intimate Ties in Transnational Spaces: The Life Trajectories of Japanese Women Married to Pakistani Migrants

Masako Kudo

Introduction

The phenomenon of cross-border marriage has attracted scholarly attention both inside and outside Asia in the last two decades (Charsley 2012; Constable 2005; Wang et al. 2009; Williams 2010; Yang et al. 2010). The lives of women who move from the global south and marry men of the global north have been documented by a number of studies, including Suzuki (2005), Sunanta and Angeles (2013) and others. However, there is a paucity of studies on the experiences of women in the global north who marry men from the global south. Hence, this study explores the marriages between the women of the global north and the men of the global south by examining the life trajectories of Japanese women who are married to Pakistani men in particular. This type of cross-border marriages increased with the flow of Pakistani labour migrants into Japan during the late 1980s. Using longitudinal data drawn from in-depth interviews of Japanese wives over a decade-long period that began in the late 1990s, this study explores the complex ways in which the lives of these women expanded across national boundaries.

The following discussion is structured as follows. The first section provides basic statistical data related to the increase in the number of marriages between Japanese women and Pakistani men in Japan. It also explores the women's motivations for marrying Pakistani men and the socio-economic status of the couples. The second section explores the ways in which family relationships expanded beyond national boundaries during the early stages of the marriage. Of particular importance is the emergence of the transnational family when the Japanese wives and their children relocated to Pakistan or to a third country while their Pakistani husbands remained in Japan. In this form of transnational family arrangement, family members are separated across national borders, and yet they maintain emotional as well as economic ties as families. The factors that contributed to this type of transnational family dispersal and the experiences of the Japanese women who relocated are scrutinized. The third section examines the various ways by which the families evolved as their life cycles progressed. By exploring the complex trajectories of family formation, this study seeks to highlight both the possibilities and the limitations of the mixed-couples' strategies to disperse the family members beyond national boundaries and to show how the husbands and wives negotiated and eventually reconciled their differing desires and ideals regarding family life and child-raising.

This study is based on my interviews with Japanese wives of Pakistani men who lived in the Kanto area of Japan (Greater Tokyo), where most Pakistani migrants reside. Most of the interviews were conducted between 1998 and 2001, although follow-up interviews were also done after that period. Initially, 40 women were interviewed.[1] Most of them had converted to Islam upon marrying their Pakistani spouses; thus, religion became one of the main factors that affected the family formation process.[2] In the first round of interviews, four of the women were residing in Pakistan[3] while the rest lived in the Kanto area. The interviewees were recruited mainly via the snowball method. I was introduced to additional women mainly by the women who I originally met during my visits to mosques.[4] While this recruitment strategy may indicate that the women who I initially met were more religiously oriented than those who seldom attended mosques, my longitudinal research data strongly indicate that the women's religious views and practices were quite diverse and that they changed considerably over time. Within each "Muslim family", the family members often did not agree on what it meant to be a Muslim. Rather, the meaning of being Muslim was contested and negotiated throughout the family formation process, as will be discussed later in this chapter.

The Emergence of Japanese-Pakistani Marriages in Japan in the 1990s

With the influx of migrants from Pakistan to Japan in the late 1980s, the number of cross-border marriages between Japanese women and

Pakistani men increased considerably during the 1990s. These migrants were predominantly men who were in their twenties and thirties, and most had formerly resided in urban areas in Pakistan such as Lahore and Karachi. Upon their arrival in Japan, the majority of the men worked illegally for small-sized enterprises that were located mainly in the Kanto area. These men engaged in manual work because labourers were in great demand at that time. A significant number of the Pakistanis overstayed their visas, especially after the Japanese government rescinded the visa exemption agreement with Pakistan in 1989. Following a peak period in 1988, the number of incoming Pakistani nationals dropped sharply.[5]

Although Japan's economic decline in the 1990s accelerated the departure of the Pakistanis, a significant number of them remained in the country and legalized their status by marrying local women. During the 1990s, the number of marriages between Pakistani men and Japanese women increased steadily, and many of the spousal visas that were obtained by Pakistani men were later converted to permanent resident visas (see Figure 1.1). In 2011, Pakistani men who held either spousal or permanent resident visas accounted for approximately 40 per cent of the total 10,849 Pakistanis registered in Japan (JIA 2012).[6]

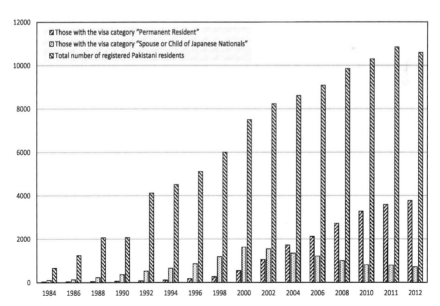

Figure 1.1 Number of registered Pakistani residents in Japan, 1984–2012
Source: Japan Immigration Association, 1985–2013.

Profile of the Japanese Wives

The Japanese wives who were interviewed had varying levels of education (Table 1.1). The majority (24 out of 40) had gone beyond a high school education, and of these 10 had entered four-year universities, reflecting a 1995 national trend. (Official figures for 1995 show that 22.9 per cent of females in Japan had entered four-year universities (Ministry of Education, Culture, Sports, Science and Technology [MOECSST] 2006.)

Table 1.1 Educational levels of Japanese wives interviewed

Educational Level	*Number*
Secondary School (education up to the age of 15 years)	1
High School	11
Vocational College	11
Junior College	3
University	9
Post-Graduate School	1
No Reply	4
TOTAL	40

The Japanese women who were interviewed met their Pakistani husbands at their workplace, at venues such as sports gyms, or through introductions by mutual friends. Although the women's personal motivations varied, two common reasons for their decision to marry a Pakistani migrant were noteworthy. First, many of the women had developed a keen interest in the world outside of Japan before they met their husbands. Second, the women felt that Pakistani husbands "took care of and showed concern for the family", unlike the widely held image of a Japanese husband who works long hours and leaves most domestic matters to his wife. For the Japanese women, the Pakistani migrants offered an alternative form of partnership and the possibility of experiencing a world beyond Japan (Kudo 2008).

Occupational Transformations

After marriage, the Pakistani husbands tended to start their own business (Kudo 2007, 2008). Many became involved in exporting used cars, an economic niche that was filled particularly by Pakistanis in Japan. By 2001, 28 of the 40 husbands had become self-employed. Most of them were involved in exporting used cars, while the others opened Indian/Pakistani restaurants and *halal* (lawful in Islam) food shops. In contrast, most of the wives ceased working after they got married. This tendency to become a full-time housewife was especially common after the women had children. In fact, only 7 of the 40 interviewees kept their full-time jobs (Kudo 2012). Their decision to stop working was partially influenced by their husbands' religio-culturally derived belief in the value of gender segregation. In this regard, it should be noted that among Japanese women in general there is a tendency to place careers on hold during the child-rearing years and to return to work later in life. This persistent trend is evidenced by the well-known "M-shaped Curve" which appears when women's labour force participation rate is graphed by age. There is a sharp drop in the rate of labour participation among women in their early thirties who are starting to raise children. The bottom of the "M" has risen in recent years, although the basic M-shape has been retained (Cabinet Office, Government of Japan 2013).

Follow-up interviews conducted after 2001 revealed that some of the women found it difficult to find employment after their children no longer needed full-time care. One reason is the age and gender discrimination that exists in the Japanese labour market. Another reason is that some of the women whose husbands were self-employed had to spend time processing business documents for their husbands who were unable to read and write Japanese, which prevented the wives from engaging in regular employment.

Becoming Muslim

Because Pakistani men who live in Japan are typically self-employed, they tend to form close networks with compatriots who manage or work in similar businesses. Mosques are one of the important sites where Pakistani entrepreneurs build their religio-ethnic networks. The self-employed Pakistani husbands of the interviewees were able to perform religious duties as their work schedules were more flexible than those of Pakistani men who worked in factories. However, the way the husbands practised their religion varied greatly. The processes involved in the reconstruction of a Muslim identity within a migrant context seem rather complex. For instance, a husband of one of the women interviewed founded an Islamic organization. He stated that he returned to his Muslim roots when he migrated to Japan, indicating that the hardships he experienced as a migrant caused him to reflect upon Islam and encouraged him to form an Islamic organization with his compatriots. Additionally, many of the women interviewed remarked that their husbands became more observant of religious duties after they got married and had children.

What were the Japanese wives' perceptions of their own newly acquired religious identities after converting to Islam? Many of the women initially believed that conversion was merely a part of the legal marriage arrangement. Nevertheless, a significant number of the women became more religious as time passed. Some of them even began to wear the *hijab* (scarf or veil that Muslim women use to cover their head and the upper part of the body). These were not necessarily due to their Pakistani husbands' influence. Rather, these changes occurred because some of the women formed close ties with other Japanese women who were experiencing "the same circumstances". In the early 1990s, many of the women began to establish connections with other Muslim women in the community by attending Islamic or other classes, such as Urdu language classes. This emergent community of Japanese Muslim women produced three outcomes.

First, the religious gatherings provided the wives with opportunities to share their often painful experiences of marginalization within their own country. For example, the women spoke about their families' strong opposition to their marriage to "Asian foreign workers". The wives also described the discrimination their husbands experienced in the wider society and how their husbands' low status contrasted sharply with that of the Westerners' higher status in the Japanese hierarchically structured image of the "Other". Second, within these gatherings the wives discussed family issues, including the difficulties they experienced when remitting money to Pakistan and the issues involved in raising Muslim children in a non-Islamic environment in Japan. Thus, a network of mutual help was established and feelings of solidarity developed among those who shared their experiences with each other. Third, the discourse of "true Islam" versus "local customs of Pakistan" emerged when women talked about their personal experiences in Japan and Pakistan. For instance, in the women's gatherings that I witnessed in the late 1990s and early 2000s, the wives would frequently question the legitimacy of certain Islamic practices which they had heard from their husbands and in-laws (Kudo 2007). The wives tended to redefine themselves as "converts" who attempted to practise what is written in the Qur'an and the *Hadith*, (records of the words and deeds of the Prophet Muhammad). Some of them believed that they differed from those who were "Muslims by birth" who tended to follow local customs without deeply reflecting on whether or not they were in accord with "true Islam". Such a stance contrasted sharply with the women's previous perceptions of themselves as "paper Muslims" or "Muslims in name only".

The Japanese women's quest for "true Islam" repositioned them within the home as well as in the wider society. Some of them disagreed with the beliefs of their husbands and in-laws about female modesty, which they were expected to follow. For example, in one of the Islamic gatherings for Muslim women attended mostly by wives of Pakistani men and which I attended, one woman remarked, "My husband tells me to keep my hair long. Is that part of Islamic teaching?" In this way, the woman had challenged her husband's request by invoking "true Islam". At the same time, she had questioned the asymmetrical gender relationships that exist between husbands and wives in Pakistani society (Kudo 2007: 19-20). Additionally, some women emphasized that although they had become "Muslim", they had not become "Pakistani" upon marriage.

Negotiating Muslim-ness within the Shifting Contexts of Women's Lives: Child-rearing in the Local Community

Many of the women who were interviewed several years later had stopped visiting mosques on a regular basis. A major reason was the increased interaction with non-Muslims in the local community as a consequence of their children entering school. To nurture their children's Muslim identity in their non-Islamic environment, the women had to negotiate with the non-Muslim majority, including the staff of their children's school, regarding issues such as the special preparation of food and appropriate clothing for female children during physical education classes. In some cases, these requests were regarded as deviations from the norm of cultural homogeneity of the non-Muslim Japanese. More critically, the Japanese mothers had to negotiate their Muslim-ness in ways that were significantly different from that of their "foreign" husbands, whose differences were more easily accepted by Japanese society in general. To facilitate these negotiations, the women resorted to careful modifications of their Islamic practices. For example, some of the women who previously covered their heads either ceased this practice or began to cover their heads more loosely. Nevertheless, they still maintained the importance of Islam despite the changes in their behaviour. When describing their negotiating experiences, they would refer to themselves as "Japanese Muslim" (Kudo 2007: 21–3).

Border-crossings in the Early Stages of Marriage

The Pakistani husbands' acquisition of legal status in Japan meant that they could resume face-to-face relationships with relatives in their home country. As described in Kudo (2007), the families traveled to Pakistan for various purposes, including attending the marriage ceremonies of the husbands' siblings or celebrations of *Eid* (Islamic festivals). For those with self-employed husbands, the families tended to remain in Pakistan longer because the husbands' flexible work schedule enabled them to do so. Some of the Japanese wives and children stayed in Pakistan for a few months before the children reached school age. During their stay, events such as a son's circumcision and other children's life rituals, such as *aqiqa* (sacrifice made on the occasion of the birth of a child), took place. Some of the children also learned to recite the Qur'an from the female members of the household. Hence, the children's religious identities were nurtured across national boundaries.

The lives of the Japanese women who lived with their husbands' joint family members were shaped by the norms of gender segregation that are widely observed among the middle- and lower-middle classes in Pakistan. Therefore, the women normally spent their time at home. Their status within the family was largely determined by seniority and gender, although it was potentially elevated due to their direct and indirect economic contributions through remittances sent from Japan (Kudo 2007, 2008, 2012). Members of the husbands' joint family, particularly the males, were brought to Japan to assist the husbands in their newly established businesses. This joint economic activity played a crucial role in further developing transnational families, as discussed towards the end of this chapter.

Relocation of Mother and Child: Dispersal of the Family across National Boundaries

When the children of Pakistani-Japanese couples approached school age, a new development occurred in the formation of their families across national boundaries. For instance, some of the wives and their children relocated to Pakistan or to a third country while their Pakistani husbands remained in Japan to operate their businesses. In the first round of interviews conducted in 1999, four of the participants were already residing in Pakistan. An additional seven participants relocated to Pakistan later. A variety of motivations contributed to the emergence of this type of transnational dispersal. Most often it involved the husbands' desire to have their children, particularly their daughters, educated in an Islamic environment (Kudo 2012). This desire was linked to religio-cultural notions of female modesty in Pakistani society: upon reaching puberty girls are expected to cover their bodies and be physically segregated from unrelated males. However, the ways in which these gender norms are interpreted and practised within Pakistani society differ significantly depending on factors such as class and region. Another reason for the transnational dispersal of the family was to provide the children with an English language education. Many of the families who moved to Pakistan sent their children to prestigious schools that offered English-mediated learning environments. Although international schools were available in Tokyo, these prestigious schools in Pakistan were much more affordable for the families because they could take advantage of the favorable currency exchange rates between the two countries.

The families sometimes struggled with the decision to relocate abroad. Many of the Japanese mothers were aware of the challenges they would face in Pakistan, such as the limitation on women's physical mobility and the fact that they would have to reside in joint households. They also had concerns about the climate and safety in Pakistan. Furthermore, the women did not necessarily agree with their husbands' point of view that Pakistan was the best place to nurture their children's Muslim identity because some of the Japanese mothers believed "Islamic" practices in Pakistan to be somewhat conflated with local customs. However, the Japanese mothers also faced difficulties in their efforts to raise their children as Muslim in non-Islamic Japan (Kudo 2007, 2008). In addition to the pressure to conform to the prevailing discourse of homogeneity in Japan, no institutional support was available for people who wished to practise Islam because the Japanese educational system had not yet taken steps to meet the needs of children from different religious backgrounds (Hattori 2008: 220). Given these circumstances, the burden of developing their children's Muslim identities fell mainly on the Japanese mothers. Thus, they tended to accept, albeit sometimes reluctantly, migrating to Pakistan or another country.

Evolving Forms of Transnational Families and the Changing Roles of Japanese Wives

For many of the wives, the form of the transnational family described thus far was fluid. The following sections explore the complex trajectories of family-formation across boundaries depicted in Figure 1.2 and show how the roles of the Japanese wives evolved as their life cycle progressed.

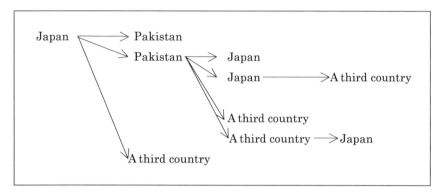

Figure 1.2 Various trajectories of relocation observed among the Japanese wives and their children

Reuniting in Japan: Negotiation within Transnational Households

Although some of the Japanese women who relocated to Pakistan with their children settled there on a long-term basis, others returned to Japan after a few years. Of the 11 Japanese wives and children who relocated to Pakistan, 5 returned to Japan and reunited with their husband.[7] The case study of Mrs. Tayab, one of the wives, illustrates the complex factors that led to such a return. Her case also demonstrates how a husband and wife negotiated and reconciled their differing needs and desires as the process of family formation evolved across national boundaries.

The Case of Mrs. Tayab

Mrs. Tayab and her husband had two daughters and a son. She and her children migrated to Pakistan when the children were very young, while her Pakistani husband stayed in Japan to tend his business. Mrs. Tayab and her children relocated because her husband had a strong desire to have their children educated in an Islamic environment. The overseas move was originally intended to be long-term. However, the family reunited in Japan after a few years. Mrs. Tayab cited various reasons such as the difficulties that women faced when they were outside the home because of the social norm of sexual segregation in Pakistan. She emphasized that in comparison with the freedom that men have in Pakistan, women have very limited mobility. Another reason was the hardships that her children experienced in adjusting to Pakistani schools. In addition, Mrs. Tayab realized that the lifestyle in Pakistan did not necessarily align with the "true" teachings of Islam.

Although her husband was unhappy with her decision to return to Japan, he was placated when he learned that she had learned to recite the Qur'an in Arabic while she was in Pakistan and that, therefore, she now had the ability to teach this to their children. Furthermore, Mrs. Tayab took the children to a nearby mosque on a nightly basis to attend after-school Qur'anic lessons, which further pacified her husband.

After returning to Japan, Mrs. Tayab began working in a local shop on a part-time basis, primarily because it offered flexible work hours that allowed her to fulfill her maternal responsibilities. As the children grew older, she gradually extended her work hours to save money for her children's education. Mrs. Tayab had yet another reason for working. According to her, "It is possible that my earnings allow my daughters and myself to remain in Japan. If my husband had earned enough, and if I did not have to work, I might have succumbed to the pressure to take my daughters to live with the joint family in Pakistan." Although her husband owned a business, he experienced financial difficulties during the ongoing recession. Thus, Mrs. Tayab's earnings contributed significantly to the remittances that the couple regularly sent to the joint family in Pakistan. This situation undoubtedly gave Mrs. Tayab some bargaining power when negotiating with her husband about where their children (particularly their two daughters) would be educated.

Relocating to a Third Country

Of the 40 women interviewed, 4 took up residence in a third country. Interestingly, of these four only one mother and her children moved directly from Japan to a third country. In the three other cases, they initially migrated to Pakistan and before moving to a third country. Of these three, one case involved the mother and her children first moving from Pakistan to a third country before finally returning to Japan after several years abroad. In the remaining two cases, the mother and her children returned to Japan from Pakistan and then moved to a third country.

The third country to which the women and their children moved included the United Kingdom (UK), the United Arab Emirates (Takeshita 2008, 2010), Malaysia and New Zealand. These countries were chosen because they could provide the children with both an Islamic and English education. (Although the UK and New Zealand are not Islamic countries, they have far larger Muslim communities than Japan. Hence, the children could receive Qur'anic lessons from nearby mosques or private teachers.) The women discovered that it was much easier to live in a third country than in Pakistan because the third country tended to have better infrastructure and a milder climate. The third country also allowed the women greater physical mobility, although this varied from place to place. An additional benefit was the women's ability to form an autonomous household, one that was free from the control of the joint family.

To relocate to a third country, the couple mobilized their ethno-religious networks that extended globally (Kudo 2015). This network mobilization is evidenced by the fact that the women who migrated to English-speaking countries resided in areas with significant South Asian and/or Muslim populations. The transnational business connections developed by the husbands also facilitated the initial stage of the settlement of the wives and the children.

While the couples were able to utilize their resources to relocate, sometimes there were obstacles to long-term settlement in the third country. A major obstacle was the difficulty of securing visas for family members who could not meet the country's strict immigration requirements. In one case, the family members were unable to renew their visas, so the wife and children moved to Pakistan and then returned to Japan, where the Pakistani husband resided. In addition to immigration barriers, the women struggled with other problems. They had to operate in an unfamiliar environment using a foreign language (primarily English) without their husbands' assistance. Additionally, some of the women and children encountered racial and religious discrimination. Furthermore, for many of the women the global economic stagnation adversely affected the husbands' businesses, and the cost of living continued to rise in the country to which the families relocated. In fact, financial difficulties deterred the women from visiting Japan. These issues indicate that although the Japanese wives and their Pakistani husbands benefitted from their global networks and resources, they were still unable to freely cross national boundaries.

Various Trajectories of Transnational Family Formation

The patterns of transnational family formation exhibit even greater variety over time. Four cases drawn from recent follow-up interviews highlight these new developments in family formation. In the first case, a joint family was formed in Japan. Initially, the couple arranged for the husband's younger brothers to move to Japan to work. One of the brothers then married a woman from Pakistan and formed a joint household with the Japanese-Pakistani couple in a city outside Tokyo. The Japanese wife advised her Pakistani sister-in-law on work issues and matters related to children's education in Japan. The Pakistani husband's parents were deceased, and his sisters had married and moved out of the family. Therefore, the husband, who had acquired Japanese citizenship, stated that he had "no reason to return home". In the second case, a woman who had resided with her children in Pakistan for nearly a decade returned alone to Japan to care for her aging parents.[8] Although she had a sibling who lived in Japan, she was the only family member who could care for her parents. Consequently, she left her children in the care of the joint family in Pakistan. She noted that had her family been based in Japan, she would not have been able to provide the same full-time care for her parents, as there would have been no one to care for her children on a long-term basis.

In the last two cases, the transnationally dispersed families were reunited in a third country when the husbands joined the wives and children there.[9] This reunion did not necessarily mean that the husbands were able to secure an economic base in the third country. Rather, the husbands were able to relocate because their brothers who were based in Japan continued to operate their used car export business there while the husbands managed the business in the receiving country. In one of these cases, the husband was the eldest son in the family. He continued to oversee economic and other issues that developed within the joint family in Pakistan via frequent phone calls and visits to Pakistan as needed. In both cases, transnational business networks jointly operated by male kin became indispensable in sustaining the economic base of the household that was dispersed across national boundaries.

Conclusion

The following conclusions can be drawn from this research. First, family-forming processes in cross-border marriages consisting of Japanese wives and Pakistani husbands rarely involved a straightforward process in which the spouse from a country in the global south became a citizen of the country in the global North through marriage, and eventually settled there. Rather, the families were formed across national boundaries through various circulatory movements, reflecting the families' attempts to survive shifting socio-economic conditions. Although seemingly contradictory, families dispersed so that they could maintain both their economic base and their family ties. Furthermore, they hoped to nurture their children's Muslim identity by relocating to another country.

Second, various issues were contested within the families. For example, the concept of what it meant to be Muslim was negotiated between husbands and wives. These processes of negotiation were interwoven within changing power relationships that were shaped by the interplay of gender, religion and nationality, as the case of Mrs. Tayab demonstrated.

Third, the apparently flexible and fluid form of family-formation that occurred across national boundaries reflected both the possibilities and the limitations of this type of mixed marriages. Although they could maximize socio-economic and religious resources that extended across national boundaries, these families also struggled to overcome a variety of constraints, including immigration controls, racial and religious discrimination, and economic hardship.

Fourth, the roles of the Japanese wives evolved as their life cycle progressed. Some returned to wage labour in Japan, while others crossed national borders again to assume the responsibility of caring for their aging parents. This added another dimension to the dynamics of transnational family-formation.

Finally, the diverse ways in which these Japanese-Pakistani families formed across national boundaries highlight the varied experiences of the children in these families. Exploring how these children will situate themselves socio-economically in Japan or in transnational spaces and how they will forge their religious identity may shed insights on the ways in which the boundary between "us" and "them" becomes blurred, contested, and possibly reconstituted within Japan and beyond.

Acknowledgement

I would like to express my gratitude to all the participants in my study.

Notes

1. The first round of interviews was done with 40 women, among whom 22 were interviewed for the second round before 2007. I continued to conduct follow-up interviews among key informants after 2007, while also recruiting new interviewees.
2. In Japan, to obtain a spousal visa for a husband a couple must complete marital procedures in accordance with the laws of both countries concerned. This requirement for Japanese who marry Pakistanis includes entering into the religious marriage contract (*nikah*) required by Pakistan. Islam allows a male Muslim to marry "people of the Book", that is, mainly Christians

and Jews. Because the majority of Japanese women are neither Muslim nor "people of the Book", they must convert to Islam to marry Muslim men.
3. In 1999, 4 of the 40 women were residing in Pakistan with their children; the rest were living in the Kanto area of Japan. The number of interviewees living abroad fluctuated since then, as discussed later in the chapter.
4. In this study, I used pseudonyms and changed some personal data to maintain the anonymity of the interviewees.
5. In 1989, the number of arrivals from Pakistan was 7,060 (a reduction of 65 per cent from the previous year). In the following year, the number of arrivals decreased further to 5,544 (MOJ 1989, 1990, 1991).
6. Some acquired Japanese citizenship and are no longer included in the total number of Pakistanis registered in Japan.
7. Of the five cases in which the mothers and the children returned to Japan, three were divorced.
8. In another case, one woman who sent her children to reside with the joint family in Pakistan for educational purposes remarked that she had decided to remain in Japan to care for her aging mother.
9. In 2 of the 11 cases in which Japanese women and children relocated to Pakistan, the husbands later reunited with their wives and children in Pakistan.

References

Cabinet Office, Government of Japan. 2013. *Toward Active Participation of Women as the Core of Growth Strategies: From the 'White Paper on Gender Equality 2013', Summary*. Available at http://www.gender.go.jp/english_contents/about_danjo/whitepaper/pdf/2013-01.pdf [accessed 25 October 2015].

Charsley, Katherine, ed. 2012. *Transnational Marriage: New Perspectives from Europe and Beyond*. New York: Routledge.

Constable, Nicole, ed. 2005. *Cross-Border Marriages: Gender and Mobility in Transnational Asia*. Philadelphia: University of Pennsylvania Press.

Hattori, Mina. 2008. "Self-help Education for Muslims: Practices and Conflicts Relating to Child Education in Nagoya City." In *Indonesian Community in Japan*, ed. Mika Okushima. Tokyo: Akashi Shoten, pp. 215–32.

Japan Immigration Association. 1985–2013. *Statistics on the Foreigners Registered in Japan*. Tokyo: Japan Immigration Association.

Kudo, Masako. 2007. "Becoming the Other in One's Own Homeland? The Processes of Self-construction among Japanese Muslim Women." *Japanese Review of Cultural Anthropology* 8: 3–27.

———. 2008. *An Anthropology of Border-Crossing in Japan: Japanese Wives of Pakistani Muslim Migrants*. Tokyo: University of Tokyo Press.

———. 2012. "Mothers on the Move: Transnational Child-Rearing by Japanese Women Married to Pakistani Migrants." In *Wind Over Water: Migration in an East Asian Setting*, ed. David W. Haines et al. New York: Berghahn Books, pp. 150–60.

———. 2015. "Transnational Families in a Global Circulation Context: The Case of Cross-border Marriages between Japanese Women and Pakistani Migrants." *Bulletin of the National Museum of Ethnology* [Kokuritsu Minzokugaku-hakubutsukan Kenkyu Hokoku] 40(1): 71–84.

Ministry of Education, Culture, Sports, Science and Technology (MOECSST). 2006. *The Report on the Basic Survey on Schools*. Tokyo: Ministry of Finance, Printing Bureau.

Ministry of Health, Labour and Welfare Japan. 2010. *Vital Statistics of Japan*. Tokyo: Health and Welfare Statistics Association. Available at http://www.e-stat.go.jp/SG1/estat/List.do?lid=000001082331 [accessed 30 Nov. 2012].

Ministry of Justice (MOJ). 1989, 1990, 1991. *Annual Report of Statistics on Legal Migrants*. Tokyo: Ministry of Justice.

Sunanta, Sirijit and Leonora C. Angeles. 2013. "From Rural Life to Transnational Wife: Agrarian Transition, Gender Mobility and Intimate Globalization in Transnational Marriages in Northeast Thailand." *Gender, Place & Culture: A Journal of Feminist Geography* 20(6): 699–717.

Suzuki, Nobue. 2005. "Tripartite Desires: Filipina-Japanese Marriages and Fantasies of Transnational Traversal." In *Cross-Border Marriages: Gender and Mobility in Transnational Asia*, ed. Nicole Constable. Philadelphia: University of Pennsylvania Press, pp. 124–44.

Takeshita, Shuko. 2008. "Muslim Families Comprising Pakistani Fathers and Japanese Mothers: Focusing on the Educational Problems of their Children." *Journal of Women of the Middle East and the Islamic World* 6: 202–24.

———. 2010. "Transnational Families among Muslims: The Effect of Social Capital on Educational Strategies." In *Asian Cross-border Marriage Migration*, ed. Wen-Shan Yang et al. Amsterdam: Amsterdam University Press, pp. 221–39.

Wang, Hong-Zen and Hsin-Huang M. Hsiao, eds. 2009. *Cross-border Marriages with Asian Characteristics*. Taipei: Center for Asia-Pacific Area Studies RCHSS.

Williams, Lucy. 2010. *Global Marriage: Cross-Border Marriage Migration in Global Context*. New York: Palgrave Macmillan.

Yang, Wen-Shan et al., eds. 2010. *Asian Cross-border Marriage Migration*. Amsterdam: Amsterdam University Press.

CHAPTER 2

Unintentional Cross-cultural Families: The Diverse Community of Japanese Wives in Shanghai

Chie Sakai

Introduction

Globalization has increased peoples' opportunities to cross national borders and exchange information with other cultures. However, it is difficult to obtain a clear understanding of these exchanges because they are extremely diverse and complex. Currently, women tend to cross national boundaries more frequently than men. Yet in the mid-1980s, several scholars noted that very little research had been done on women's transnational migration experiences (Carstles and Miller 1993; Kofman et al. 2000; Morokvasic 1984). Since then, however, many scholars have studied women's experiences of crossing national boundaries, although only a few have examined women migrating from the developed global north for reasons other than economic necessity. Yet, increasing numbers of migrating women have been observed not only in North America and Europe but also in Asian countries (Piper 2003). Even in Japan, which has relatively few emigrants, the number of Japanese female citizens has exceeded the number of male citizens living abroad since 1999.[1]

Additionally, women's migration experiences tend to be considered less important than those of men. This is because women often move with their family members as mothers, daughters or wives and they are, therefore, considered dependent migrants. Further, women who migrate for work purposes or studies abroad are often considered separately from those who migrate for reasons of marriage or family. Although the distinction between labour migration and family migration is rarely considered when men's migration patterns are discussed, this is not the same for studies on women's migration. In their editorial introduction to *Diversity*, a 2011 UNESCO publication on female migration, Piper and French (2011: 2) state that numerous factors indicate that "women have significantly different migration motivations, patterns, options and obstacles from men".

Marriage migration is considered one of the most feminized types of migration worldwide. In fact, Constable (2005) argues that more women than men migrate after marriage. However, labour migration is usually prioritized over marriage migration when discussing women's migration experiences. This is because female labour migrants contribute to economic, political and social changes in both countries of origin and new countries of residence.

Two reasons are typically given to explain why more women in cross-national marriages migrate beyond their national borders. First, couples in which the partners have different nationalities tend to reside in the husband's native country. This is because women are more often required to accept their family members' decisions and adjust to their husbands' societies and cultures, especially in Japan. However, this tendency is also evident among marriages between people from the same country. Second, because of gender disparities in labour and social roles in the sending countries, women have relatively limited opportunities to migrate, so they tend to marry to go abroad more often than men. Cross-border marriages are, therefore, considered an option for women who desire to leave their countries. Studies on marriage migration have demonstrated that women in developing countries (the so-called global south) tend to marry more affluent men from developed countries to raise their social status, a phenomenon known as "global hypergamy" (Constable 2005; Kamoto 2008).

In Japan, the number of men who marry women from other Asian countries has been increasing. A similar phenomenon has been observed in Taiwan and Korea. However, although they migrate from relatively poor countries, many of these women marry working class men from rural areas in developed countries and are, therefore, not actually "marrying up" or living in affluence (Yokota 2008).

Constable (2005) argues that the concept of "global hypergamy" could be partially applied to marriage migration, provided potential paradoxes are first considered. For example, marriage migration from Japan to China does not clearly comply with this model, as the economic gap between these two countries has been shrinking since the 1990s. In fact, currently little economic difference remains between Japanese and Chinese metropolitan areas. Thus, Japanese-Chinese marriages usually do not result in "hypergamy".

This chapter examines cases of marriage migrants who move between areas with less of a socio-economic gap but are nevertheless at the forefront of the contradictions induced by cross-border marriage migration. It focuses on the types of problems that occur when the spouses in a cross-border marriage share a similar economic status. In particular, it presents data obtained from a study that examined the diverse experiences of Japanese women who married Chinese men and who currently live in Shanghai.

In this chapter, the current context of cross-border marriages is briefly described before focusing on Japanese women who married abroad and their strategies for managing the problems and anxieties caused by their moves.

Data Collection

The primary data collection method used in this study was semi-structured interviews, which were conducted from September 2011 to September 2012 in Shanghai. Each interview lasted from one to three hours. A total of 16 wives were interviewed, 13 of whom were Japanese women married to Chinese men. In addition, there was one Chinese woman married to a Japanese man and two Japanese women married to men from a third country (see Appendix).

The questions I asked each woman in the interviews included how she met her husband and why she decided to marry him; her motivation for moving to Shanghai; and where she intended to live in the future. I encouraged the women to talk freely and did not interrupt their narratives.

The interviewees had differing demographic characteristics because marriages between Japanese women and Chinese men include people of various ages, occupations and networks. It also turned out that a number of the interviewees were acquainted with other Japanese women with Chinese husbands or with mothers of children growing up in families with multi-cultural backgrounds.

It was unrealistic to conduct a quantitative survey. Mixed methods (including the triangulation method) which involve multiple approaches and collaborators, were used instead to recruit interviewees for the study (Denzin 2010, 2012), resulting in a relatively diverse group. First, I recruited five women who had participated in previous studies which I conducted between 2004 and 2009. These studies focused on Japanese women who had moved to Shanghai on their own initiative and worked in local companies or were self-employed entrepreneurs. Some of the interviewees in those studies were married to Chinese men. I contacted them via email and asked them to share their experiences once again, this time focusing on their marriage- and family-based decisions. In addition, I asked several previous interviewees, married and unmarried, to introduce me to their friends and colleagues who were married to Chinese men. Some provided their friends' contact information while others introduced me to their friends in person (Method 1 in Appendix). I distributed questionnaires among the cross-cultural couples living in Shanghai with the help of one of my participants. The aim of the survey was to collect basic information about and understand the attributes of people with spouses of different nationalities. This information was used identify interviewees for the current study as well as to formulate questions for the interview.

It was challenging to analyze the survey results because of the limited number of responses and only a few of the survey respondents were eligible for this study. For example, some of the respondents were men; others had spouses who were not Chinese. Although the questionnaire results were not directly used in this study, some of the women who had completed the survey volunteered to be interviewed. In addition, some of them distributed questionnaires through the *Laopohui* (Chinese for "the wives' club") mailing list, an association of Japanese women with Chinese husbands (Method 2 in Appendix). Some of the interviewees introduced me to their friends or brought a friend to the interview. I met five additional interviewees in this manner. However, two of them had husbands who were not Chinese (Method 3 in Appendix). Finally, I interviewed a Chinese woman who had married a Japanese man while she was living in Japan but she subsequently moved to Shanghai like the other female Japanese interviewees (Method 4 in Appendix). Most of the interviews were recorded with the interviewee's permission. However, some of the interviews conducted in informal settings were not recorded. Most of the interviews were conducted one-on-one, but focus groups were also held involving two or three participants at a time.

Cross-border Marriage between Japanese Women and Chinese Men

Marrying and starting a family are usually considered extremely personal decisions, but the decision to move to a different country and form a dual-nationality family is usually socio-economically motivated. Marriages between Japanese and Chinese citizens are no exception. Though neighbours, Japan and China did not have a diplomatic relationship until 1972. Since the 1980s, when China adopted an open-door economic policy, Japanese manufacturers have been seeking to diversify offshore, where labour costs are lower. In addition, in the 1980s, an increasing number of Chinese citizens went abroad to study and work. One of their destinations was Japan.

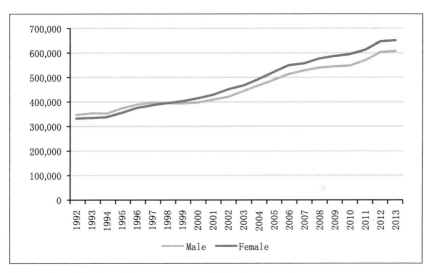

Figure 2.1 Number of Japanese nationals living abroad

Source: Ministry of Foreign Affairs, 1995–2013.[2]

Figure 2.1 shows that the number of Japanese citizens living overseas has increased since the 1990s. It also shows that the number of Japanese women living abroad has exceeded the number of Japanese men since 1999, especially in Oceania, North America and Western Europe. Particularly in neighbouring countries in Asia the number of resident Japanese males is still 60 per cent of the total number of all Japanese residents (Figure 2.2). The number of female Japanese residents in Asia has risen more than three-fold since the early 1990s. This growth rate in Asia was second to that in Oceania. Compared to Oceania, North

America and Western Europe, the Japanese community in Asia is still male dominated. However, the growth rate in the number of Japanese female residents in Asia has been as fast as the number of Japanese male residents (Figure 2.3).

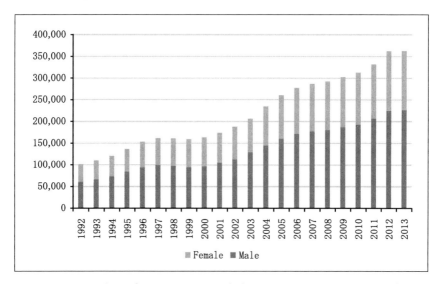

Figure 2.2 Number of Japanese nationals living in Asian countries, excluding Japan
Source: Ministry of Foreign Affairs, 1992–2013 (Upper: women, Lower: men).

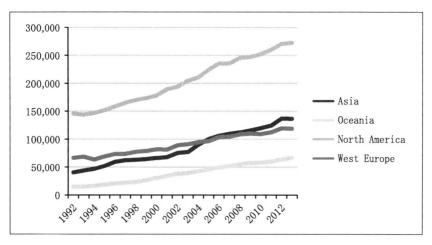

Figure 2.3 Number of female Japanese nationals living in foreign countries
Source: Ministry of Foreign Affairs, 1992–2013.

Currently, more than 650,000 Chinese nationals live in Japan (Ministry of Justice 2013), and approximately 135,000 Japanese nationals live in China (Ministry of Foreign Affairs in Japan 2014). In 1972, only 994 Chinese citizens migrated to Japan; however, this figure rose to more than 100,000 in 1985. A decade later, the number of Japanese residents in Hong Kong also rapidly increased. This trend has since continued in other large Chinese cities. In 2013, 64,000 Japanese citizens resided in Shanghai and the surrounding area, creating in Shanghai the fourth largest Japanese community abroad after Los Angeles, New York and London.

Relatively few Japanese women marry Chinese men; more Japanese men marry Chinese women.[3] The vital statistics published by the Japanese Ministry of Health, Labour and Welfare (2013) show that marriages between Japanese women and foreign men constitute 1 per cent of marriages annually. Further, Japanese women tend to marry Western men, such as Americans, Australians and Britons (Kamoto 2008). Figure 2.4 shows that Japanese men typically marry Asian women from countries such as China and the Philippines. However, Japanese women typically marry U.S. citizens and Koreans,[4] which prompted Kelsky (2001) to state that Japanese women's "occidental longings" have a long history dating back to the late nineteenth century. Nevertheless, only a few studies have focused on marriages between Japanese women and Asian men of

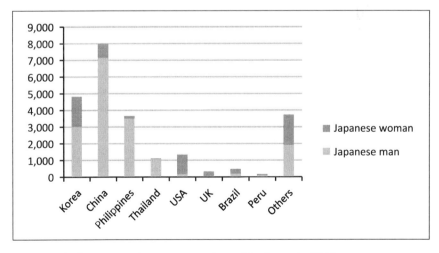

Figure 2.4 International marriages registered in Japan in 2012
Source: Ministry of Health, Labour and Welfare, 2013.

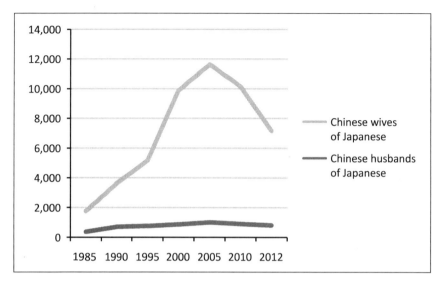

Figure 2.5 Marriages between Japanese and Chinese citizens
Source: Ministry of Health, Labour and Welfare, 2013.

other nationalities.[5] Figure 2.5 shows that in 2012 the number of Japanese women with a Chinese husband was less than 1,000. However, this number has been increasing steadily, while the number of Japanese men in such relationships has decreased by as much as 40 per cent.

Reasons for Moving to China

Japanese women who married abroad tend to migrate accidentally and individually. Since the mid-1980s, an increasing number of people have been migrating between China and Japan. Female marriage migrants are usually categorized as "dependents" in government statistics,[6] despite their participation in multiple decision-making processes in their country of origin and their cultural and economic contributions in their adopted society. Although family migration is considered a personal decision, it reflects differences in norms between the sending and receiving countries.

All 16 of the women interviewed resided in Shanghai. For purposes of analysis, they were broadly divided into three groups based on their marriage and migration dates. The first group (G1) included women who met and married their husbands in Japan before moving to Shanghai. The second group (G2) included women who moved to Shanghai or another Chinese city alone, and met then married their husbands there.

The third group (G3) included women who met their husbands in a third country, such as a country in Europe or Australia, and together they moved to Shanghai. G1 consisted of six women, including one Chinese woman, who married in Japan and subsequently moved to Shanghai between 1996 and 2011. G1 interviewees had all been married for more than 10 years at the time of the interviews. G2 consisted of seven women who moved to Shanghai or Beijing alone to work or study in China. Two of these women moved to China (particularly Shanghai and Beijing) in the 1990s, and five moved to Shanghai during the 2000s. In addition, two women, including one woman whose husband is not Chinese, met their husbands outside of China (United Kingdom and Australia) and moved to China with their husbands between 2002 and 2007. One of these women met her husband in Germany and then returned to Japan because of her husband's work. The couple eventually moved to Shanghai in 2002. Though the decision to go abroad was originally made by these women independently, the decision to move to China was made by their husbands.

Of the 16 interviewees, 13 moved to Shanghai in the 2000s. While this large cohort is indicative of the increasing migration between the two countries, it is also a sampling bias. This is because the Chinese economy grew at a record-setting rate in the late 1990s. Consequently, many Japanese citizens involved in the service industry, real estate, education, and the restaurant and retail sectors moved to Shanghai. China's economic boom and its growing Japanese community made it easier for Japanese citizens to live in China. Therefore, more Japanese labour migrants moved to China and more Japanese companies employed Chinese nationals, which increased the possibility of encounters between Japanese and Chinese citizens.

Couples Who Met in Japan

Among the couples who met in Japan (G1), the decision to move to Shanghai was made primarily by the husband. Most of the husbands had lived in Japan for several years but they decided to leave because of employment opportunities in Shanghai. While the wives' motivations for migrating to China were similar, their responses to the decision to move were diverse. Some Japanese wives accepted the decision to move to China unquestioningly; others were taken aback by it. Almost all of the couples that met and married in Japan viewed their marriage as indistinguishable from that of other Japanese couples. The husbands spoke

Japanese fluently, and most had once worked in Japan. When the family was residing in Japan, the language typically spoken within the family was Japanese. The husbands usually held permanent Japanese resident visas. One of the interviewees indicated that her husband had become a naturalized Japanese citizen, and another interviewee mentioned that naturalization was common among the Shanghai couples she was acquainted with. Sometimes Japanese parents demanded that a Chinese fiancé become a naturalized Japanese citizen before marrying their daughter. The children born to these couples in Japan only have Japanese citizenship. One couple's children were born in China, but the parents chose to give them Japanese citizenship.[7]

Some of the interviewees who had married in Japan were positive about the move to Shanghai, though others had made the move reluctantly. This difference in attitude was strongly correlated with the reason the husband provided for the move to China. The husbands of those who were positive about the decision to move had quit their jobs in Japan and immediately found new employment in Shanghai, thus enabling their wives to launch their own new lives after the move. The interviewees who viewed the move more negatively had husbands who had been assigned to work in branches of Japanese companies in China. In these cases, the family typically had little time to prepare for the move. Generally, these men who are assigned to work overseas do not have a say as to where they will work nor do they generally have the option to refuse the move. Chisako,[8] one of the interviewees, mentioned that her husband received a letter from his company informing him about his transfer to Shanghai only one month before the move; thus, there was no opportunity to fully discuss her feelings about the move. She and their children followed her husband a year later. In the case of Eriko, another interviewee, the news of the move was totally unexpected. She accused her husband of disrespecting her wish to continue to live in Japan. She is convinced that he negotiated with his company to return to China without consulting her.

The sudden decision to move to China upset these Japanese wives. Moving to an unfamiliar society radically changed their lives. For one thing, they had to quit jobs that they had exerted great effort to maintain after marrying and having children. However, the move was a welcome opportunity for the Chinese husband to return to his home country; he knew the language well and had a useful local network there. Itsuko, another interviewee, moved to Shanghai without her Chinese husband, who was a naturalized Japanese citizen and an employee in a Japanese company in Japan. Itsuko did not intend to move to Shanghai. However, in 2011, an earthquake and tsunami hit north-eastern Japan, causing a major nuclear accident at the Fukushima power plant. Itsuko's husband was concerned that their children would be affected by radioactive contamination and asked her and their children to move to Shanghai. Itsuko opposed this idea because she did not consider radioactive contamination from Fukushima a serious threat, as their home was far from the site of the disaster. Nevertheless, she eventually agreed with him and moved to a location near his parents' house.

Couples Who Met in China

The women who met their husbands in China (G2) more frequently moved to Shanghai or another Chinese city, such as Beijing, to study Chinese. Two of the interviewees moved to China in the 1990s and five others did so during the 2000s, when the number of Japanese residents in China was rapidly increasing. Most of them attended Chinese language schools when they first moved to China, and all except one found employment as a locally hired worker[9] in a Japanese company. Each became acquainted with a male Chinese colleague or customer and subsequently married in China. One interviewee met her husband while attending a language school in Beijing, and another met her husband while working as a Japanese language instructor at a university in Shanghai. Another interviewee met and married a man, who was neither Japanese nor Chinese, in Shanghai while she was studying Chinese. The most distinguishing feature of this group was that these women decided to move to China of their own accord, and unlike the women in the other two groups, who moved to Shanghai because of their spouses' decisions, these women were interested in China, the Chinese language and Chinese culture before meeting their husbands.

Couples Who Met Abroad

The third group (G3) consisted of women who met their husbands abroad. These women had left Japan to study in Europe or Australia. In Japan, women tend to go to western countries, particularly English-speaking countries, for studies abroad. However, an increase in the number of young, single women moving to China or other Asian countries for the same purpose has recently been observed. For instance, one of the three women in this group was in her forties. She had gone to Germany in 1987, where she married a Chinese man and had a child. In 1996, the couple moved to Japan with their infant and eventually moved to Shanghai in 2002. The other two women in G3 were in their thirties. One met a Chinese man in England while completing a Master's degree in linguistics. Another met her Australian husband while studying in Australia.[10] Both couples moved to Shanghai because their husbands found employment there. The women in G3 did not choose to move to China with their husbands, nor did they share an interest in China. Like the women in the G1, they accepted their husband's decision to move to China; however, they felt that their decision to live abroad had been a personal one.

Difficulty of Obtaining a Chinese Work Visa

Though their husbands are Chinese, the Japanese women who were interviewed confronted many challenges in Shanghai. They had to adjust to a new social environment and help their children adapt. They also had difficulty finding paid employment. Thirteen of the interviewees had Chinese spouses, but the types of visas they themselves held varied according to their own employment status. The spouses and children of Chinese citizens can apply for an L visa to visit relatives, but unlike those holding spousal visas in Japan, L visa holders in China are not allowed to work. If the non-Chinese spouses of Chinese citizens wish to seek employment in China, they must apply for the same work permit visa as other foreign nationals, namely the Z visa. While L visa holders who are spouses of Chinese citizens must renew their visas annually,[11] some interviewees mentioned that their children, who are Japanese citizens with a Chinese father, only had to renew their visas bi-annually.

In 2004, the Chinese government established a permanent residency system known as the "Chinese green card". Under this system, spouses of Chinese citizens who have lived in China for longer than five years can apply for a green card. Some of the interviewees had already obtained one. The green card is more efficient and less troublesome than an L or Z visa. However, green card holders are still required to renew them every ten years.[12]

Reluctance to Work in China

The strict Chinese immigration laws prevented several Japanese wives from taking up formal employment. In fact, most of those who joined their husbands in Shanghai were unemployed. Large Japanese companies abroad typically prefer the wives of their male employees to be full-time homemakers and usually pay an additional family allowance to compensate for the wives' lost income. The interviewees who were full-time employees in Japan often gave up their careers reluctantly. One of them, Chisako, worked as a public relations officer before moving to Shanghai. Her job was the reason she hesitated to move to China with her husband. She remained uncomfortable with her new role as a full-time homemaker. Below is her account of this experience.

> I did not want to move to China. We used to be a dual-income family, and I thought I was definitely not going to quit my job.... Our children went to a day-care centre after my return to work from maternity leave, but I was unwell after giving birth to our second child when my husband was transferred to Shanghai. I returned to work for a while, but I felt I was out of my depth. Therefore, the move was actually well timed, and I quit that job as soon as it was possible....I suddenly stopped working, and I did not expect to be out of work, but I was exhausted after I did, and I therefore stayed with our children for a year....When I got married, I told the person who acted as our matchmaker at our wedding that I would never quit my job, and I, therefore, still have not fully accepted that I eventually quit. I enjoyed working in an organization, as well as working as part of a team. Compared to employment that finishes at five o'clock, domestic chores are never-ending.

It was difficult for the Japanese wives to find jobs in Shanghai because of visas, their lack of language skills and their limited knowledge of Chinese culture. Thus, those who moved to China after marriage usually started learning Chinese after their move to Shanghai. For instance, Chisako studied basic Chinese for a year. Further, although compared to Japanese homemakers with Japanese husbands, the women interviewees had numerous opportunities to interact with local Chinese people. Nevertheless, the acculturation process has not been easy. Below Chisako states why she currently does not want to work in China.

> If I start working here, I think I would need to acquire more language skills. Actually, I do not work here because there are numerous differences between China and Japan. For example, people frequently fail to respect appointments and promises here.

Another interviewee, Eriko, also quit her job before moving to Shanghai. She said that she had been working in Japan after her children were born and she could have continued working had she stayed there. However, Eriko felt that she had to protect her children from culture shock brought on by their move to Shanghai; hence, she stopped working before moving there.

In 2010, Eriko, worked as an assistant convention guide at the Shanghai World Expo and thoroughly enjoyed the experience. She worked with several Japanese women, approximately 20 of whom remained in Shanghai to work after the expo. Most of them were young, single women. Eriko praised their openness and bravery, but she was not keen to follow their example.

Marrying a Steady-income Husband and Forming a Single-income Household

The Japanese women who married in Japan regarded the decision to marry a Chinese man in Shanghai a risky decision. They argued that Japanese women should avoid marrying local men in China who were unable to earn as much as their Japanese counterparts, otherwise these wives would not be able to return to Japan. Itsuko, who was comfortable being a full-time homemaker, mentioned that she had never heard of Japanese wives with paid employment in Shanghai. When Eriko mentioned the approximately 20 Japanese women who continued to work in Shanghai after the World Expo, the interviewees' reactions were varied. Whereas Eriko praised these women for their positive attitudes, Itsuko believed that they should return to Japan as soon as possible. She asserted that locally employed staff of Japanese companies in China earned approximately CNY10,000 per month (USD1,600). It would be difficult to live in Shanghai on such a low salary, she said, and unless Japanese women married someone with a higher salary, they may not have the financial means to return to Japan if they stayed in China too long.

Masako, another interviewee who has been a full-time homemaker since her marriage also held a similar view. She and her husband met in Beijing in the early 1990s. He was originally from Hong Kong. She was studying Chinese and he was managing his family's business in Beijing. After their marriage, Masako complied with his decision to move. Before moving to Shanghai, they had lived in Hong Kong and Chengdu. In Shanghai, she decided to stay at home as a full-time mother and homemaker. Masako reckoned that few of the Japanese wives who were in paid employment held jobs out of necessity. As for herself, she thought that she did not need to do so.

Generally in Japan, the norms governing the gender division of household roles have changed considerably. Thus, the younger interviewees were not averse to formal employment, though they believed that the husband should be the main breadwinner. Yoshiko and her husband met while they were studying abroad. She worked as a Japanese language instructor at a university when she first moved to Shanghai. Before they married, her fiancé was still looking for a job; thus, she needed to keep her job so that she could qualify for a visa to stay in Shanghai. She worked at the university for a year and a half, but when her employer told her to move to a different school,[13] she decided to quit her job and marry her fiancé to obtain an L-visa. After leaving her teaching position, she obtained a certificate to teach Chinese tea ceremony, which she taught to Japanese homemakers. In addition, she taught Japanese to a father at her daughter's kindergarten; she also planned to teach English to Japanese children. Yoshiko stated that she loved spending time with her daughter; she did not intend to work and instead prioritized her role as a mother. Her daughter was attending a kindergarten, where the mothers were expected to collect their children in the early afternoon. She did not want her daughter to go to a day-care centre with longer hours nor to hire a nanny. She regarded her husband as the primary source of income in the family, though she could work as a skilled teacher.

Working in Shanghai

Despite the difficulties they encountered, many of the Japanese wives eventually found jobs in Shanghai. Although they had moved to Shanghai to accompany their husbands, some of the interviewees obtained formal employment several years after their arrival there. These women expected a long-term stay in China because their husbands' primary source of employment was in China. Namiko, who moved to Shanghai in the mid-1990s, at first helped her husband manage his newly established company. She also established a consulting firm for Japanese business owners interested in investing in new branches or factories, and this endeavour gradually became more important to her. In addition, she created an association for Japanese women working in Shanghai, which meets several times each year. Yasuko and Risako also found employment after learning basic Chinese. Yasuko worked as a freelance Japanese instructor, and Risako formed a partnership with an old acquaintance. Risako explained her situation as follows:

> When we moved to Shanghai, our daughter was in the first grade. We sent our two-year-old son to a kindergarten, and both children stayed at school until five o'clock. Therefore, after attending Chinese language classes for half a year, I had nothing to do, except to have lunch with other Japanese wives in Shanghai. When I became bored, one of my German friends asked me to help set up a new branch of their business in Shanghai. I accepted her offer and started working. Those who worked in Shanghai had been working most of their adult lives, but admitted that the primary household income was their husbands'. Nevertheless, their personal preference was to continue working. While we were living in Germany, it was common for women who had children to return to work after their maternity leave.
>
> Several women selected shorter working hours. However, upon returning to Japan, I realized that the majority of my husband's colleagues' wives were full-time homemakers, and it seemed strange to them that that I still wanted to work despite my husband earning a sufficient income.... In Japan, we often think that women should not work outside the home because it would not be good for the children. This situation affected my husband and he asked me why I had to work... In China, his mother and sisters are all working and women in Shanghai tend to think that it is boring to stay at home or that staying at home is like playing. My husband sometimes says that my income only covers the cost of gifts to my Japanese relatives, but I do not want to quit, and he does not ask me to do that.

In addition, an increasing number of Japanese women are marrying local Mainland Chinese men and working full-time after their marriages. Taeko studied Chinese for two years because she thought one year of study would not make her proficient enough in Chinese to work in Shanghai. She also worked as a part-time translator while studying in Beijing, where she had a Chinese man for a colleague. They moved to Shanghai together and married several years later. Another interviewee, Ayako, quit her job after working in Japan for three years. She studied Chinese for six months in Shanghai and began working at a Japanese company, where she met her husband. Most of the interviewees who followed this path did not change their lifestyles and kept their Z visas (work visas). If they had quit their jobs, they would have had to apply for an L visa. Sachiko, for example, quit her job after giving birth to her first child. She wanted to breastfeed and care for the baby herself. After the child's first birthday, she resumed work. She mentioned that her income was essential to their household and that she did not intend to quit her job.

The women who had worked in Japan prior to moving to China provided various reasons for their move. Many had considered their lives in Japan at an impasse because they were not expected to seek promotions or assume greater responsibilities in their workplaces. They also mentioned that in Japan it would have been difficult to raise children while working. In China, it is common for women to continue working after marrying and having children. However, because of the lack of government support for working mothers,[14] they are forced to hire an *amah* (domestic help) or rely on their parents-in-law for childcare. Hanako's case exemplifies this situation. Her son's primary caregivers were her in-laws, although she got the impression that they did not like to let her take care of him anyway. On the weekends, she sometimes went on excursions with her son without them. She added that conflicts often arose over him, but because she was far from her own parents, she had to rely on her in-laws.

Taking Care of Children in a Multicultural Environment

Regardless of whether or not a mother was engaged in paid employment, the parents' priority was to raise their children without outside assistance. Because the women's experiences in Japan differed from their husbands' and in-laws', their approaches to parenting often differed. For example, a diverse selection of schools is available in Shanghai. In choosing which school to put the children, schools must be compared and their relative benefits discussed with the Chinese family. Masako mentioned that her children and those of several of her friends had attended several different schools. However, it was not always possible to transfer to a new school because it was extremely challenging to switch the children to a different language of instruction halfway through their education. Thus, these mothers had to decide early on as to whether their children would be educated in Japanese, Chinese or English. In the end, eight of the interviewees chose to educate their children in Japanese, five in English and two in Chinese schools. One interviewee had a toddler; she was still in the process of selecting the most appropriate school. These choices reflected the interviewees' own perspectives on the schools and they were indicative of their intention to either stay in China or return home. It also showed their concern for the children's sense of belonging.

Educating Children in Japanese Schools

The majority of the interviewees (8) selected a Japanese education for their children. They expressed two main reasons for this choice. First, they considered it a more appropriate option for their children because they would eventually return to Japan. Second, some of them believed that Japanese schools offered a better education than Chinese schools, regardless of whether the parents intended to return to Japan or not. Shanghai has one of the largest Japanese schools in the world. The school has approximately 3,000 students who are educated in two elementary schools and one junior high school.[15] In addition, in 2011, the first Japanese high school was established for students who had finished their compulsory education. The Japanese school is the centre of the Japanese community, and numerous institutions and facilities have been established for Japanese residents near these schools, including the Japanese Embassy, high-rise apartment buildings whose tenants are almost exclusively Japanese, supermarkets, preparatory schools for Japanese entrance exams, a piano school and a ballet studio for Japanese children.

The Japanese schools are designed to offer an education similar to that available in Japan, which motivated interviewees who planned to return to Japan to select a Japanese school. The curriculum complies with Japanese teaching guidelines, and most of the teachers are from Japan. Chisako and Itsuko planned to return to Japan after their oldest children had taken the high school entrance exams, even if this decision was against their husbands' wishes. Itsuko had recently moved from an apartment near her in-laws to one closer to the Japanese schools to ease the burden of commuting to and from the school and the preparatory school everyday. She mentioned that she was unconcerned about her child's exams because the prep school managed the entire process. Chisako had intended to return to Japan as soon as her older son entered junior high school, but because her husband was still working in Shanghai, she changed her plans and decided to stay in Shanghai for three more years. Her primary consideration in selecting their children's school was to educate them in an environment that would effectively prepare them to return to Japan and re-adjust there easily. Other interviewees selected Japanese schools because they regarded these schools as an excellent option for their children. Several interviewees also wanted to mitigate the cultural shock their children might experience in school. Some of the children had moved to Shanghai as reluctantly as their mothers. Living in a foreign country was stressful for them, regardless of whether the country was the homeland of one of their parents. The following is Itsuko's account.

> For my husband, China is his homeland, and although he lived in Japan for 20 years and hardly ever went back. He still considers China a wonderful place. He had told our children about the beauty of China and they believed him, but the area we moved to in Shanghai did not fit his descriptions. People's manner and the environment outside our apartment near their grandparents' home were completely different from our home in Japan. It was therefore quite challenging for them.

Generally, most of the Japanese students in China are children of Japanese assigned workers employed by Japanese companies, but the number of students with at least one non-Japanese parent has increased. Some interviewees mentioned that the Chinese education system laid too much emphasis on competition, which worried their husbands. They therefore discussed several options but eventually decided that their children should attend a Japanese school, even if they did not have specific plans to return to Japan. Xiaoli, a Chinese woman from Shanghai who married a Japanese man while attending graduate school in Tokyo, moved to Shanghai in 2010 because her husband changed jobs. She also selected a Japanese school for their 9-year-old daughter. Although her daughter understood casual conversation in Chinese and Shanghainese,[16] Xiaoli regarded her daughter's identity as Japanese, and she was convinced that her daughter would not adjust well to a local Chinese elementary school. She commented,

> I thought her Chinese writing, reading and grammatical skills would not be on par with Chinese children of her age, especially if we selected a school with a good reputation. My daughter attended a local school in Shanghai for a while, and she therefore knew that Chinese schools usually give students a lot of homework. In addition, she was unhappy with the school lunches and bathrooms. Given all these circumstances, I believed it would be difficult for her to have a good time in a local school.

Interviewees with young children said that only Japanese kindergartens taught children proper manners, which convinced them to choose a Japanese education for their children. Yoshiko selected a Japanese kindergarten for her daughter after visiting Japanese, English and international kindergartens. She had studied English from an early age and initially believed that it was more appropriate for her daughter to attend an international school. However, her husband preferred Japanese schools because he considered discipline to be vital to a child's early education. She agreed with her husband because some of the local kindergartens she visited did not make a favourable impression.

> When I visited some local English schools and kindergartens, I noticed that several kids were inconsiderate towards others' feelings, and I thought that it might be because they were from wealthy families and they were spoiled. In Japanese kindergartens, teachers encouraged the kids to share their toys and clear up after playing. In local or international kindergartens, teachers approved of the "first come, first served" rule and hired cleaners to clean and arrange the toys. I therefore believed that a Japanese kindergarten was a more appropriate fit for my daughter.

However, the wives' expectations of the Japanese schools were not fully realized. First, children still experienced culture shock, even though the schools' environments resembled those of Japanese schools. Chisako's son was extremely depressed because he could not play with his friends in the park after school. Japanese parents do not allow their children to play outside because it could be dangerous, so the children have to spend much time indoors. In addition, the interviewees' children had to endure the frequent and painful experience of losing friends who moved back to Japan earlier than they, because unlike these friends, their Chinese fathers tended to stay in China longer than their Japanese colleagues.[17] Furthermore, the children could not plan for their future when their parents did not intend to return to Japan. Students in Japanese schools usually attend university in Japan because Japanese is their primary language.

Attending a Chinese School and a Mother's Struggle to Maintain her Child's Japanese Language Proficiency

Only two of the interviewees sent their children to Chinese schools. In both families, the Chinese father took the initiative to ensure that his children received a Chinese education. His wife, Kazuko, had been living in China for more than 20 years and spoke Chinese fluently. She had a full-time job and employed Chinese domestic help. Thus, Chinese became the family's home language, although her husband could speak Japanese because he had lived in Japan for seven years. Kazuko was concerned about her daughter's Japanese language development because she would have to communicate in Japanese with her maternal grandparents when they visited them in Japan. Kazuko considered sending her daughter to a Japanese school, but her husband considered their daughter as Chinese, despite her Japanese citizenship. He thus insisted on sending her to a Chinese school. However, Kazuko considered sending her daughter to a Japanese language school.

In Eriko's case, the daughter was sent to a Chinese school. When the family moved to Shanghai from Japan, Eriko's husband decided that their 3-year-old daughter should attend a Chinese kindergarten. Eriko wanted her daughter to attend a Japanese school, but she eventually agreed. The daughter's kindergarten teachers requested that the family speak Chinese at home, so since then Eriko's husband had been speaking Chinese with their daughter. Eriko continued to converse with her daughter in Japanese to maintain her Japanese language ability. However, when she returned after six months of receiving medical treatment in Japan, her daughter had lost her Japanese language proficiency. In Eriko's words,

> After living apart from my daughter for six months, she became a Chinese girl. She always spoke in Chinese; she had forgotten her Japanese. One day I said something to her in Japanese. She turned to her father and asked what I was saying, which shocked me.

Eriko realized that she would have to make an effort to develop her daughter's Japanese proficiency, so she enrolled her in after-school Japanese classes once a week. In addition, she sent her daughter to a Japanese summer school near her parents' home.

Both women who put their children in a Chinese school felt the need to improve their children's Japanese language skills, but their husbands were indifferent to this issue.

Providing Children with the Opportunity to Go Beyond China and Japan

For the parents who planned to send their children to a university outside of Japan, a Japanese primary school was not the best option. This is because children with a Japanese-only education have fewer opportunities to continue their studies outside of Japan because of their limited English. In addition, children who are not Chinese nationals are treated as foreign students in China, even if they had completed their formal education in China. Consequently, one-third of the interviewees sent their children to an international program at a Chinese school or to an international school where classes were taught in English, so that they would have the option to study in countries other than Japan and China. Interviewees who themselves had been educated in English were typically indifferent to the idea of returning to Japan. Their husbands who owned their own companies or who worked as co-managers of their own businesses were similarly unconcerned about being transferred to another branch in a different country without being consulted first, Additionally, some of the husbands did not speak Japanese, so they did not consider returning to Japan as a viable option. The interviewees in this group expressed several concerns. First, because numerous English education options existed it was difficult to make a choice; hence, they desperately needed information to help them select a school. Second, they felt compelled to maintain and develop their children's Japanese language abilities. Third, universities in the United States, Australia and Europe are more expensive than those in Japan and China.

Masako mentioned that not all families could afford to send their children to study abroad, but it was also challenging to take courses in several different languages. In addition, students attending an international program in a Chinese school communicated with each other in Chinese, so they were not as proficient in English as the students attending international schools or those who had been educated in English-speaking countries. Therefore, some of the interviewees had decided to transfer their children to international schools or to schools in English-speaking countries. Nevertheless, these options were extremely expensive. To facilitate the sharing of information about schools in Shanghai, the interviewees established a network that included mothers of Japanese children and Japanese-Chinese couples. Masako was a leading member of this group before her family moved to Australia for her children's education.

Changing Relationships with Chinese Society

In this study, the diverse experiences of women in international marriages who were living in Shanghai were analyzed. The women had lived in this city for a period 2 to 15 years or more, during which their lives and relationships with Chinese people and society at large tended to change drastically. The interviewees who considered their stay in the city to be short-term and who had aligned their identities and affiliations with the Japanese community did not regard themselves as typical Japanese mothers. For one thing, their lifestyles were different from those in other Japanese families, even if their Chinese husbands worked in Japanese companies and their children attended Japanese schools. They got together with their in-laws at least once a month, and they had limited knowledge of Chinese society. For example, they used public transport, such as buses, and they did not agree with Japanese mothers who deemed public buses dirty and dangerous. In addition, some Japanese wives felt that they were different from Chinese mothers. In Itsuko's words,

> My children and I always discussed the lunch boxes students brought every day to the Japanese school. We could tell a mother's nationality based on the lunch. Japanese mothers created beautiful lunches and they all included the same items that were popular among Japanese housewives in Shanghai. Chinese mothers put stir-fried meals on rice.... I asked my children what nationality our lunches were. They said that their lunches were in-between, because they were sometimes like the other Japanese kids' lunches, but some dishes that were prepared by their grandmother were completely Chinese.

Just like her children's school lunches, Itsuko also experienced her family as being in the middle. Some interviewees lived with or near their in-laws, which strengthened their relationship with Chinese people. However, the mother-in-law did the household chores, such as cooking, cleaning and caring for the grandchildren for them, the interviewees experienced cultural dissonance. They realized that they needed this help, yet there were differences in the Japanese and Chinese ways of doing things that they found difficult to reconcile. Nevertheless, they sought ways to reduce the tension between themselves and their in-laws. Ayako was thankful for her mother-in-law's assistance when she gave birth to her first child in Shanghai, although Chinese traditions, such as the taboo on washing hair for a month after childbirth, perplexed her. Since moving to Shanghai, Yasuko had accepted living with her in-laws, but she still preferred to eat a simple breakfast, such as bread and tea, with her daughter and husband rather than eating a Chinese breakfast with her in-laws.

Most of the interviewees strongly identified themselves as Japanese, although some regarded their children differently. Chisako sent her children to a Japanese school, but the protagonist of an animated Japanese movie who had half-human, half-wolf children forced her to reflect on her situation. Other interviewees whose children attended Chinese schools, such as Kazuko and Eriko, considered their children more Chinese than Japanese. Kazuko always encouraged her daughter to describe herself as both Japanese and Chinese rather than as exclusively Chinese. Except for those who intended to return to Japan and whose children attended Japanese schools, the remaining interviewees did not expect their children to live in Japan, though almost all of them had Japanese citizenship.[18] Interviewees worried that if their children did not learn to speak proper Japanese, it might be difficult to renew their Japanese passports. Thus, they insisted on speaking in Japanese at home.

At the time of the interviews, Japanese residents in Shanghai were becoming increasingly concerned about political tensions between Japan and China. In September 2012, the Japanese government nationalized uninhabited islands known as the "Senkaku Islands" in Japan and the "Diaoyu Islands" in China, which precipitated a politically tense situation. It was rumoured that a group of Chinese people had physically attacked several Japanese residents in Shanghai in protest, prompting the Japanese school to temporarily close on 18 September, the date of the Manchurian Incident. This particular group of Chinese people were unhappy with the Japanese government's move and with public opinion in Japan. However, they also disagreed with the Chinese government's approach to the conflict.

Some interviewees worried that their children might feel anxious about the situation, given their Japanese connection. Others indicated that their families discussed the situation. One interviewee told me that she was glad when her husband switched off the TV when it was covering the territorial dispute. Their family usually watched a TV show about the Sino-Japanese war at suppertime, though it always depressed her because the Japanese in the show were depicted as cruel enemies of the Chinese, a common theme in Chinese TV shows. The coverage of the territorial dispute was similar, hence her relief when her husband turned off the TV. She believed her husband understood her feelings. On the other hand, Chisako realized that her Chinese husband tended to be on the side of the Chinese government when they discussed the territorial dispute.

Most of the interviewees were also concerned about their future. In particular, the wives of assigned workers definitely wanted to return to Japan, but they were frustrated because they could not decide when to return to Japan. Some of the women who moved to China to study

Chinese and work in Shanghai were also concerned about whether or not they would eventually return to Japan. They had chosen to move to Shanghai but they imagined that they would return to Japan after a few years. Marriage provided them with opportunities to deepen their involvement in Chinese society; however, it also tied them to China and their families. Some interviewees believed that their move to China was permanent. Yasuko mentioned that her friends had talked about death and dying. Though not the majority, interviewees expressed similar anxieties, primarily in relation to when they would return to Japan and where they would live in the future.

Conclusion

The analysis of the experiences of 16 Japanese marriage migrants in China revealed that they were extremely diverse and complex.

Several of the interviewees had decided to move to Shanghai to study or work; others merely complied with their Chinese husbands' decisions. Some of the women intended to stay in China permanently, while others planned to return to Japan as soon as possible. The latter, therefore, constantly worried about their living arrangements and anticipated their move. A number of interviewees lived among other Japanese residents and associated with their in-laws in Shanghai, while others were only acquainted with a few Japanese residents nearby. In addition, the interviewees had extremely diverse experiences with regards to employment, language and their children's education.

Despite the diversity, however, the interviewees' experiences had much in common. Firstly, their residence in China reflects the increasing economic and cultural relationship between China and Japan. Some interviewees viewed the opportunity to work in China positively, but others felt that it was difficult to take control of their lives in this foreign land. They had accidentally or unintentionally moved to Shanghai. Those who married Chinese men in Japan had not intended to move to China. Those who moved to China for work and study purposes had not intended to marry a Chinese man and live in Shanghai for such a long time.

Secondly, regardless of their reasons for migrating to Shanghai, moving to and living in a foreign country had affected their family, especially their children. Previous studies on migration emphasize that the experiences of women migrants are considered less important than those of migrant men because women move across national borders with their families. However, unlike men, women's migration with their families forces such women to become more responsible for their children, if there are any. Many interviewees in this study felt that their careers had been suspended because of the difficulties involved in obtaining work permits and adjusting to cultural and linguistic differences. In addition, mothers shouldered more of the responsibility of caring for their multicultural children to lessen the effect of culture shock and educational problems on them. Some interviewees accepted that they had to prioritize family life over their own careers, although others were dissatisfied with this decision. Some indicated that they loved taking care of their children, but they were also frustrated because having been educated in the Japanese system, they were unable to fully help their children who were being educated in the Chinese or international system.

Class hierarchy may be a critical factor in these marriages. Interestingly, many interviewees said that there were no differences between marriage with a Chinese man and marriage with a Japanese man. They believed that in their case, they just met someone whom they liked and married him. However, several of the interviewees insisted that Japanese women should not marry foreign partners whose incomes are not equal to their Japanese counterparts, otherwise they would not be able to maintain the same standard of living as other Japanese residents in Shanghai.

Finally, in their multicultural households of the Japanese women who were interviewed, they were usually able to minimize conflict. Nevertheless, these efforts prevented women from pursuing their own careers. Several interviewees intentionally or unintentionally married men who earned more than them, thus avoiding the possibility of downward mobility. Even though cross-border migrations are considered personal decisions, multicultural families need to develop ways of coping with the difficulties they encounter. In this study, the responsibility to manage these difficulties fell primarily on the women. The study participants all lived relatively comfortable lives, but they shared similar difficulties.

By scrutinizing the lives of the Japanese women married to Chinese men, we can begin to understand how dual-nationality married couples who have migrated, particularly the women in these relationships, make enormous sacrifices to live in foreign countries, in this case China. These women are at the forefront of the contradictions induced by cross-border marriage migration, even if it is migration between equally developed countries.

Appendix: Summary of informants' characteristics

Name (pseudonym)	Method	Year Arrived in China	Year of Marriage	Where the Couple Met	Current Job
Ayako	1	2006	2008	Shanghai	Employed
Kazuko	1	1986/96	2003	Shanghai	Employed
Sachiko	1	2001	2008	Shanghai	Employed
Taeko	1	2000 (Beijing)	2009	Beijing	Employed
Namiko	1	1996	1996	Japan	Entrepreneur
Xiaoli	4	2010	2001	Japan	Employed
Hanako	2	2003	2010	Shanghai	Employed
Masako	3	1992 (Beijing)	?	Beijing	Housewife
Yasuko	3	2003	1999	Japan	Freelance
Risako	2	2002	1988?	Europe (Germany)	Employed
Wakako	2	2004	2006	Europe (UK)	Housewife
Chisako	2	2007	the 1990s	Japan	Housewife
Eriko	2	2005	2000	Japan	Housewife
Itsuko	3	2011	?	Japan	Housewife
Fumiko	3	2006	2008	Shanghai	Housewife
Rika	3	2005	2007	Australia	Housewife

Notes

1. In the *Annual Report of Statistics on Japanese Nationals Overseas* published by the Japanese Ministry of Foreign Affairs, Japanese residents overseas are divided into primary movers and family members.
2. The Japanese Ministry of Foreign Affairs collected statistics about Japanese citizens abroad from all of its embassies and legations in foreign countries and published them in the *Annual Report of Statistics on Japanese Nationals Overseas*. The report shows that the number of Japanese women abroad exceeded the number of men for the first time in 1999. This trend has continued, and there are now 43,000 more women than men overseas.
3. The figures available through the Shanghai Civil Affairs Bureau suggest that it is not common for Chinese men to marry foreign women. In 2008, only 428 Chinese men in Shanghai were married to wives who were not Chinese nationals. This number is one-fifth of the number of Chinese women with foreign husbands (2,125).
4. Most Koreans who live in Japan are belong to the third or later generation. Thus, Japanese-Korean marriages are different from other cross-cultural marriages.
5. Research on Japanese women's marriages to Asian men of other nationalities has been conducted. For example, Yamashita (1996) shows that many

Japanese women went to Bali and married local men in the 1990s. Kudo (2008) researched the marriage between a Japanese woman and a Pakistani man. In addition, popular TV dramas and films have depicted romantic relations between a Japanese woman and an Asian man. For example, NHK aired the drama "Shanghai Typhoon" in 2008. The drama described the romance between a Japanese woman, who had moved to Shanghai to open her own business, and a wealthy Chinese man. Such plots have become more popular since Korean dramas have become widely accepted in Japan.

6. In the *Annual Report of Statistics on Japanese Nationals Overseas* published by the Japanese Ministry of Foreign Affairs, Japanese residents overseas are divided into primary movers and family members.
7. Both Japan and China have single citizenship systems. Therefore, the interviewees in this study did not consider dual citizenship for their children. For this reason, their attitude towards their children's citizenship may be distinctly different from that of Japanese marriage migrants in countries where it is possible to obtain multiple citizenships, such as Canada, Australia and the United States (Kamoto 2006, 2007; Hamano 2011).
8. All names used in this chapter are pseudonyms.
9. In Japanese companies abroad, there are typically two types of workers. The first type includes those assigned from the headquarters in Japan (assigned workers). The second type includes those who have been hired locally. These workers are called "local" or "locally hired workers". The salary gaps between the two types are usually large.
10. He was not a Chinese man, but China now attracts people and companies from all over the world.
11. The website of the Chinese embassy in Japan states that the visas typically held by Japanese residents are the F visa (visiting and interchange), J visa (journalists), L visa (travel), Q visa (visiting Chinese relatives), X visa (students) and Z visa (work permit). Available at http://www.china-embassy.or.jp/jpn/lsfu/hzqzyw/t1071920.htm [accessed 26 Nov. 2015].

    One of the interviewees, who has a Chinese husband, told me that she applied for the L visa but that there is also a Q visa for visiting Chinese relatives. The Chinese visa system for foreign residents is difficult to navigate and has recently undergone substantial changes. Some interviewees said that they relied on information provided through mailing lists of Japanese residents in China when they applied for a Chinese visa as the spouse of a Chinese citizen.
12. The Chinese government established a permanent resident status (D visa; Chinese green card) in 2004. By the end of 2011, more than 4,700 foreign citizens held green cards. *Renming Ribao*, a Chinese newspaper, reported that the government was now preparing to reform the system (*Renming Ribao* Japanese edition, 29 Jan. 2013). Available at http://j.people.com.cn/94475/7978742.html [accessed 26 Nov. 2015].

13. She explained that universities in China often ask foreign teachers to change schools every two years because the administrative staff did not want the teachers to become over-familiar with the students.
14. For Japanese women who want to continue working after childbirth, China seems to be more accommodating. However, my interviewees realized that in China a more traditional way of raising children that includes the help of extended family is preferred. Mothers usually have to return to work after several months of maternity leave, and public day care institutions are far from satisfactory. Taeko, one of the interviewees, said that these institutions were for those who had no other options.
15. In 1975, a supplementary Saturday school was established in Hongqiao; it became a full-time school in 1979. A new elementary school opened in Putong in 2006 because of the increasing number of students.
16. She took her daughter to Shanghai to attend a local school there while her family was living in Tokyo. She had several acquaintances in Shanghai because she had been a teacher there before moving to Japan.
17. Pollock and Van Reken (1999) argue that children who grow up in foreign cultures because their parents have taken jobs abroad not only experience cultures distinctly different from their native cultures; they also tend to have unstable relationships with their friends.
18. The decision about which citizenship to give their children created the biggest difference between Japanese wives in China and those who migrated to countries where dual-citizenship is available.

References

Castles, Stephen and Mark J. Miller (2008). *The Age of Migration: International Population Movement in the Modern World*. London: Macmillan Press.

Chinese Embassy in Japan website. http://www.china-embassy.or.jp/jpn/lsfu/hzqzyw/t1071920.htm [accessed 26 Nov. 2015].

Constable, Nicole, ed. 2005. *Cross-border Marriages: Gender and Mobility in Transnational Asia*. Philadelphia: University of Pennsylvania Press.

Denzin, Norman K. 2010. "Grounded and Indigenous Theories and the Politics of Pragmatism." *Sociological Inquiry* 80(2): 296–312.

Denzin, Norman K. 2012. "Triangulation 2.0." *Journal of Mixed Methods Research* 6(2): 80–8.

Hamano, Takeshi. 2011. "Japanese Women Marriage Migrants Today: Negotiating Gender, Identity and Community in Search of a New Lifestyle in Western Sydney." PhD diss., The University of Western Sydney.

Kamoto, Itsuko. 2006. "In Quest of 'Someday': A Study of Cross-national Marriages in Montreal, Canada (1)." *Contemporary Society* 9: 93–119.

———. 2007. "In quest of 'Someday': Case Studies of Cross-national Marriages in Montreal, Canada (2)." *Contemporary Society* 10: 77–104.

———. 2008. *Kokusai Kekkon Ron?* [The Theory of International Marriages?]. Kyoto: Houritsu Bunka Sha.

Kelsky, Karen. 2001. *Women on the Verge.* Durham, NC: Duke University Press.

Kofman, Elenore et al. 2000. *Gender and International Migration in Europe: Employment, Welfare and Politics.* London and New York: Routledge.

Kudo, Masako. 2008. *Ekkyo no Jinruigaku* [Anthropology of the Crossing the Border]. Tokyo: University of Tokyo Press.

Ministry of Foreign Affairs, Japan. 2014. *Annual Report of Statistics on Japanese Nationals Overseas.* Available at http://www.mofa.go.jp/mofaj/files/000049149.pdf [accessed 26 Nov. 2015].

Ministry of Justice, Japan. 2013. *White paper on 2013 Immigration Control.* Available at http://www.moj.go.jp/nyuukokukanri/kouhou/nyuukokukanri06_00042.html [accessed 26 Nov. 2015].

Ministry of Health, Labour and Welfare, Japan. 2013. *Vital Statistics of Japan.* Available at http://www.mhlw.go.jp/toukei/list/81-1a.html [accessed 26 Nov. 2015].

Morokvasic, Mirjana. 1984. "Birds of Passage are also Women…." *International Migration Review* 18(4): 886–947.

Piper, Nicole. 2003. "'Birds of passage' Also in Asia: Women and Labour Migration from a Regional Perspective." *Development Bulletin* 62: 30–3.

Piper, Nicole and Amber French. 2011. "Do Women Benefit from Migration? An Editorial Introduction." *Diversities* 13(1): 1–4.

Pollock, David and Ruth Van Reken. 1999. *Third Culture Kids: Growing Up Among Worlds.* Yarmouth, Main: Intercultural Press.

Yokota, Sachiko. 2008. "Global Hypergamy? A Case Study of Vietnamese Female Spouses in Taiwan." *Intercultural Communication Studies* 20: 79–110.

CHAPTER 3

Marriage "During" Work Migration: Lived Experiences of Filipino Marriage Migrants in Malaysia

Linda A. Lumayag

Introduction and Conceptual Framework

Globalization and increased mobility across national borders have greatly altered the forms and levels of human interaction in society (see, for example, Yeoh et al. 2013: 139). They have also created opportunities for women, particularly those from the global south. This mobility is based on various motivations: work, education, travel, study grant exchange (Jones 2012a, 2012b; Toyota 2008) and business meetings abroad. One important motivation is migration for international marriage. International marriages are defined here as marriages engaged in by two consenting adults from two different nation-states, hence affecting issues related to citizenship, children's access to education, social welfare, and other basic civil and cultural rights.

Studies on migration reveal common research perspectives of transnational marriages or international marriages, including the following: (1) men from modern and economically advanced societies seek marriageable women from poorer and less economically advanced societies (Hsiao 2010, 2012); (2) there is an industry of legitimate and mediated matchmaking agencies that facilitate connections between potential candidates for marriages involving two countries (Chee 2010); (3) potential grooms are often poorer men from rural areas who initially experience difficulty finding prospective local brides because of the changing perception of marriage and women's emphasis on obtaining higher education (Suzuki 2003); (4) men have a preconceived perception that women from less developed countries are poor and subservient (Jones and Shen

2008; Suzuki 2003) and can provide additional domestic labour in the household social reproduction, such as in the care of the elderly; and (5) potential brides search for men who are modern, rich and *possibly* white. These perspectives are clear in various narratives identified in studies conducted in the United States, Germany, Australia, Canada and Japan (Chee 2010). The phenomenon of international marriage has also engendered new concepts and images. An example is "mail-order brides", a term that is commonly associated with Filipino women who engage in commercial matchmaking transactions to find their future husbands (Constable 2003; Piper and Roces 2003; Suzuki 2003). Glodava and Onizuka define "mail-order bride" quite broadly as

> ...women who found their spouses through the mail. The process may be initiated by an introduction service agency through the use of a catalog, newspaper or magazine advertisement, or videotape service. It may also be initiated through [an] introduction made by a friend or relative. (Glodava and Onizuka 1994, cited in Constable 2003: 68)

The phenomenon of "mail-order brides" did not arise from a vacuum. The concept is the product of a particular need of the community to find alternative strategies to forge new social relations (Suzuki 2003: 401). In addition to the common perspectives of international marriage mentioned above, there is a long-standing belief that the predominance of this activity is focused on the unidirectional movement of women from the global south to the global north and, similarly, from third-world to first-world economies. This activity reflects a straightforward commercial transaction of marriage of women from China, the Philippines, Thailand and Vietnam, to name a few, to advanced countries such as the United States, Japan, Australia and Canada (Jones 2012a; Hsiao 2010; Lu 2008; Wang and Chang 2002). The 2010 United Nations Secretary General's Report (2012) showed an increase in the number of international migrants from 155 million in 1990 to 2,014 million in 2010. In the span of 20 years, the number of international migrants in northern developed countries grew by 46 million, or 56 per cent, whereas immigrants in southern countries increased by 13 million, or 18 per cent.

The Commission on Filipinos Overseas (CFO) revealed that from 1989 to 2013, of the 455,458 Filipino spouses and other partners of foreign nationals by gender, 91.44 per cent were females (CFO 2013). In terms of distribution of Filipino spouses by major country, the United States recorded the highest increase in such marriages, 42.52 per cent;

Japan, 25.77 per cent; and Australia, 7.98 per cent from 1989 to 2013 (CFO 2013). According to Gavin Jones, an eminent sociologist from the National University of Singapore, marriage migration from the Philippines is considerable. From 1989–2014, between 14,000 and 25,000 Filipinos left the country annually as spouses or partners of foreign nationals, based on data collected by the Commission on Filipinos Overseas (2015).

Despite the emerging "global south-global south" framework in international marriages, there is a need to consider new theoretical perspectives and practical approaches to understand the associated complexities and challenges. Thus, in addition to work migration, the present study observed migrants who left their home countries for the purpose of education, travel or marriage. The marriage migration phenomenon, like the phenomenon of work migration, is also no longer limited to the south-north framework of analysis; rather, there is a clear phenomenon of marriage migration within the south-south divide. Particularly in Asia, cross-border marriages, also known as international marriages, have become an important segment of the globalized migration stream (Cahill 1990; Sung 1990, as cited in Wang and Chang 2002). Hugo expressed an earlier conception of cross-border marriages:

> …groups of recruiters, lawyers, agents, organizers, travel agents and intermediaries of various kinds, often comprising complex networks linking origin and destination, have become important gatekeepers in global immigration processes, both legal and illegal. (Hugo 1996: 109)

Earlier patterns of marriage migration involved marriage first, then migration, as occurs in the "mail-order bride" strategy, in which romantic relationships were expected to develop within a few days of the first meeting. Empirical research results presented in this chapter shows, however, that migration occurs first, then marriage—as observed in work migrants, travellers, international students and business expatriates. In fact, dramatic changes in migration patterns can be observed in the phenomenon of south-south migration; however, these patterns remain poorly understood, largely because data on migration in developing countries are incomplete and unreliable (Ratha and Shaw 2007).

Thus, migration as a process is not simply a matter of crossing borders for different motivations. Migration is also a well-organized and structured process which supplies labourers and marriage migrants from less developed economies to affluent, modernized and developed nation-states. Global economic circumstances have altered the once traditional landscape of global migration in such a manner that migration is no longer confined to Western countries such as the United States, Australia and Canada (Jones 2012a, 2012b; Hsiao 2010; Castles and Miller 2009), or what is called the "south-north" migration. Hence, the global phenomenon of migration for marriage must be understood as a by-product of capitalist development—"one manner in which men and women cope in societies distorted and marginalized by capitalist globalization" (Hsiao 2010: 5). If migration occurs within nation-states, that migration is dictated by the same formula, that is, poorly developed rural economies pushing available labour to find opportunities in cities and towns.

This chapter attempts to locate the position of female marriage migrants in Malaysia, one of the increasingly developed economies in Southeast Asia, along with Singapore, Thailand and Brunei. Specifically, the chapter examines the social location of Filipino female migrants in relation to their everyday experiences as foreign wives in an ethnically diverse Malaysia. It aims to understand their position as foreign wives despite the degrading of their professional status because of being marriage migrants. It presents the case that marriage migrants who do not match *global marriage-scapes* are easily left behind in academic discussions and policy-making. Cases of Filipino marriage migrants who came to Malaysia to work or to study and eventually married Malaysian men are examined.

Methodology

This chapter is part of a larger study that examines the concept of belonging with regard to foreign wives who reside in Malaysia (UMRG Project BK209-2011A). The participatory observation and informal interviews were carried out from 1994 until 2014 in Kuala Lumpur, Malaysia. Interview comments were gathered through this participatory observation.

I have been involved with migrants' issues and causes since 1994, when I contemplated pursuing my doctoral degree at a public university in Malaysia. In those days, labour migration policies were either ambiguous or rules were non-existent; quite often, foreign domestic workers (FDWs) from the Philippines ended up being exploited by their employers, employment agents or even their co-ethnics. Soon, I began to learn that some FDWs settle in Malaysia by marrying local men. I spent a significant amount of time on numerous Sundays interacting with foreign wives and listening to their stories. I performed purposive sampling to identify a small sample of 18 women who could participate in my

Table 3.1 Summary of the characteristics of interviewed Filipino women married to Malaysian men (N = 18)

Characteristics	Number
Age	Youngest: 30 Oldest: 57
Type of visa upon first entry	Student: 2 Professional: 5 Domestic worker/unskilled: 11
Type of visa held at the time fieldwork was conducted (2011–12)	(1) From unskilled visa to Social Pass/Dependent Pass (2) From Student to Social Pass/Dependent Pass (3) From Professional to Dependent Pass
Number of years living in Malaysia	Longest: 35 years Shortest: 3 years
Number of years married	Longest: 33 years Shortest: 5 years
Marital status upon first entering Malaysia	(1) Married with dependent children in the Philippines: 3 (2) Single parent with dependent children: 7 (3) With common-law husband in the Philippines: 5 (4) Single: 3
Level of education	High School graduate: 8 College graduate: 6 Vocational School graduate: 2 Postgraduate: 2
Type of work at the time fieldwork was conducted (2011–12)	(1) From full-time domestic work to part-time domestic work (2) From full-time student to freelance tutor (3) Professional work maintained (4) From domestic work to operating own small-scale business (5) Full-time housewife
Marital status of Malaysian men before contracting marriage to Filipino women	Divorced: 13 Single: 4 Second wife: 1
Number of children with Malaysian husband	Minimum: 1 Maximum: 4

study, which involved in-depth interviews and informal conversations. These women ranged in age from their thirties to their fifties and had been married between 5 and 33 years. I observed these women in their residences and in the community, particularly during their "socialization" activities. Interviews were recorded, and data scripts were transcribed. Categories and themes were identified, analyzed and interpreted. The characteristics of the FDWs as drawn from informal interviews conducted in Kuala Lumpur from 1994 to 2014 and participant observation are summarized in Table 3.1.

International Marriages in the Global South

This section describes the general picture of international marriages in Malaysia. It then discusses the salient features of marriages between Filipino women and Malaysian men.

International Marriages in Malaysia

Of the ten destination countries to which Filipinos migrated in 2013, Malaysia ranked number four, with the United States, Saudi Arabia and United Arab Emirates occupying the first three places, respectively. Malaysia is the only country in Southeast Asia in which there is a greater Filipino presence (Table 3.2). This figure is likely rather conservative as

Table 3.2 Top 10 countries of destinations of Filipinos (based on the 2013 Stock Estimate of Overseas Filipinos)

Rank	Country	Number
1	United States	3,535,676
2	Saudi Arabia	1,028,802
3	United Arab Emirates	822,410
4	Malaysia	793,580
5	Canada	721,578
6	Australia	397,982
7	Italy	271,946
8	United Kingdom	218,126
9	Qatar	204,550
10	Singapore	203,243
Total		8,1978,993

Source: Commission on Filipinos Overseas, 2015.

it does not include the thousands of undocumented immigrants in East Malaysia. The large population of Filipinos in Malaysia can be explained by its proximity to the Philippines, similarity in cultural characteristics and ethnic backgrounds and even social networks that in one manner or another help facilitate cross-border migration.

Thus, if we examine the national statistics of international marriages specific to Malaysia, the number is quite high, as shown in Table 3.3. Malaysian Deputy Minister of the Interior Dato Sri Dr. Haji Wan Junaidi Tuanku Jaafar, in a Parliament meeting held in April 2015, revealed that from December 2004 to 2014, there were 16,702 marriages of Malaysians to other nationalities, with Indonesia topping the list with 5,992 marriages, India with 2,374, Thailand with 1,409 and "Others" at 6,927. The "Others" category appears high and includes 30 other nationalities, based on the information provided to the minister by the National Registration Department of Malaysia in April 2015.

Table 3.3 Number of registered marriages between foreigner and Malaysian citizen, 2004–14

Nationality of Wife	Number of Marriages	Percentage
Indonesia	5992	35.8
India	2374	14.2
Thailand	1409	8.4
Others	6927	41.4
Total	16,702	100.0

Source: Hansard of Parliament of Malaysia, 21 April 2015.

However, previous marriage statistics data published by the Malaysian Department of Statistics (2007: 49, 51, cited in Chee 2010) indicate that there were 61,144 registered non-Muslim marriages in Malaysia in 2005 and 60,477 in 2006 compared with 112,736 registered Muslim marriages in 2005 and 116,159 in 2006. The discrepancy in terms of the latest statistics is glaring, and I surmise this figure reflects non-Muslim couples, including those coming from Vietnam and the Philippines. Conversely, if we examine cross-border marriages in Sabah in East Malaysia, nearly 20,000 Filipino and Indonesian Muslim foreigners have married locals since 2000, according to the data revealed during the 2013 Royal Commission of Inquiry that investigated the arbitrary issuance of identification cards (ICs) to undocumented Muslim immigrants in the state. In addition, an increasing number of foreign Muslim women married local Muslim men, from 222 in 2000 to 1,302 in 2012. Furthermore, without considering the religious affiliation of these marriages, 10,922 foreign women opted to marry local men, whereas only 8,859 foreign men married local women between 2000 and 2012 (*Daily Express*, 23 May 2013).

Sustained efforts have been made to obtain data on international marriages from at least three Malaysian government bodies: the Department of Statistics, National Registration and the Department of Islamic Development Malaysia (JAKIM); however, such efforts failed to achieve the desired results. In most cases, statistics related to migration, inter-ethnic marriages or cross-border marriages are deemed "sensitive" information, and researchers rely on Parliamentary meetings and hearings when official statistics are distributed to the media and placed in the public domain.

Focusing on Filipino marriages in Malaysia, the Embassy of the Republic of the Philippines revealed that from 2012 to the first half of 2015, there appears to have been a steady number of marriages between Filipinos and Malaysians, peaking at 937 marriages by mid-2015. Table 3.4 shows a consistently high number of marriages between Filipino women and Malaysian men from 2012 to 2015. It also shows the propensity of Filipino women to marry local Malaysian men rather than for Filipino men to marry Malaysian women, with 832 marriages compared with 105 over the last four years. These data, however, do not indicate which of the three major Malaysian ethnic communities Filipino women mostly marry into. These data only capture those marriages registered at

Table 3.4 Filipino marriages in Malaysia, 2012–15

Year	*Number of marriages between Filipino men and Malaysian women*	*Number of marriages between Filipino women and Malaysian men*	*Total*
2012	25	262	287
2013	27	232	259
2014	28	209	237
2015*	25	129	154
Total	105	832	937

Note: *Data captured from January to May 2015 only.
Source: Embassy of the Philippines, Kuala Lumpur, June 2015.

the Embassy of the Philippines in Kuala Lumpur and do not include those couples who decide to register their marriages in the Malaysian National Registration Department.

Marriage Migration in Malaysia: Salient Features of Marriages between Filipino Women and Malaysian Men

This section describes a particular phenomenon of marriage "during" work migration, which suggests that female migrants were married after arriving in Malaysia to work in the service sector of the economy. In the present study, I examine more closely the cross-border marriages occurring in West Malaysia, where a considerable number of Filipino women worked as migrants before marriage. Some of the women I met during fieldwork had passed through the East Malaysia en route to Kuala Lumpur, the capital city of Malaysia.

It has been noted that during the mid-1980s, the demand for foreign domestic labour in Arab countries declined. Simultaneously, the Mahathir administration embarked on a full-scale industrialization scheme that allowed Malaysian women to participate in the country's economic development. This entry of the Malaysian women into the labour force created space for non-Malaysian women to perform household chores. Industrialization also facilitated the employment of women from neighbouring countries. Toward the end of the 1980s, a deluge of foreign domestic workers (FDWs) entered Malaysia from the Philippines and Indonesia. Studies have shown that Malaysia, as a host country, also created a market environment by choosing source countries that could provide the cheapest FDWs.

Therefore, the Philippines and Indonesia became primary suppliers of FDWs for middle-class Malaysian households (see Table 3.5). Market economies are oriented toward competition. In effect, Indonesia's salary ceiling has always been lower than the Philippines' salary ceiling. By contrast, the Philippines established a minimum wage that Malaysian employers were required to follow because most Filipino FDWs can speak English. Conversely, most Indonesian FDWs speak minimal English. Since the 1980s, the Philippines has regularly been sending FDWs to Malaysia. However, the Philippines has reduced these efforts in recent years because Malaysia reopened other sectors of its economy, such as information and communication technology (ICT), education and the hotel and restaurant industry. Thus, the migration of Filipinos to work in Malaysia has created new types of social relationships within the country's multi-ethnic and multicultural settings. For instance, some Filipino domestic workers possess considerably greater physical mobility because of their insistence on enjoying a weekly day off, although this is an exception rather than the rule. This mobility allows them to engage in a variety of social relationships (friendships and casual encounters) outside their employers' homes. Consequently, this physical visibility opens them up to more relationship opportunities.

Table 3.5 Number of overseas Filipino workers (new hires and rehires), 2009–13

Year	2009	2010	2011	2012	2013
Number of OFWs	7,256	9,802	16,797	25,261	34,088

Source: Philippine Overseas Employment Administration (POEA) website. Available at http://www.poea.gov.ph/stats/2013_stats.pdf, "Table 3: Number of Deployed Land-based Overseas Filipino Workers by Top Ten Destinations, New Hires and Rehires: 2009–2013" [accessed 3 August 2015].

The salient features of cross-border marriages contracted in other developed countries can also be observed in Malaysia. However, four distinguishing markers are noteworthy. First, the non-adoption of marriages arranged by commercial matchmaking agencies illustrates Filipino women's perceptions of Malaysia when they attempt to find future Malaysian husbands, which they are unable to do with potential husbands from Canada, New Zealand or the United States. Thus, the traditional "mail-order bride" phenomenon, which triggered a deluge of international marriages among Filipino women within the "global south-global north" framework in the 1980s, has not been observed in Malaysia. The following factors may contribute to this non-observance of the "mail-order bride" phenomenon. Religious differences between the two societies provide one reason why organized matchmaking marketing transactions are not known, in the cases examined in this chapter. Additionally, Malaysia was not known as a destination for work or marriage until the 1980s, when the country began to recruit Filipino FDWs to work in middle-class Malaysian households. This juncture in the economic development of Malaysia opened some doors to international marriages between Filipino women and Malaysian men. Furthermore, migration before marriage appears to be more prevalent in Malaysia—and perhaps in many labour-receiving countries—than marriage before migration, as observed in the global south-global north framework.

The second marked difference in international marriages in Malaysia is the similarity of cultures between the contracting parties. Whereas religion can be a barrier to forging marriages between Christian Filipinos and Muslim Malaysians, the similarity in language systems, cultural practices and values may nevertheless be a contributing factor to the growing number of cross-border marriages. Prior knowledge of the social conditions of the locality allows women to optimize different personal support channels and friendship networks if they are to pursue marriage plans.

The third marker observed from my investigation is that most marriages within the ranks of Filipino domestic workers are contracted across the ethnic divide and that these marriages tend to be to economically disadvantaged Malaysian men. Although Malaysian work contracts stipulate that FDWs are not allowed to marry or become pregnant in Malaysia during the time they possess employment passes (*Straits Times*, 19 February 2006), sexual relationships and cohabitation continue to occur.

Fourth, while the concept of hypergamy, that is, foreign women marrying to "move up the ladder" of social classes and positions, can be observed in certain international marriages contracted in Western countries (for example, Constable 2005), the case of Malaysia may be a different story if, indeed, there is upward social mobility. Filipino women in Malaysia appear to marry local men who belong to the lower working class, rendering it quite difficult for them to move up the economic and social ladder, as also observed in Taiwan and South Korea (see, for example, Hsiao 2010, 2012*)*. It should be noted that Filipino women have a greater propensity to marry Malaysians of Indian or Chinese descent. Nevertheless, in this particular study there are also cases of professional Filipino women marrying Malay Malaysians, a marriage that in itself creates a distinct and complex issue associated with Islamic practices, class and ethnicity.

Filipino women who possess professional qualifications in the Philippines but who ultimately become domestic workers (for one reason or another) may not necessarily improve their lives after they marry. In the past, Malaysian law stated that foreign spouses were not allowed to work. However, after 2010 Malaysia began issuing spousal visas that permit foreign spouses to work. It is uncertain whether individuals who marry in Malaysia "marry up" or "marry down". Once a marriage is legal, a Filipino woman can convert her work/employment visa to a dependent/social pass. In one sense, when a woman holds an employment visa, she is in a better position than a woman who holds a dependent pass and works illegally as a domestic worker. Until recently, dependent pass holders were not permitted to work if potential employers offered wages of less than MYR1500 (USD380[1]) (circa the mid-2000s). However, because work for spousal visa holders was recently legalized, the situation may have changed, assuming that women have been informed of the visa changes.

Marriage "during" migration occurs, despite the fact that FDWs in Malaysia are not permitted to engage local men in relationships with the goal of marriage. In this study the Filipino women who married Malaysian men tended to have lived in Malaysia for some time prior to marriage. In particular, the Filipino FDWs in this study met their Malaysian partners at least two years before they finally decided to marry. This period approximately coincides with the duration of these domestic workers' first work contracts. Individuals who hold domestic worker visas must have their visas cancelled, return to the Philippines and re-enter Malaysia with social passes stamped on their passports. Based on the Association of Southeast Asian Nations (ASEAN) agreement that regulates travel within Southeast Asian countries, Filipinos can enter Malaysia without visas and remain in the country for 30 days. Simultaneously, their future husbands can process all the documents required to register marriages at the National Registration Department in Malaysia. Future wives of Malaysian spouses must hold valid passports and visas before the solemnization of marriage can occur. Foreign wives generally receive social passes that are renewable annually, although in some cases, their passes must be renewed every three or six months or every two years.[2] Malaysia demands an array of secular and religious permits that foreigners must obtain not only for marriage but also for residence and work. Indirectly, fewer than 2 per cent of all Malaysian marriages involve a foreigner compared with nearly 40 per cent in neighbouring Singapore (*Economist*, 12 November 2011). In 2009, it was estimated that there were 100,000 foreign spouses in Malaysia. However, only 8,600 entry permits were issued to foreigners, including the spouses and children of Malaysians, to stay in the country between 2001 and 2008 (*New Straits Times*, 12 March 2009).

Filipino Women Married to Malaysians: Issues and Concerns

This section examines the different aspects of marriage as influenced primarily by migration.

Based on the type of visa that they held when they first entered Malaysia and the highest level of education they attained prior to leaving the Philippines, the Filipino women married to Malaysian men fall into four groups: (1) documented/undocumented workers; (2) women with exposure to local cultures; (3) women married to men with complex marital relationships; and (4) women with careers. To fully understand the experiences of these foreign wives, it is crucial to determine into which group the women fall as it affects their position in society on a personal, social and cultural level from the moment they decided to marry Malaysian men.

Documented versus Undocumented Workers

The extent of the women's access to and participation in legal rights protection, their access to job opportunities, their children's education and their social networks generally hinged on the type of visa they held prior to marriage. In this study, I attempt to deconstruct the Filipino women's lives based on the type of immigration visa they held when they initially entered Malaysia. For many years, a policy was in effect in Malaysia that prevented individuals from marrying when they possessed unskilled work visas (Chee 2011: 8). This may be simply a question of procedure when women possess employment passes and convert these passes into social passes the moment they are declared legally married.

However, there are issues that pertain to Filipino women's undocumented status as foreign workers. Thus, their legal rights remain unprotected in the strictest sense. Women's undocumented status can result from changes in employers, escapes from employers, situations in which employment agents or employers withhold passports and lapsed work permits. If women are undocumented, they cannot register their marriages. Although the Malaysian immigration regulation is clear regarding the requirements for the issuance of social passes to foreign wives, individual experiences can be complicated and varied. Frequently, the number of months or years allowed in the visa for foreign spouses can differ widely. Occasionally, foreign wives are requested to leave Malaysia when their social visas are about to expire. In these cases, foreign wives must leave through the nearest exit point, such as Singapore, Thailand or the Philippines. Upon re-entry, they are allowed to remain in the country from 15 to 30 days. During that period, Malaysian husbands must return to the immigration department and have their wives' social passes stamped as renewed.

On other occasions, depending on how well foreign wives can convince front desk officers, they are not required to leave Malaysia and re-enter the country. In these cases, the husbands will escort their foreign wives to the immigration counter. The couples will also bring letters stating that, at the time of renewal, they have remained married. Husbands must be physically present at the time of visa renewal to give the impression that the husbands and wives remain married, even if this is not necessarily true. Husbands may accompany their wives and renew visas although in reality, the spouses now live separately, which suggests that the husband may live with another woman. This can occur when children are involved. Husbands do not want to lose their children simply because they refuse to cooperate during visa renewal.

Women with Exposure to Local Cultures

It is interesting to note that foreign wives in the second group have had prior exposure to "different" cultures, religions and languages—social aspects that could serve as benchmarks in their married lives. Women who have worked as FDWs, factory workers or entertainers may have qualitative advantages in terms of the depth of knowledge they have acquired with respect to Malaysia. FDWs' everyday relationships with their employers' families and with individuals outside their employers' households may be considered outstanding advantages that can help them better understand the similarities and differences between Filipino and Malaysian cultural practices.

The Philippine "mail-order bride" industry, which is quite popular in countries such as the United States, Japan, Canada, Australia, Sweden and Denmark, is not available in Malaysia. This may be explained by differences between the cultural and religious backgrounds in Malaysia and the Philippines and by the fact that Malaysia is a multi-ethnic society. Commercial matchmaking agencies do operate in Malaysia; however, such agencies tend to support Chinese Malaysian men's attempts to meet future brides in Vietnam (see also Yeoh et al. 2013) and China. By contrast, Indian Malaysians utilize agencies that specialize in Indian brides, although this is not currently considered a widespread phenomenon. Thus, it is understandable that marriages between Filipino women and Malaysian men are based on one or both partners' prior exposure to the other partner's cultural orientation. The fact that the husband, the wife or both had opportunities to discover their spouse's cultural and religious differences prior to marriage becomes a central component of the relationship. The partners' ability to understand one another's differences, particularly with respect to the types of languages spoken in their communities, can provide safety nets because wives can then communicate with local community members, their husbands' families and their friends.

The Filipino women observed in this study demonstrated a high degree of language competence. They could either speak Bahasa Malaysia, Cantonese, Hokkien, Mandarin or Tamil. Bahasa Malaysia is the dominant language spoken at all levels of social interaction in Malaysia. The women in this study were confident in their ability to speak this language, particularly when their in-laws were unable to speak English.

Married with Complex Marital Relationships

The third group of Filipino wives comprise those who married currently "married" or divorced men. Interesting marital relationships occur in all modernizing societies. These relationships can be even more intriguing in the fluid, mobile and fast-changing global environment. However, marital relationships or combinations engaged in by migrants/immigrants deserve their own analysis. In this particular category, Filipino women tend to marry Malaysian men as second wives. Take the case of Sybil.

Sybil

Sybil, 43, worked in a government office in Manila before she decided to pursue her studies in Malaysia. She entered Malaysia in 2001 as a doctoral student in a public university. She met her future Malay Muslim husband when they attended a conference in Manila. After a whirlwind romance, an *imam* (a Muslim priest) married the couple in a Muslim ceremony in Manila. Sybil was unfamiliar with Islam and believed everything was fine until she discovered that her husband had not officially divorced his first wife. Although the Muslim rite was valid in the Philippines and, to a certain extent, in Malaysia, the first wife claimed that her husband contracted the second marriage without her permission.

Sybil had entered Malaysia with a student pass because she was pursuing her doctoral degree at a public university. She experienced difficulties obtaining a social pass when her student pass expired because the government had refused to validate her marriage in Manila. Sybil and her husband hired a lawyer to fight their case, transferred the case to another court and legitimized their marriage rites in Manila. Only then was she permitted to obtain a social pass. Of course, the couple spent a huge sum of money on legal fees.

In certain Malaysian states, including the federal territory of Kuala Lumpur, Muslim men are not permitted to register for second marriages until they receive express permission from their first wives. Circumstances like these affect all future undertakings, such as applications for social passes and permanent residence and simple tasks such as opening bank accounts.

When husbands and wives live together with husbands' parents and siblings, spousal issues can rapidly arise. The cases of Maricel and Rosa are interesting in this regard.

Maricel

Beginning in 1997, Maricel worked for two years as an FDW. During that time, she met a Chinese Malaysian man, who worked as a chauffeur for a rich Chinese family. When she left the Philippines, she also had an estranged husband and two children who remained there. Maricel married the Chinese Malaysian. She claimed that although her husband was a very good man, she would have preferred that they lived independently from her ailing mother-in-law. Although Maricel had two sisters-in-law who could have cared for the elderly woman, the family placed all care responsibilities on Maricel. She greatly lamented this situation. However, she justified it because her husband was the only son; thus, the care responsibility for his aging mother fell on his shoulders. In addition, Maricel's mother always reminded her to take good care of her mother-in-law because she was her husband's mother.

Maricel was a very enterprising woman. She woke up early every morning and bathed and fed her mother-in-law. Then, she would drive to downtown Kuala Lumpur to sell food that she had prepared the night before. She also dabbled as a hairstylist and beauty products promoter. Recently, she opened a beauty salon in one of the popular destinations for migrant workers in Kota Raya.

Rosa

Rosa originated from Cotabato in Mindanao, Philippines. She came via Sandakan, Sabah. She was devastated to find that Sabah was just like Mindanao because she had thought it would be a place where the climate was cool, that it would have a winter season. She was mentally prepared to live in a very cold place.

She started as a cook in a logging company whose workers came from west Malaysia. She met her husband, who was a foreman of the logging company. Rosa and her husband lived together as husband and wife and they decided to go to Johor with their young children. The couple lived together as husband and wife without the benefit of marriage for 22 years because she did not have the proper documents to show to the National Registration Department. Rosa and her husband had attempted to get married; however, because she lacked the proper documents or proof of legal residence in Malaysia, her marriage registration could not proceed. Her husband nevertheless managed to register their three children at the National Registration Department, naming Rosa as their mother.

Because her husband was the eldest in the family, Rosa had the difficult task of caring for her mother-in-law and her husband's siblings, who all lived together in one house. Rosa performed all of the tasks that a domestic worker would perform. Her husband was the eldest son in a family of four. Prior to meeting Rosa, he had worked as a foreman at a palm oil company in Sabah. At that time, Rosa worked as a cook for the same company. Rosa wanted to live separately from her husband's family; however, her husband lacked the financial means to buy or rent a house for their own growing family. When she completed her household duties like washing, cleaning and cooking, she worked at a nearby salt factory to earn a meagre income. She believed that this was better than not earning at all. When the children returned home from school, they joined her at work in the salt factory, where the children were known as "salt packers". Rather than being based on the employees' time, payment was based on the number of packets that each worker could finish in one day. With her children's assistance, Rosa was thereby able to help pay for food and school costs. Before Rosa's mother-in-law died, she convinced Rosa to pray to Buddha. Initially, Rosa was uncomfortable praying with her mother-in-law. For example, Rosa had to bow to the "*datu*" (Buddha) when she was making an offering to the gods. Rosa was required to do this because the old woman was unable to pray because of her physical immobility. Rosa recalled that prior to that time, when she kowtowed to perform the prayer, she actually thought about her "own" god. As time passed, she realized that the more she prayed to the "*datu*", the more frequently she received what she prayed for. One day, she asked her children to join her in prayer.

One particular event convinced Rosa that her prayers to the "*datu*" were more effective than the prayers she performed when she practised the faith in which she had been raised. On that occasion, the family lacked sufficient funds to pay for the children's tuition. She prayed hard to the "*datu*". On a regular schedule, she spent a part of her earnings from salt packing to buy lottery tickets. After her prayers on that day, she bought a lottery ticket—and luck must have been on her side because she won. She became more convinced that her newfound "religion" was the religion she would die with because it answered her prayers. For financial reasons, Rosa had not returned to Cotabato City in the Philippines for more than 20 years.

The third group also includes women who had families or bore children out of wedlock prior to leaving the Philippines. Work migration has created a condition that forces women, particularly those in the domestic sector, to leave their children and spouses in the Philippines, and they may not see these families again for at least two years. After Malaysia initially opened its doors to FDWs, these workers returned home every two years, after signing new contracts. These infrequent return trips to the Philippines, coupled with the stresses involved in maintaining long-distance spousal relationships, have created varied relational situations. The cases of Asuncion and Olivia are examples of such a situation.

Asuncion

Asuncion left her four young children with her common-law husband in Davao in 1990. She entered Kuala Lumpur via Sabah in 1991 and worked as a domestic worker in a local policeman's household. Along the way, she met someone who promised her a Malaysian identification card (IC). She paid MYR1,500 (USD380) to that person and got her IC; however, she never used it for finding employment. She believed that it was not genuine. The only time she used it was when she entered Kuala Lumpur from Kota Kinabalu. She found it frightening to be holding two different identification documents: a Malaysian IC and a Philippine passport. In Kuala Lumpur, she went out of her way to make new friends and obtained employment as a domestic worker for an expatriate family. In 1998, she met her Malaysian husband and married him in Manila, Philippines, even though her common-law husband and their children continued to live in Davao. Because she had children and an "ex-common-law husband" to feed and clothe, she continued to work as a domestic.

Olivia

Olivia was married when she left three children and a philandering husband behind in the Philippines. She was employed as a laundry woman in Manila prior to her departure for Kuala Lumpur in 1991. She worked as a domestic worker in Kuala Lumpur, and it was on a day off that she met her current Malaysian husband, who was unmarried.

Women with Careers

The fourth group of women comprise those who have had a career back in their home country.

Filipino women who possess higher education and can pursue professional jobs may achieve better lives by creating, expanding and sustaining their social networks. These networks can help them develop a sense of family and community during the time in which they live apart from their own support networks. However, until 2010, foreign spouses were not supposed to engage in any form of employment or enterprise while holding social passes. This rule had implications for many Filipino women who married Malaysians. The women who had had professions that they could pursue or educational qualifications that would have allowed them to start careers outside the Philippines were effectively barred, sidelined and isolated from the workforce by this rule. Sybil had a master's degree in food technology in the Philippines. She worked as a junior scientist in a government agency. In her own words, she described her experience as follows:

> ...I came here, and I sort of, like, got shocked because the first thing, the first thing in the morning, I had to wash, wash all the clothes, and iron clothes. Oh my God, I never did this in the Philippines when I was there, you know, because somebody ironed and washed my clothes for me. So it was a big shock. And then I was not busy. I didn't do anything. I was, like, in.... I was, like, just in the house, I was waiting for.... I'm just waiting for my husband to come home and all that. So, I got depressed at the start, so I was like okay, wait for my husband to come home, and I don't know what time he's coming home.

Prior to 2010, foreign spouses were barred from the pursuit of any gainful employment other than employment with large multinational companies, companies that employed more than ten workers, or companies that provided work contracts that itemized the basic salaries of potential employees. Penalties were enforced in the form of imprisonment and/or fines when social or dependent pass holders were caught working without valid work permits. That rule has changed; spousal visas are now renewable every five years.[2] Spousal visas entitle holders to work or seek work. However, thousands of social pass holders in Malaysia remain unaware of these changes related to immigration visas. Concepcion wanted to work as a kindergarten teacher in Kuala Lumpur. At that time, this type of employment was not open to non-citizens. She did not accept a job because she was afraid that she would be caught working illegally although other Filipino spouses worked as preschool teachers in many of the rapidly developing communities located in the Klang Valley. Good employment was the only manner in which middle-class Filipino spouses could maintain their status and economic positions in Malaysia. When they were denied work, their potential as human resources was wasted in the process. By contrast, Filipino women who marry upper-middle-class or wealthy Malaysian men can pursue lives of leisure, develop entrepreneurial skills, and maintain "high" social status in Malaysian society although this is the exception rather than the rule.

Social Conditions of Filipino Women Migrants Married to Malaysian Men

This section examines four issues that influence and affect the well being of Filipino women as foreign spouses in Malaysia, namely, poverty and access to work opportunities, language competency, husband-wife relationships and emerging household dynamics.

Poverty and Access to Work Opportunities

Poverty among immigrant families is a major problem in Organization for Economic Co-operation and Development (OECD) countries (Harttgen and Klasen 2008). No data are available in Malaysia that reveal the extent to which families of marriage migrants suffer from poverty and deprivation. However, my field observations revealed that marriage migrant families struggle to cope with the rising cost of living, particularly in Kuala Lumpur. The Filipino women I interviewed presented varied portraits of their social lives with their Malaysian husbands. When I asked whether they preferred life in Malaysia to life in the Philippines, the general sentiment expressed by these women was "at least there is work here in Malaysia". They stated that although wages were not sufficiently high, if they worked hard, they were repaid with the continuous renewal of service. As previously mentioned, the women's future was, in some ways, determined by the type of visa that they obtained when they first came to Malaysia. Their future was also influenced by their degree of familiarity with the environment and the quality of the social interactions that they had with their circle of friends.

Women who initially worked as FDWs in Malaysia never left domestic service once they married. In fact, they continued to work as domestic workers, lacking both proper documentation and legal protection. However, I did observe some rearrangements wherein prior to their marriages, the women had worked full-time for one employer. These employers were primarily foreign expatriates. At the time of the interviews, the majority of the women held several part-time jobs that they generally obtained through personal support networks comprising Filipino domestic workers. Once these women were in the loop, they connected with their friends in the circle and began to exchange a variety of information, including employment opportunities. The women thereby built small communities of FDWs who married local men. These women celebrated their children's birthdays, enjoyed lunches and dinners with friends, or spent Sundays in church with their children. In 2010, there was a regulation pertaining to working foreign wives: If these women were discovered working illegally, they could be charged in court. However, I was unable to find any newspaper coverage of this issue or discover reports of women being penalized in court for working illegally.

Observation of the nature of these women's jobs and their husbands' jobs suggests that these couples fall well below the levels of what might be considered the middle-class. According to actual information provided by the women, some did not own houses, and others never had the opportunity to bring their entire families back to the Philippines for regular vacations. For most Filipino women, returning home at least once a year to visit their families and relatives appeared to be uncommon. For instance, Rosa did not return to Mindanao until she had been married for 22 years, and Olivia did not return for 5 years. These women worked part-time in Kuala Lumpur in the salt factory and as a domestic worker, respectively. By contrast, Maricel, who operated a beauty salon, drove her own car. She also worked part-time as a domestic worker and returned to the Philippines whenever money was available.

Language Convergence and Ethnic Identity

It is interesting to note that the Filipino women I interviewed were able to embrace the language spoken in their communities. Their ability to communicate in the local language facilitated their entry into their in-laws' families, who frequently were unable to speak English. The decision to use a variety of languages depends on the speaker's intention. These women's decision to speak Bahasa Malaysia to Malaysians represented a means of convergence. The women decided to speak this language to identify with Malaysians. Conversely, the women might have switched to their mother tongues when they did not want to identify as Malaysians. This is known as divergence. However, because Malaysia is a multilingual society and because these women were foreigners, the women generally opted for convergence. Once the women became fluent in Bahasa Malaysia, the language spoken outside their homes, some women even began to learn Mandarin, Hokkien, Cantonese or Tamil. In a multilingual society such as Malaysia, the fact that these women learned to speak different languages to engage in their everyday activities shows their adaptability. More importantly, becoming multilingual demonstrates the possession of a survival skill, particularly for Filipino women. In fact, from the local community's perspective, Filipino women's ability to communicate in Bahasa Malaysia was considered a marker of acceptance into the community because the majority of the local people were unable to speak English during that time.

Therefore, in Malaysia, it is possible to observe Filipino women fluently speaking in Bahasa Malaysia with taxi drivers, hawkers, shopkeepers and other people in their neighbourhoods. The Filipino wives' ability to learn a variety of languages with ease helped them assimilate into their "new" homeland. However, it is interesting to note that Filipino mothers feel uncertain or express mixed emotions when they must decide whether to teach their mother tongues to their children. They do not believe that it is practical or useful to teach their children Cebuano, Tagalog, Bicolano or other Philippine languages because their children live and study in Malaysia. Even within the home domain, the preferred language will either be the husbands' ethnic language, which is typically Bahasa Malaysia, or English. The promotion of Bahasa Malaysia in public schools throughout Malaysia and the less-than-inspired interest of Filipino mothers in teaching their mother tongues to their children will in all likelihood cause children of mixed-marriage couples to lose one of their parents' mother tongues. Although couples may be interested in teaching their children their mother tongues, the children face limited pressure to practise those languages daily. Certainly, a language must be regularly spoken and practised to maintain facility in it.

Trivialization of Gendered Husband-Wife Relationships?

In West Malaysia, Filipino women marry into one of three major ethnic communities: Indian, Chinese and Malay. The type of married life that a Filipino woman might experience based on the group into which she marries tends to be associated with stereotypical portrayals of these ethnic groups, even if these stereotypes are untrue. These stereotypes are so prevalent that once an individual learns the ethnic background of a woman's husband, the next question or observation tends to reflect the prevailing stereotype of that ethnic group in Malaysia.

Amelya

Amelya was 23 when she entered Malaysia as a domestic worker. She had a degree in commerce and business administration in the Philippines but decided to work overseas because of a lack of opportunities back in Mindanao. Her story causes us to reflect on how long she might be able to bear the heartaches and suffering caused by her Indian Malaysian husband of 19 years. She stated that after two years of marriage, her husband began to court another woman. He then began to live with the second woman. However, he continued to come home to Amelya occasionally, acting as if nothing had occurred. At the time of her first interview, Amelya's husband was living with three women, all of whom had different ethnic backgrounds—a Malay businesswoman and two Indonesian FDWs. Amelya's husband worked as a security guard at a diplomatic mission in Kuala Lumpur and earned a basic pay of MYR1,800 (approximately USD460) monthly.

Amelya continued to work as an FDW to address the high cost of living in Kuala Lumpur. She provided her husband with a regular MYR10 (USD2.5) food allowance. She continued to wonder why she clung to the relationship when she knew her husband constantly cheated on her. Amelya could not explain or even understand the situation but stated that her interests did not lie with her husband. Rather, Amelya remained focused on her children's future. Her husband threatened that if Amelya were to decide to return to the Philippines, he would buy her a one-way ticket; however, she would not be allowed to take her children with her. For Amelya, leaving her children behind in Malaysia would never be an option, particularly because her children were "the only focus of her life". What was strange in this situation was Amelya's ability to rationalize her subordinate position and avoid doing anything to stop her husband's philandering.

Dynamics of New Household Issues

In this study, the Filipino women who married Malaysian men experienced distinctly novel household issues that demand examination. First, these women left children, husbands or common-law husbands behind in the Philippines. These actions had legal, economic and personal implications for the management of household issues. The results of several observations revealed that these women's financial obligations to children —and, at times, to ex-husbands/ex-common-law husbands—whom they had left behind in the Philippines continued, even if the women had ended their relationships as legal wives or partners. Asuncion left her aging ex-common-law husband in Davao in the care of her three children. While he was alive, she sent monthly remittances sufficient for subsistence. When her ex-common-law husband died, Asuncion returned home to perform her last duty, which was to provide him a decent burial. Although she already had a Malaysian husband, at her children's insistence, she returned to the Philippines and paid all expenses incurred during the wake.

Maricel took everything in stride when she responded to her children's incessant demands for money. Initially, they asked for money to pay for their college education. According to Maricel, "They study as if they will never graduate." She very much wanted her son and daughter to graduate, obtain degrees and move on with their lives. However, her financial obligations never seemed to end: the children continued to demand money for food, university fees, and eventually, to support the newborn baby of her daughter, who became pregnant at age 18. Some of the women's Malaysian husbands help provide financial assistance for children from their previous marriages/relationships. Olivia's struggling husband, who worked as a small-time contractor, responded to Olivia's children's financial needs related to education, daily subsistence and hospitalization.

Conclusion

Cross-border marriages within the "global south-global south" framework —in this case, Malaysia—display a degree of complexity. The need to examine in close detail many issues confronting marriage migrants, their local husbands and the role of Malaysia's socio-political structures as a nation-state is pertinent because the marriage migrants' position in their new homeland is precarious and dependent on the compassion of the state (Lauser 2008). Marriage and migration are thus linked to "citizenship and to relations of power created and sustained by the law" (Constable 2003; Piper and Roces 2003: 15). In the area of labour participation, none of the women I interviewed had left the labour force after marriage, which indicates that they "enjoy" relative "economic autonomy" vis-à-vis the status of other women in Malaysia, even with the type of domestic work in which they engage. These women have relative economic autonomy in the sense that they remain active in the labour force and do not have to depend on their husbands for their financial needs, particularly if they are sending remittances to the Philippines. Another pertinent issue is "global hypergamy" (Constable 2005: 10), which has traditionally assumed that cross-border marriages could bring about an upward shift in women's social location by virtue of their marriage to men from other countries and/or ethnic groups. Examining the situations of the Filipino women observed in this particular study indicates that those women who were working as domestic workers when they first entered Malaysia several years ago have never "shifted" or changed their occupation; in fact, they have become undocumented domestic workers because, unlike before, they now hold dependent passes and not employment passes. However, the possession of a dependent pass entitles one to a "higher" position, commanding more respect from friends and social networks, which shows that a dependent pass is "much better" than being admitted as a foreign domestic worker. This pass also reinforces their new position as the wife of a Malaysian, who will most likely be given citizenship sooner or later; this, again, sets them apart from the rest. Therefore, the idea of "global hypergamy" becomes a more interesting assumption when we place the roles of class, gender, power or ethnicity in context to understand the current social position of foreign wives within the particular socio-political structure of a nation-state.

Immigration policies in Malaysia do not consider the presence of foreign wives who may be able to contribute their professions and skills to the economic development of the country. In the case of Filipino women (and of many others in this category who have a foreign spouse), before 2010, migrants who held dependent passes were not allowed to be gainfully employed, even migrants with the academic qualifications to join the skilled labour force. This occurred with foreign women who had careers to pursue but were barred from engaging in any form of gainful employment because of their dependent visa status. The seeming exclusion of foreign wives denied them the right to work during their peak productive years. Thus, it is clear that marriage did not pose an immediate remedy to formal rights. In other words, it did not grant them legal rights, such as access to residential, political or labour rights, nor substantive citizenship rights, such as non-discrimination and children's access to education (Lauser 2008: 103). In reality, the female migrants' marriages to local men engendered a host of complex problems related to such issues as access to employment, the division of property, and the rights to children in cases of separation or divorce.

Furthermore, foreign women who may have been married before but are now divorced or separated or foreign women who may have cohabited with their Malaysian partners and have produced children during cohabitation present a different picture of the social reality that affects their well-being. It would be unwise to focus solely on marriage migration because that would constrain or limit the study of women within this scope. Marital stresses and tensions have revealed that for women involved in these relationships, during times of extreme difficulty, their only option was to leave their marital homes and assume full responsibility for their children's future and their own well-being. Because of inadequate information and a lack of national or state aggregated data that focus on marriage or on divorce/separation in international marriage, the picture remains incomplete. Preliminary field observations revealed a challenging reality comprising issues of infidelity, harassment, domestic violence and extreme isolation from the support network of women's nation-states.

Another challenging issue is the visa status of marriage migrants. It is extremely difficult to obtain permanent residence status (PR) once a marriage migrant is contracted in marriage to a Malaysian man. Thus, if no PR is given within the first two or three years after marriage and the women have previously held domestic worker visas, the women cannot engage in gainful employment beyond domestic work. In this particular study, none of the women I interviewed moved beyond the domestic work sector. In fact, they became more marginalized than before, although the type of marginalization may be difficult to understand. Could marriage migration within the south-south framework create a better condition than, say, conditions in the south-north? It is safe to assume that the differences in these marriage migration patterns do not imply a better situation in the international marriage equation. Global migrations for work and marriage fundamentally follow the identical path dictated by the capitalist nature of our economy, as do the social relationships that develop in the process of migration.

Finally, international marriage as an area of concern may be too narrow given the complex issues and challenges surrounding marital relationships. One cannot safely continue to believe that migrants' problems are solely related to issues such as husband-wife relationships and differences in lifestyles or behaviour. In conducting this study, what struck me was the extremely limited boundaries of the application and conceptualization of international marriage, cross-border marriage and transnational marriage. I strongly suggest that the breadth and depth of the phenomenon be captured by widening the scope to include divorce and other forms of intimacy that influence and affect or are affected by migration processes. "Intimacy" migration does encourage and facilitate discussions related to issues such as marriage, cohabitation, divorce, citizenship, property rights and children's education. Thus, the politics of "intimacy" migration indicate the inclusion of critical issues that otherwise would have been downgraded or assumed to be less meaningful in the migration process.

Acknowledgement

I would like to publicly recognize the assistance afforded to me by the Embassy of the Philippines in Kuala Lumpur. The Coordinator of the Foreign Spouse Support Group also provided assistance in the procurement of statistical data for this article. This study was funded by the University of Malaya Research Grant (UMRG) Number BKP209-2011A.

Notes

1. According to the exchange rate of August 2015.
2. No clear-cut policies address the number of years allotted to foreign spouses. In my fieldwork, I observed that some women were allowed an initial three months, then six months, and one year, two, three or five years thereafter. This condition itself can be confusing to affected individuals because of its ambiguity and may be the vacillating attitude of the Immigration Department.

References

Cahill, Des. 1990. *Intermarriage in International Contexts: A Study of Filipina Women Married to Australian, Japanese and Swiss Men*. Manila: SMC Press.

Castles, Stephen and Mark Miller. 2009. *Migration in the Asia Pacific Region*. New York: Migration Policy Institute, New York.

Chee Heng Leng. 2010. "International Marriages in Malaysia: Issues Arising from State Policies and Processes." In *Changing Marriage Patterns in Southeast Asia: Economic and Social Dimensions*, ed. Gavin Jones, Terence Hull and Maznah Mohamad. London: Routledge.

Cheng, Sealing. 2011. *On the Move for Love: Migrant Entertainers and the U.S. Military in South Korea*. Philadelphia: University of Pennsylvania Press.

Constable, Nicole. 2003. *Romance on a Global Scale: Pen Pals, Virtual Ethnography and "Mail-Order" Brides.* Oakland: University of California Press.

———— ed. 2005. *Cross-Border Marriages: Gender and Mobility in Transnational Asia.* Philadelphia: University of Pennsylvania Press.

Commission on Filipinos Overseas. 2015. *Global Mapping of Overseas Filipinos.* Available at http://www.cfo.gov.ph/index.php?option=com_content&view=article&id=1342:statistical-profile-of-spouses-and-other-partners-of-foreign-nationals&catid=134:statisticsstock-estimate&Itemid=814 [accessed 27 Nov. 2015].

————. 2015. *Number of Filipino Spouses and Other Partners of Foreign Nationals by Major Country: 1989–2014.* Available at http://cfo.gov.ph/index.php?option=com_content&view=article&id=1342:statistical-profile-of-spouses-and-other-partners-of-foreign-nationals&catid=134:statisticsstock-estimate&Itemid=814 [accessed 27 Nov. 2015].

Daily Express. 2013. *20,000 foreigners married locals.* 23 May 2013. Available at www.dailyexpress.com.my/news.cfm?NewsID=85418 [accessed 15 June 2015].

Economist. 2011. Herr and Madame, Señor and Mrs. 12 Nov. 2011.

Glodava, Mila and Richard Onizuka. 1994. *Mail-Order Brides: Women For Sale.* Fort Collins, CO: Alaken.

Parliament of Malaysia. 2015. *Hansard of Parliament of Malaysia, 21 April 2015.* Available at www.parlimen.gov.my/hansard-dewan-rakyat.html [accessed 5 Aug. 2015].

Harrtgen, Kenneth and Stephan Klasen. 2008. *Well-being of Migrant Children and Migrant Youth in Europe.* Available at http://globalnetwork.princeton.edu/bellagio/Harttgen%20Klasen%20Final.pdf [accessed 15 June 2015].

Hsiao Chuan Hsia, ed. 2010. *For Better or For Worse: Comparative Research on Equity and Access for Marriage Migrants.* Hong Kong: Asia Pacific Mission for Migrants.

Hsiao Chuan Hsia. 2012. "Reproduction Crisis and Marriage Migrants in Taiwan." Paper presented at the International Conference on Dynamics on Marriage/Divorce-related Migration in Asia, Tokyo University of Foreign Studies, Tokyo, Japan, 15 December 2012.

Hugo, Graeme. 1996. "Asia on the Move: Research Challenges for Population Geography." *Journal of Population Geography* 2: 95–118.

Jones, Gavin. 2012a. "Marriage Migration in Asia: An Introduction." *Asian and Pacific Migration Journal* 21(3): 287–90.

————. 2012b. *International Marriage in Asia: What Do We Know, and What Do We Need to Know?* Asia Research Paper Series 174. Asia Research Institute, National University of Singapore.

Jones, Gavin and Hsiu-hua Shen. 2008. "International Marriages in East and Southeast Asia: trends and research emphases." *Citizenship Studies* 12(1): 9–25.

Lauser, Andrea. 2008. "Philippine Women on the Move: Marriage Across Borders." *International Migration* 46(4): 85–110.

Lu, Chia-wen Lu. 2008. "Commercially Arranged Marriage Migration: Case Studies of Cross-border Marriages in Taiwan." In *Marriage, Migration and Gender*, ed. Rajni Palriwala and Patricia Uberoi. New Delhi: SAGE Publications, pp. 125–51.

New Straits Times. 12 Mar. 2009.

New York Times. 10 May 2012.

Philippine Overseas Employment Administration (POEA) website. Available at http://www.poea.gov.ph/stats/2013_stats.pdf. [accessed 2 Aug. 2015].

Piper, Nicola and Mina Roces. 2003. "Introduction: Marriage and Migration in an Age of Globalization." In *Wife or Worker: Asian Women in Migration*, ed. Nicola Piper and Mina Roces. Lanham, Maryland: Rowman and Littlefield, pp. 1–22.

Ratha, Dilip and William Shaw. 2007. *South-South Migration and Remittance.* World Bank Working Paper 102. Washington: World Bank.

Straits Times. 19 Feb. 2006.

Sunday Times. 12 Sept. 2013.

Sung, Betty-Lee. 1990. *Chinese-American Intermarriage.* New York: Center for Migration Studies.

Suzuki, Nobue. 2003. "Transgressing 'Victims'—Reading Narratives of 'Filipina Brides in Japan'". *Critical Asian Studies* 35(3): 399–420.

Toyota, Mika. 2008. "Editorial Introduction: International Marriage, rights and the state in East and Southeast Asia." *Citizenship Studies* 12(1): 1–7.

United Nations General Assembly Report. 2012. *International Migration and Development.* A/67/254, 67th session, New York. Available at http://daccess-dds-ny.un.org/doc/UNDOC/GEN/N12/452/13/PDF/N1245213.pdf?OpenElement [accessed 27 Nov. 2015].

Wang, Hong-zen and Chang Shu-ming. 2002. "The Commodification of International Marriages: Cross-border Marriage Business in Taiwan and Viet Nam." *International Migration* 40(6): 93–116.

Yeoh, Brenda S.A., Chee Heng Leng and Vu Thi Kieu Dung. 2013. "Commercially arranged marriage and the negotiation of citizenship rights among Vietnamese marriage migrants in multiracial Singapore." *Asian Ethnicity* 14(2): 139–56.

PART II
Reversed Geographies of Power

CHAPTER 4

"Centre/Periphery" Flow Reversed?: Twenty Years of Cross-border Marriages between Philippine Women and Japanese Men

Ikuya Tokoro

Introduction

In the last two decades, international marriages (*kokusai kekkon*) between Filipino women and Japanese men have become one of the main types of cross-border marriage in Japan. Before 2005, the majority of Filipino women who married Japanese men entered Japan as entertainers working in bars and nightclubs. While working, they met men whom they decided to marry. Many studies have examined cross-border marriages between these former entertainers and Japanese men from sociological, anthropological, gender and feminist perspectives. For example, a number of researchers have conducted comprehensive studies examining various aspects of this cross-border marriage migration in terms of its social and historical backgrounds, and other related issues (Ballescas 1992; Constable 2005; Faier 2007; Parreñas 2001, 2008; Suzuki 2005; Suzuki 2008; Yang 2010). In recent years, and especially since 2005 (as noted by Parreñas 2008), the patterns and trends of Filipino-Japanese cross-border marriages have gradually yet significantly changed due to the tightening of Japanese immigration policies in response to a global anti-human-trafficking campaign led by the United States (Parreñas 2008: 135–7; U.S. Department of State 2005).

This chapter describes events up until 2013 that relate to issues affecting Filipino-Japanese cross-border marriage. The first half of the chapter describes changing patterns in Japanese-Filipino cross-border marriage with a focus on the effects of the global anti-human-trafficking campaign. The second half of the chapter explores the following issues: cross-border divorce, remittance and the so-called *konkyu houjin* (impoverished Japanese marriage-migration men) problem. The problems that Japanese men encounter in cross-border marriages with Filipinas have been neglected by previous studies of cross-border marriage migration in Japan. This author examines the konkyu houjin problem in order to demonstrate the emergence of an interesting phenomenon that questions core assumptions underpinning the work of other scholars of cross-border marriages. Previous studies have focused on the Filipina marriage migrants leading them to describe the movement of Japanese marriage migration in terms of periphery-to-centre and poor third world-to-rich first world dichotomies. However, descriptions of konkyu houjin marriages suggest that a hitherto unstudied reversed centre-to-periphery/rich first world-to-poor third world movement is at work and must be described to adequately explain the flow of cross-border marriage migration between Japanese men and Filipino women.

Recent Marriage Trends between Filipinas and Japanese Men

This section examines the various factors that contributed to a significant decrease from 2006 to 2012 in cross-border marriages between Filipino women and Japanese men. This decrease was a direct consequence of Japanese immigration policies developed in response to strong criticism from the U.S. government in 2005, which described the migration of Filipina entertainers to Japan as a form of human trafficking (Parreñas 2008: 135–7, U.S. Department of State 2005). See Table 4.1.

Table 4.1 Number of Filipina-Japanese marriages (and divorces) registered in selected years between 1995 and 2013

Year	Number of Marriages	Number of Divorces
1995	7,188	1,456
2000	7,519	2,816
2005	10,242	3,485
2006	12,150	4,065
2008	7,290	4,782
2009	5,755	4,714
2010	5,212	4,630
2013	3,118	3,574

Source: Ministry of Health, Labour and Welfare, 1996, 2011.

In 1993, Filipino women and Japanese men entered into more than 6,000 cross-border marriages. The majority of these women worked as hostesses to serve customers in establishments known as *Filipin Pubs* in Japan. Others worked in other establishments as entertainers who sing and perform dance routines. In practice, being an entertainer or a hostess is the same job for all intents and purposes. In 2000, there was an increase in the number of marriages between retired (pensioned) Japanese men and Filipinas. In 2005, as mentioned above, the U.S. Department of State claimed that the migration of Filipina entertainers to Japan was tantamount to human trafficking. In response to this criticism, the Japanese government revised its policies to restrict the number of Filipina entertainers in 2006 resulting in a dramatic decline in the number of Filipina entertainers in Japan. For example, the total number of Filipina entertainers living legally in Japan was 50,691 in 2004. However, by 2010 the number had dropped to 6,319. The number of cross-border marriages registered between Filipino women and Japanese men also declined dramatically due to this change in policy (see Table 4.1).

The year 2006 marked the last time that Filipina entertainers could apply for marriage visas that would secure their entry into Japan. This led to large numbers of prospective couples marrying to beat the deadline, resulting in a total of 12,150 marriages being registered. However, by 2013 the number of registered marriages between Filipino women and Japanese men had declined to 3,118.

The dramatic decrease in the issuance of entertainer visas, however, has not been the only recent significant change in the visa situation of Filipinas in Japan. In addition to the Immigration Department's limitations on the issuance of marriage visas, the department has also restricted the issuance of Certificates of Eligibility (COEs) to Filipinas who have already married Japanese men and are residing in Japan. These restrictions are enforced because the Japanese Immigration Department suspects that a number of marriages registered between Filipina women and Japanese men are false; that is, Filipinas and willing Japanese men register nonexistent marriages so that these women can work in Japan.

In recent years, for example, the Immigration Department has detained many marriage brokers in the Philippines who arrange false marriages, as well as Filipinas who have migrated to Japan on the strength of falsely declared marriages. The increase in false marriages has been a result of restrictions placed on the issuance of Japanese entertainer visas to Filipinas. During an interview with the staff of a Manila-based visa facilitation agency, I learned that in 2006 Filipina entertainers had rushed to marry Japanese men to gain entry into Japan before this window of opportunity closed forever. Since 2007, the number of these agencies' clients has decreased because of the above policy changes. However, false marriages have become the new dominant method for Filipino women to enter Japan. Some of these women find marital partners by searching social media sites such as Facebook, Twitter and Internet chat portals. Others find partners by accessing their social networks of friends and family. For instance, Filipino wives of Japanese men sometimes attempt to introduce their sisters or cousins to the friends or relatives of their Japanese husbands in the hopes of finding a partner for them. These new patterns in cross-border marriage have gradually emerged and accelerated in recent years due to the restrictions on entertainer visas. In addition, it has become increasingly difficult for non-entertainer Filipinas to acquire marriage visas and COEs. In general, they must successfully pass through a number of stressful institutional and legal processes before they are granted marriage visas and/or COEs. In the next section, we will examine these processes in detail.

Institutional Barriers in Cross-border Marriages

Non-entertainer Filipinas face several institutional barriers when they attempt to legally remain in Japan and apply for marriage visas and/or COEs. They must pass through the many steps of the visa process so that the Immigration Department can scrutinize visa applicants to eliminate fake marriage claims. Marriage brokers or visa-facilitation agencies typically require Japanese citizens to visit the Philippines at least three times prior to becoming engaged. These visits make the relationships seem real and provide evidence that the marriages are not fake. As part of the application process for a marriage visa, applicants must submit records of phone calls made, emails sent or copies of letters exchanged between the Filipinas and their Japanese fiancés to prove that their relationship is based on mutual love rather than the desire to obtain a Japanese visa. If a prospective couple hopes to live in Japan, the couple must undergo a complex and time-consuming procedure to acquire a valid visa. First, they must secure various documents for the wife from a variety of local and central government offices in the Philippines. These documents include a birth certificate authorized by both the local Civil Registrar and National Statistics Office (NSO), baptismal certificate, Certificate of Legal Capacity and Certificate of Marriage authorized by the NSO.

Then, the couple must apply for a Japanese COE. Once the wife receives her COE, she must apply for a valid visa that will allow her to remain in Japan.

In recent years, even women with valid visas have found that the visa renewal process has become increasingly difficult. Interviews conducted with the representative of a visa-facilitation agency located in Manila revealed that this process has become quite difficult because of the increasing instances of some Filipino women applying for Japanese marriage visas while still legally married to Filipinos. These women do this because divorce is illegal for all Philippine citizens, except Muslims. Married Philippine citizens can only legally separate by annulling their marriages. However, the annulment process is time consuming and very expensive for ordinary Filipinos. Therefore, many couples do not apply for an annulment. They simply live separately from each other.

Fake Marriages

A significant number of Filipina marriage migrants are introduced to their future husbands by sisters or relatives who are already married to Japanese men and have settled in Japan. In part, changes to Japanese immigration and border control policies have made this an increasingly popular way of meeting a husband in order to work in Japan. In addition, partly because the economic situation for ordinary people in the Philippines has deteriorated in recent years, the families of some migrants encourage them to find husbands for sisters, nieces and other female relatives in order to increase the remittances they receive from overseas family members. As a consequence, the boundaries between marriage migrants and migrant workers have become blurred.

Although the institutional barriers remain high for Filipinas wanting to marry Japanese men, there are personal barriers as well. Individual emotions and affections, particularly love, also play an important role in cross-boundary marriage migration. During my research, I have become aware of several cases in which Japanese men had to cancel their planned marriages with Filipinas at the last minute, even after these women had successfully passed through the stressful institutional procedures. In many cases, the women stated that they were unable to marry men they did not truly love. In many of these cases, the age gap between the women and their prospective Japanese husbands was very wide. In typical cases, the women were in their twenties or early thirties, while their Japanese partners might be in their fifties or sixties.

The need to be sincerely in love with, and affectionate towards, one's husband seems to play an important part in decisions to enter a fake marriage or continue with one. Some Filipinas hesitate to accept marriage offers from brokers because they are afraid or feel a sense of discomfort when they consider living with a man whom they do not know or love. The following case studies describe the situations of several Filipinas who hesitated to enter into "fake marriages" to travel to Japan.

The Case of Maya

I interviewed a young Filipina, Maya (pseudonym), in 2012. She was working in a karaoke bar/club in Manila to contribute to her family's finances when she was invited by a "promoter" (marriage broker), who visited her club as a guest, to work in a club in Japan where she would earn a monthly salary of USD1,300. However, as part of her employment agree, she had to participate in a fake marriage and the possibility of living with her "husband" to fool immigration officers into concluding that the marriage was real. However, Maya found it unacceptable to live with an unfamiliar man even if the marriage was false. She had seen a photograph of her would-be "husband" who was over 50 years old and not very attractive, according to the then-21-year-old Maya. The huge age gap between her and her Japanese husband made her not particularly eager to accept the broker's offer, even though she was only being asked to enter into a fake marriage. In the end, she declined the offer.

The Case of KC

This case describes a 24-year-old Filipina who had just ended a fake marriage in Japan. I interviewed KC (pseudonym) in Manila in March 2012 after she returned from Japan, where she had been in a fake marriage. She was born and raised in Davao on the island of Mindanao, in the southern part of the Philippines. She had worked for some time in a karaoke bar/club in Manila. Between 2009 and 2010, she accepted a proposal from a broker who had approached her in the club to enter into a fake marriage with a Japanese man. She lived in Japan for approximately two years as the "wife" of an unfamiliar man who lived in the city of Fukuoka on the island of Kyushu. She also agreed to work as a hostess in a bar/club in Fukuoka.

After she moved to Fukuoka, KC met her Japanese husband on several occasions. However, they never lived together in the same house.

At that time, Immigration Department inspections were rare, and Filipinas in false marriages were able to live separately from their husbands. However, KC had to pay a certain amount of her salary to her husband in compensation for "renting his name". The broker had originally promised KC that she would receive USD700 out of a total monthly salary of USD2,000. She was required to pay her husband USD500 per month, and her broker, USD800 per month. However, in reality, she only received about USD500 per month. Moreover, the broker failed to pay the promised amount to either KC or her husband. Instead, he kept most of the money for himself. As a result, KC's husband divorced her, and the broker confiscated her passport to prevent her from quitting her job and leaving the country. She had no choice but to work in another club in Fukuoka so that she could earn a sufficient income to remit money to her family in Davao. KC struggled in this situation for three months before ultimately escaping from the bar and the broker. First, she travelled to Kokura in the nearby city of Kitakyushu where her aunt worked as an entertainer. KC moved in with her aunt and began working as a hostess. However, she eventually had to leave her aunt's house because her aunt was in the process of divorcing her Japanese husband. Next, KC moved to Nagoya, where she once again acquired work as a hostess in a karaoke club. There, she was able to earn between USD2,500 and USD3,000 a month because no money was deducted for broker's fees. KC remitted USD1,000 per month to her family in Davao, which allowed them to build a new house. KC eventually left Nagoya and began working in a club in Tokyo. However, there she only earned USD900 per month. Finally, she surrendered herself to the Immigration Office in Tokyo, which deported her back to the Philippines.

As we can see from KC's case, the crackdown on human trafficking led by the United States has had ironic consequences. The Japanese government stopped the issuance of visas to Filipina migrants because the U.S. Department of State described the migration of Filipina entertainers to Japan as a form of human trafficking. As a result, the number of fake marriages has increased because arrangements like KC's offer an alternative method for these women to enter and work in Japan. Like KC, many Filipinas who enter Japan through fake marriages are vulnerable to exploitation and abuse by brokers—more so than the migrant workers who previously entered Japan as entertainers. Therefore, as noted by Parreñas (2008), the paradox of these anti-human trafficking measures is that they have placed Filipina migrants in an increasingly vulnerable position.

Recent Problems Related to Cross-border Marriages

A validly married couple with a visa and COE permitting the wife's legal residence in Japan might still face significant problems. The reality of these difficulties is demonstrated by the high divorce rate among Filipino-Japanese couples, which was approximately 65.8 per cent as of 2008. This high divorce rate has a number of causes. Some couples struggle with difficulties related to remittances. In many cases, Filipino women who reside in Japan are the breadwinners of their birth families, who expect substantial financial support in the form of remittances. The amount of these remittances varies widely. In my interviews, I learned that most Filipinas in Japan remit between USD400 and USD1,000 per month depending on their individual situations. In addition to these regular monthly remittances, Filipino women also send occasional remittances when their birth families experience emergencies such as sickness or damage to property due to natural calamities, such as typhoons and floods, or when tuition fees for brothers or sisters are due. One Filipina I interviewed had remitted more than USD11,000 for such purposes. Frequently, the Japanese husbands of these women are in situations where they must assist their own families as well as those of their wives. Such situations can cause marital difficulties and serve as a reason for divorce.

Konkyu Houjin: Impoverished Japanese Marriage-migration Men

An additional issue that has received relatively little attention is the migration of Japanese men and their Filipino wives to the Philippines. In recent years, the situation of konkyu houjin has become more visible in the Japanese media (Mizutani 2011). For example, in 2010 the Japanese embassy in Manila helped 332 Japanese men, the highest number of Japanese men aided by diplomatic staff in any foreign country that year. That number was an increase of 46 per cent from the previous year. Moreover, since 2001 the embassy has aided approximately 100 or 200 men annually. According to embassy staff, however, only two staff members have been assigned to address this problem. Most Japanese men in need of help are those who have travelled to the Philippines and remained there with their Filipino girlfriends or wives. When these Japanese men first move to the Philippines, they would not be considered poor or impoverished. However, after relocating, the majority of them either gradually or rapidly become impoverished due to the costs of supporting their girlfriends' or wives' families. In some cases, they might spend their savings too rapidly while not generating any additional income.

Most of these Japanese men who move to the Philippines to join their wives or girlfriends lack sufficient language skills in English, Tagalog/Filipino or local dialects, and many of them have difficulty obtaining jobs there. As a result, some of these impoverished Japanese men are abandoned by their wives or girlfriends. In many cases, the men do not know other people in the Philippines. As a consequence, some konkyu houjin ask the Japanese embassy for assistance, and they are usually advised by the embassy to return to Japan. Alternatively, the embassy may suggest that the men ask their relatives in Japan to send money. In many cases, these konkyu houjin do not have a family in Japan. In other cases, they do not have good relationships with their families who refuse to help them. As a result, some of these men become homeless in the Philippines, or are forced to rely on assistance from Filipino neighbours. The following case studies describe several tragic incidents involving konkyu houjin in the Philippines.

The Case of a Shooting Committed by a Konkyu Houjin

In July 2011, there was a shooting incident in a suburb of Metro Manila. A Japanese man in his late fifties shot at least six people, including some relatives of his ex-wife. One of the victims died instantly; at least five people were injured. According to a media report, the shooter was angry with his ex-wife and her relatives because he believed that they had cheated him out of more than PHP3 million (equivalent to approximately USD65,000) within a five-year period. He had originally met his ex-wife in a karaoke bar/club in Japan. When they met, he was still married to a Japanese woman, but he divorced her and married the Filipina entertainer in 2007. Because he did not have a very good relationship with his parents and other family members, this man decided to migrate to the Philippines. Prior to his migration to the Philippines, he sold all his property in Japan, including his house, and forwarded a significant amount of money to his wife's family to buy a car, which he planned to use to operate a taxi business after relocating. He also sent money to pay for a new house in a suburb of Manila, where he planned to live with his new wife. However, after he migrated to the Philippines, he discovered that his wife's family had already used most of the money for their own purposes. He had no car and no house. He and his wife began to quarrel about their financial problems, and ultimately they divorced. However, he remained in the country and planned to start a small business with some Filipino friends. Unfortunately, he was cheated by these friends, and he lost most of the money he had brought with him from Japan. His anger and disappointment with his ex-wife and the friends who had cheated him finally drove him to violence (*Manila Shimbun* 26 July 2012). He was jailed and is waiting for a trial and verdict.

The Case of a Konkyu Houjin Who Committed Suicide

This case study describes another tragic incident involving a konkyu houjin who committed suicide in the Philippines. I heard this story from Linda (pseudonym), the man's Filipino ex-girlfriend. In 2004, Linda was working as an entertainer in a karaoke bar/club in Chiba, Japan, where she met a Japanese man named Yasushi (pseudonym) who worked at a company office in a nearby suburb. They soon became attracted to each other, and Linda became Yasushi's girlfriend. At that time, Linda was 24 years old and Yasushi was 38. Yasushi was a jealous man. He often became angry with Linda when he watched her serving other guests in the club. When her work contract and six-month visa expired Linda informed Yasushi that she would not be staying in Japan. Yasushi decided to migrate to the Philippines so that he and Linda could be together. Moreover, Yasushi had a debt of several million yen in Japan, and he wanted to escape from having to repay this debt. In 2005, he moved to the Philippines and began living in Linda's house in Cavite Province. After several months, Linda became pregnant. However, Yasushi was unemployed and they lacked funds for the most basic daily needs. Yasushi was unable to leave the country because he had overstayed his visa and would not be allowed back if he left; he also lacked funds to buy an airplane ticket. Furthermore, he had no one in Japan he could depend on and the great burden of the several million yen he owed remained. Ultimately, Yasushi committed suicide in Linda's house when she was seven months pregnant.

The two cases described above might seem rare and exceptional. However, stories of Japanese men who fall into difficult circumstances after they move to the Philippines to live with their Filipino wives or girlfriends have become more common in recent years. There is no exact data as to the number of konkyu houjin in the Philippines, but from my own research I estimate that the number is 200 to 300 for the country as a whole. As indicated above, in many cases Japanese men have been cheated by the family members of their Filipino wives and lost their property and/or money.

During one interview, I learned about a Japanese man in his mid-fifties who moved to one of the Visayan Islands in the central part of the Philippines after he resigned from his job in Japan. He used all his retirement savings to build a house on the island. With all his savings spent, he had no other source of income. He was unable to find a job because he could not speak the local dialect or English. Ultimately, his Filipino wife and her family members evicted him from his own house. He went to the city of Cebu, the main city of the region, to ask for help; however, nobody was able to help him. He even surrendered himself to the Philippine Immigration Office, but the office was unwilling to send him back him to Japan because he had no funds to buy an airplane ticket. Thus, he had no choice other than to live as a *de facto* homeless person in the Philippines.

Conclusion

Over the last two decades, marriages between Filipino women and Japanese men have become one of several common types of international marriages (*kokusai kekkon*) in Japan. Prior to 2005, most of the Filipino women who married Japanese men entered Japan as entertainers and worked in bars and clubs. However, this pattern underwent a significant change after 2006 because Japanese immigration-control policies were tightened in response to the global anti-human trafficking campaign led by the United States.

In this chapter, I have attempted to determine what events and conditions define the recent cross-border marriages between Filipina women and Japanese men. I have found that these conditions have been influenced by the aforementioned global anti-trafficking-campaign resulting in Filipinas marrying Japanese men in order to work in Japan to support their families in the Philippines and the emergence of konkyu houjin.

This chapter has highlighted two negative and paradoxical side effects of the anti-human-trafficking campaign despite its humanitarian intent. First, the policy has caused the situation of Filipina migrants to worsen rather than improving it. Currently, many Filipino migrant women have no choice other than to depend on illegal means—such as fake marriages—to enter Japan because the formerly legal method (obtaining an entertainer's visa) is no longer allowed. As a result, Filipino women today are much more vulnerable to abuse and exploitation by illegal brokers or recruiters than they were ever before. Even Filipinas who marry Japanese men whom they truly love face institutional barriers when they attempt to acquire marriage visas and/or COEs to legally remain in Japan. Because of the proliferation of fake marriages, they have to undergo a complex and time-consuming visa process to demonstrate their legitimacy.

Second, by presenting case studies of konkyu houjin, this chapter also shows that a peculiar phenomenon is emerging which cannot be accounted for by the current assumption that cross-border marriage flows move from "the periphery to the centre" or "poor third world to the wealthy first world". This assumption asserts that the general flow of migration involves poor women from the global south (the socially, economically and technologically peripheral third world) migrating to the global north (metropolitan centres of rich, materially advanced countries) to seek better lives. This assumption might be valid to a certain degree in the case of Filipino women migrants because they engage in cross-border marriages to travel to Japan and improve their economic conditions. However, the cases of konkyu houjin examined in this chapter show ostensibly "rich" Japanese men moving to the Philippines where they become impoverished for various reasons. This constitutes a reversal in the flow of cross-border marriage migration between Japanese men and Filipina women, a flow which has accelerated since the late 1990s. This reversed migration flow from the global north to the global south has not been explained. Of course, it is possible to claim these konkyu houjin become impoverished due to a series of badly thought-out decisions. However, this does not explain why these men make these decisions in the first place or why these decisions make sense to them. This suggests that studies of cross-border marriages between Filipino women and Japanese men should widen their research scope by also examining multi-directional or reverse flows of migration.

Acknowledgement

Most of the data collected for this article was obtained during field research conducted by the author in Japan and the Philippines. Field research was conducted in the Philippines on several occasions, particularly in March and July–August 2012. This study was made possible by the provision of financial aid [(Grant Number 23251006)] from the Japan Society for the Promotion of Science (JSPS).

References

Ballescas, M.R.P. 1992. *Filipino Entertainers in Japan*. Quezon City: Foundation for Nationalist Studies.

Constable, Nicole, ed. 2005. *Cross-Border Marriages: Gender and Mobility in Transnational Asia*. Philadelphia: University of Pennsylvania Press.

Daily Manila Shimbun, 26 July 2012.

Faier, Lieba. 2007. "Filipina Migrants in Rural Japan and their Professions of Love." *American Ethnologist* 34(1): 148–62.

Ministry of Health, Labour and Welfare. 1996. *Vital Statistics of Japan*. Tokyo: Health, Labour and Welfare Statistics Association.

———. 2011. *Vital Statistics of Japan*. Tokyo: Health, Labour and Welfare Statistics Association.

Mizutani, Takehide. 2011. *Nihon wo Suteta Otokotachi: Firipin ni Ikiru "Konkyu Houjin"* ["Konkyu Houjin" in the Philippines]. Tokyo: Syueisya.

Parreñas, Rhacel Salazar. 2001. *Servants of Globalization: Women, Migration and Domestic Work*. Stanford, CA: Stanford University Press.

———. 2008. *The Force of Domesticity: Filipina Migrants and Globalization*. New York: New York University Press.

Suzuki, Nobue. 2005. "Tripartite Desires: Filipina-Japanese Marriages and Fantasies of Transnational Traversal." In *Cross-Border Marriages: Gender and Mobility in Transnational Asia*, ed. Nicole Constable. Philadelphia: University of Pennsylvania Press.

———. 2008. "Filipino Migration to Japan: From Surrogate Americans to Feminized Workers." *Transnational Migration in East Asia, Senri Ethnological Reports* 77: 67–77.

United States Department of State. 2005. *Trafficking in Persons Reports*. Washington, D.C.: U.S. Government Publications Office.

Yang, Wen-Shan and Melody Chia-Wen Lu. 2010. *Asian Cross-Border Marriage Migration*. Amsterdam: Amsterdam University Press.

CHAPTER 5

Child Return Migration from Japan to Thailand

Sari K. Ishii

Introduction

In 2009, a news story[1] spread across Thailand. A poor 9-year-old boy, who sold fish at a temple in northern Thailand to earn money so he could go to school, had been showing foreign tourists a photograph of a young man and asking them if they knew him. The boy, Keigo Sato, claimed that the man was his Japanese father. He was born on 28 February 2000 in the Phichit province in northern Thailand. His Japanese father and Thai mother had registered their marriage with the Japanese authorities on 17 January 2000. According to Japan's nationality law, the boy was a Japanese national regardless of his birthplace because he was born to a formally married couple in which one spouse was a Japanese national. After registering their marriage in Japan, his parents moved to Thailand, and the boy was born in his mother's home in a village located in northern Thailand. However, after the boy was born, his father returned to Japan and lost contact with the boy's mother. Later, the boy's mother contracted an illness and passed away in 2009. On her deathbed, she told her son to find his Japanese father by asking tourists at the temple about the father's photograph. The news about the boy's abject situation first appeared in a Thai newspaper in May 2009. Soon thereafter, several other newspapers and magazines published reports about the boy, and his story eventually became national news in Thailand. Embassies began searching for the father and eventually located him. The boy's remarkable reunion with his father on 26 October 2009 was reported in the Thai media. This symbolic event prompted many mothers and children in similar situations to submit inquiries to the Japanese embassy in Bangkok and the Consulate General of Japan in Chiang Mai, northern Thailand.[2] Notably, however, this news that swept Thailand was hardly reported in the Japanese media.

Thailand is acknowledged as a major country of origin for female marriage migrants. Although numerous studies have focused on the marriage migrants from Thai northeastern villages who immigrate to Western countries (Angeles and Sunanta 2009: 551; Ariyabuddhiphongs and Kampama 2009: 284; Esara 2009: 413; Tosakul 2010: 179), only a few studies have explored marriage immigration from northern Thailand to East Asian countries, despite the large number of marriage migrants from this region. The number of female migrants traveling from northern Thailand to Japan increased in the mid-1980s but decreased after the early 1990s, a pattern that corresponds to Japan's economic boom and subsequent recession. Following this wave of female migrants, the number of cross-border marriages between Thai women and Japanese men increased.

Not only was there an increase in the number of cross-border marriages, there was also an increase in the number of divorces between Thai-Japanese couples. The number of Japanese-Thai children born out of wedlock also increased. It was not until 1995 that the Japanese government began tracking the number of Thai-Japanese children in its official statistics. It can be safely assumed that the birth of Japanese-Thai children had already been increasing since the mid-1980s. Between 1995 and 2013, the official statistics indicate that 11,436[3] Japanese-Thai children were registered in Japan (see Table 5.1).

Despite the fact that by 2015 many of these children will be teenagers or adults in their early twenties pursuing higher education, employment and marriage, few studies have explored their current situation. Where are these children now? In which nation have they been integrated or not integrated legally, socially and economically? This chapter investigates the situation of these Japanese-Thai children to determine whether or not the gendered geography of power that marriage migrants believed in has persisted in relation to these children's long-term situation. In other words, has being Japanese indeed proven beneficial to these children?

In the following sections, the existing analytical viewpoints on Thai marriage migrants and their home villages are reviewed. Then, empirical studies conducted in rural villages in Northern Thailand are presented.

Table 5.1 Marriages, divorces and children born between Japanese men and Thai women registered in Japan (Number of Persons)

Year	Marriages	Divorces	Children Born
1992	1585	171	
1993	1926	186	
1994	1836	239	
1995	1915	315	851
1996	1760	320	827
1997	1688	362	859
1998	1699	435	852
1999	2024	540	836
2000	2137	612	736
2001	1840	682	742
2002	1536	699	670
2003	1445	678	638
2004	1640	685	579
2005	1637	782	509
2006	1676	867	512
2007	1475	831	507
2008	1338	795	446
2009	1225	823	427
2010	1096	743	380
2011	1046	665	394
2012	1089	652	325
2013	981	649	346
Total	34,594	12,731	11,436

Source: Ministry of Health, Labour and Welfare, 1992–2014.

Finally, based on the empirical research results, the gendered geography of power issue vis-à-vis these Japanese-Thai children is discussed.

The "Commodification" of Thai Women

Female Thai marriage migrants are typically discussed within the context of the relationship between human trafficking and the commodification of women connected to the tourism industry. Within this context, marriage migration is often analyzed as an extension of the tourism-oriented service industry. Such studies typically suggest that marriage migration among Thai women began with the "rental wife" phenomenon of the Vietnam War, during which some American soldiers lived with local women (Chantavanich et al. 2001: 6; Cohen 2003: 60; Esara 2009: 405; Ratanaolan-Mix 2005: 3). After the American military withdrew from the area, the leisure industry for soldiers swiftly adapted to the growing international tourism market (Chantavanich et al. 2001: 6–7; Esara 2009: 405).

Western male researchers have sometimes discussed ambiguities between prostitution and romantic love for foreign tourists on the touristic stage in Thailand (Askew 2009: 197; Cohen 2001: 256). These researchers note that because of this ambiguity, "romantic love" may sometimes lead to long-term relationships and even to marriage. In such studies, the difference between marriage migration and human trafficking/commodification of women is not always evident (Cohen 2003: 58; Esara 2009: 406; Whittaker 2009: 321).

Theories Emphasizing Female Migrants' "Own Agency"

More recent studies raise questions about the portrayal of marriage migrants as victims. These studies emphasize the women's own agency in choosing marriage migration as a strategy for securing a "better life" that is not achievable for them in Thailand (Angeles and Sunanta 2009: 571; Tosakul 2010: 197–8). Such studies analyze the ways in which women's agency is exercised within Thailand's current social system. Tosakul describes Thai village women who participate in marriage migration as follows:

> ... they are conscious social actors who aspire to attain economic success by redefining and reinterpreting their cultural values in light of their own local cultural practices and those introduced by Western thinking that would serve their current interests and positions, despite their constrained and subordinated positions within the existing system. (2010: 198)

According to these recent studies, there are many single mothers from rural villages saddled with poor social capital among Thai female marriage migrants. Because of their backgrounds, the women hold a disadvantaged position in Thai society, in which they belong to a lower social and economic class (Chantavanich et al. 2001: 17; Ratanaolan-Mix & Piper 2003: 55; Tosakul 2010: 196). Women from rural villages experience powerful social pressures. The traditional values of matrilocal agrarian communities stipulate that a daughter is responsible for taking care of her aging parents (Angeles and Sunanta 2009: 555; Sunanta 2008: 18). Additionally, some marriage migrants marry and have children with local men before their marriage migration (Angeles and Sunanta 2009: 553; Chantavanich et al. 2001: 18, 45; Ruenkaew 1999: 5, 11). Local custom holds these women also responsible for raising those children (Ruenkaew 1999: 11).

However, these minimally educated single mothers from rural areas are typically unable to enter high-income occupations (Sunanta 2008: 20) or to remarry prosperous husbands as an alternative (Esara 2009: 422; Tosakul 2010: 156). Furthermore, despite the social pressures on women to fulfil this dual responsibility, the state's social welfare system provides insufficient support for single mothers (Ruenkaew 1999: 11). Therefore, marriage migration could be regarded by such women as the only way to fulfil traditional local expectations (Tosakul 2010: 196). Through marriage migration, the women believe they can regain their identities and their relationships with family and friends at home (Chantavanich et al. 2001: 41; Sunanta 2008: 19; Tosakul 2010: 197) or even gain esteem (Ariyabuddhiphongs and Kampama 2009: 292–3) by fulfilling their duty as defined by the traditional gender ideology of family responsibility and obligations (Angeles and Sunanta 2009: 555; Sunanta 2008: 3). The women also believe that their families may acquire higher status in the community in this way (Sunanta 2008: 3). Given these circumstances, the women freely "choose" marriage migration to circumvent their subordinated position (Esara 2009: 422), which is how one strand of research explains the Thai women's agency in the phenomenon of marriage migration.

The Gendered Geographies of Power in the Long Term

Either explicitly or implicitly, both strands of the research discussed above assume that impoverished Thai women who cannot achieve upward social/economic mobility within Thailand marry men from wealthy countries to achieve socio-economic security (Ariyabuddhiphongs and Kampama 2009: 292; Tosakul 2010: 186) or to circumvent their disadvantaged social position within Thailand (Sunanta 2008: 20). These assumptions seem to correspond to what Constable (2005) calls the *gendered geographies of power*. She explains that "marriage can be used to achieve upward geographic mobility and independence (Freeman, Schein); to provide economic support for families back home (Suzuki, Oxfeld, Constable); or to escape less than ideal marital opportunities or gender constraints at home (Constable, Thai)" (Constable 2005: 15). The female migrants or former migrants from Thai villages whom the author met in the field often explained their trans-border marriage in similar terms, especially in relation to children. Their narratives often involved marrying foreign men to provide a better life for their children.

This chapter verifies whether or not the gendered geography of power to which these women subscribe actually improved the living standards of their children. Although current research increasingly acknowledges the relationship between transnational migration and the subsequent alteration of the configuration of families, which is integral to children's lives and experiences in Asia (Yeoh et al. 2012: 123), few studies focus on child migration subsequent to the marriage or divorce of their parents, whether they are bi-ethnic children or children from a previous marriage (Williams 2010: 215). This chapter empirically analyses cases in which the gendered geography of power seen in previous marriage migration studies does not persist into the children's generation.

Research Methodology and Data

Based on the background provided above, this study scrutinizes cases of Japanese-Thai children who have returned from Japan to northern Thai villages. The data were collected through empirical field research. Two complementary methodologies—a questionnaire and interviews—were used. The questionnaire was administered between June and October 2011 to 41 children born to 33 mothers in a province in northern Thailand.[4] The questionnaire was administered with the cooperation of Saphan Fan, an NGO dedicated to supporting return migrant children in the area. The questionnaire was designed by the author and it was verified by the NGO staff who had been working with the children for several years. The same staff also administered the questionnaires. The author also conducted interviews between 2006 and 2012 with the following: (1) 7 (former) female marriage migrants living in Thai cities and in Japan but whose Japanese-Thai children were being raised in their home villages in northern Thailand; and (2) 12 members of communities to which the migrant children from Japan had returned.

The Demographics of Investigated Return Migrant Children

The demographics of the investigated mixed-ethnic children who return migrated from Japan to northern Thailand are summarized in Table 5.2.

Table 5.2 Background characteristics of interviewed return migrant children (N = 41)

Items	Results
Age	Average 12.58, Maximum 19, Minimum 4
Gender	17 male (41.5%), 24 female (58.5%)
Nationality	21 Thai only (51.2%), 3 Japanese only (7.3%), 17 both Thai and Japanese (41.5%)
Place of Birth	21 from Thailand (51.2%), 20 from Japan (48.8%)
Mother's nationality at time of child's birth	37 Thai (90%) 4 with "authorized foreigner" status (10%)
Remittance	4 from Japanese fathers (9%) 7 from mothers in Thai cities/Japan (17%) 30 receive little or virtually no support (73%)
Name usage	31 Japanese names[5] (76%) 10 Thai names[6] (34%)

Source: Questionnaire designed by the author and administered by Saphan Fan, June–September 2011.

The majority of the target Japanese-Thai children were teenagers at the time of our research. This was not surprising because statistics show that the largest inflow of female migrants from Thailand to Japan occurred in the 1980s and early 1990s. There were no significant gender differences among the children: 17 males and 24 females. The relatively balanced proportions indicate that the mothers did not have a particular gender bias as is sometimes found among inter-married couples. For example, a daughter/son is more likely to take after their mother/father's side, as reported by previous studies on the children of inter-married couples (Sue and Telles 2007). This apparent lack of bias also may reflect a high proportion of children born out of wedlock; however, this factor was not included in the questionnaire.

A review of the nationality status of the target children reveals that (1) the actual number of Japanese-Thai children is approximately twice the number registered with the Japanese authorities; and (2) the children who are not registered in Japan are spared from being stateless because the current nationality code of Thailand defines nationality both by the territory and by *jus sanguinis*. Based on the questionnaire results, 17 children had both Thai and Japanese nationalities; 21 children had only Thai nationality; and 3 children had only Japanese nationality. An analysis of the children's birthplaces showed that 21 were born in Thailand while 20 were born in Japan. The number of children born in Thailand corresponds exactly to the number of children who have only Thai nationality. Of the 20 children born in Japan and currently living in Thailand 17 also acquired Thai nationality and now have dual nationality. These findings indicate that the number of children registered in Japan (and who therefore hold Japanese nationality) is the same as the number who were born in Thailand and are not acknowledged by the Japanese government (and therefore do not have Japanese nationality).

Although a significant number of the children (35 out of 41) have already lost financial support from their Japanese fathers and nearly all of them (38 out of 41) are endowed with their education/social welfare on the basis of their Thai nationality, 31 out of 41 children still use Japanese names in their daily life. Respondents explain that the reason why the children use Japanese names is because they do not have Thai names. Considering the notion that naming reflects the parents beliefs about what are appropriate children's names for persons of their status, and institutionalized norms and pressures (Lieberson and Bell 1992: 514), we can assume that at the time of the child's birth, the mother or the mother's relatives believed that "being Japanese" would be beneficial for the children in the future.

The Complex Legal Status of Return Migrant Children

Northern Thai women from rural communities often rationalize that their marriage migration will provide their children with better opportunities by endowing them with a more privileged nationality. Ms. W., a typical interviewee in her early forties who migrated to Japan in the early 1990s, illustrates this attitude. She migrated to marry a Japanese man whom she "met through a friend of a friend".[7] After entering Japan on a tourist visa, she ran away from her fiancé and began working at a shop. Soon thereafter, she married one of her customers and obtained a spousal visa. After giving birth to a son, she left her husband and sent the son to her home village. She began living with Thai friends and resumed work at a shop. She gave money to her husband every month; in return, her spousal visa was secured.[8] When I interviewed her in 2011, she had been hired to manage a shop and she was living with a Japanese boyfriend. She recognized that three households were dependent on her income: that of her husband, her boyfriend and the relatives raising her son in northern Thailand. Her husband and her boyfriend often demanded additional money from her. Her husband would threaten that if she did not comply, he would not help her renew her spousal visa. Her boyfriend would become violent if she did not comply with his requests for money. She had to comply with their demands for additional money or lose her legal status, face violence or lose her boyfriend. She said that she had always intended to send remittances to the relatives raising her son, but that this support tended to be intermittent because her priority was to give money to these two men. She explained her situation as follows:

> Even though my life is difficult, I can say that I am happy to have married a Japanese man and given birth to a Japanese boy. If I had given birth to the child of a poor local man in my hometown, my son would also have become a poor, hopeless man. At least my child is Japanese, so there are possibilities open to him in the future.

However, merely having Japanese nationality does not always result in advantages for return migrant children growing up in lower-class communities in rural Thailand. Indeed, 5 out of the 17 children with both Thai and Japanese nationalities noted that they were required to renew the residential visas issued by their local immigration office because of their status as Japanese nationals, although they were also Thai nationals.[9] The mothers of these children or the mothers' kin who cared for these children, also reported that the children must renew their visas as Japanese citizens since they once went through Thai immigration using Japanese passports. One 16-year-old girl had to renew her visa after she went to Japan for a short period when she was 12 years old. She was born in Japan to a formally married Japanese father and a Thai mother. She acquired her Japanese nationality immediately after her birth when her father registered her birth at a municipal office in Japan. Because her parents also registered her birth with the Thai embassy in Japan, she received Thai nationality as well. When she returned to northern Thailand with her mother at the age of three, she was enrolled on her mother's household registration record. She then lived in the village as an ordinary Thai national for nearly nine years. However, when she was 12 years old, she visited Japan for a short time. When she returned to Thailand, she used her Japanese passport to get through immigration. Thereafter, the local immigration bureau required her to renew her visa as a Japanese national, if she chose to remain in Thailand. Her mother inquired about this matter at the main immigration bureau in Bangkok, where she was informed that her daughter was not required to extend the visa if she was a documented Thai national. Despite being cognizant of the fact that her daughter did not require a visa extension, the mother renewed the daughter's residential visa by paying a renewal fee[10] every 90 days[11] because she wanted to avoid trouble with the local immigration bureau. This case shows that return migrant children who live in marginalized border villages and who have Japanese nationality may actually be disadvantaged compared to ordinary Thai children. Legally, it is more advantageous for return migrant children in rural Thai villages to have only Thai nationality not Japanese nationality or dual nationality.

In fact, the most difficult cases are those of return migrant children who have only Japanese nationality. Of the 41 interviewed children, 3 did not have Thai nationality. Rather, they only held residential permits issued by the Thai government because they were born in Japan of mothers who do not have Thai nationality because they belong to the ethnic minority. According to observations made in the field, ethnic minority women are among the "Thai female migrants" from northern Thailand. Since the 2000s, minorities have been increasingly granted Thai nationality by the Thai government. However, many female marriage migrants left Thailand before this development occurred. As a result, the three children mentioned earlier had only Japanese nationality. The current nationality code of Thailand authorizes the granting of Thai nationality by birth according to the principles of parental *jus sanguinis* and territorial privilege.[12] However, children born outside of Thailand to ethnic minority mothers who were not Thai nationals[13] cannot acquire Thai nationality by *jus sanguinis* or by the principle of territorial privilege. Children, who grew up in the Thai border areas with only Japanese nationality, face the most difficulties. Not only must they periodically pay a fee to renew their residential visas as foreigners, they are also not entitled to an education visa after they grow up and finish their schooling. As adults, therefore, if they become unemployed, do not marry a Thai national or divorce a Thai national, they may not be eligible for any type of residential visa. They will then be considered illegal Japanese migrants although they grew up in Thailand, speak only Thai and have no practical connection to Japan. In short, holding only Japanese nationality worked against the returned children raised in rural Thai communities.

The Unstable Economic Status of Return Migrant Children

The economic status of the return migrant children tended to be as low as that of ordinary single mothers' households in the community, unless they received substantial remittances from Japan. Only 4 of the 41 interviewed children periodically received sufficient remittances from their Japanese fathers at the time of the research and only 7 received remittances from their mothers, who worked either in Japan or in urban areas in Thailand. However, these remittances were not always adequate. A typical case is described by a mother's relative who was raising return migrant children as follows:

> At first, their Japanese father built a fancy house in the village for the children; in those days, the father sent remittances to the children regularly. After a couple of years, the remittances became sporadic and then they ceased. The mother tried to make contact with the father, but she could not reach him. The mother sold her fancy house to obtain money for the children and moved into a tiny rented room. It was not long before the money was gone. Now, the mother has left the children with us and re-migrated to work in a major city in Thailand. The mother sends remittances to the children sometimes, but not regularly, because she now has a new family in the city. We are now baffled and anxious about how to care for the children.

Unlike studying or working abroad, going abroad as a marriage migrant is unlikely to result in acquiring qualifications or practical skills that improve one's economic stability after returning home. Usually, the only difference between ordinary single mothers in the community and single mothers returning from Japan seemed to be the complaints and pressures the latter endure from their relatives, who sometimes feel as if their expectations had been "betrayed". The results of our investigation showed that many returned single mothers did not have the ability to earn enough money to support their children. Among the 33 mothers of the 41 surveyed children, only 2 gained economic advantages after returning from Japan. One of them bought a large field with the money she brought back from Japan and is now the manager of a rubber plantation. The other mother set up a general store that she now runs. Sadly, the majority of the mothers did not have the ability to invest their money as wisely as these two women. After their return to the home villages, their expectations that marrying a foreigner would raise their economic status depended on the receipt of remittances from their foreign husbands. A number of the return migrant mothers simply waited to receive their husband's remittance, which sometimes seemed hopeless. In other words, the economic geography of power wanes when the intimate relationship ends.

The Vulnerable Social Status of Return Migrant Children

The social status of return migrated children may sometimes be more vulnerable than children of ordinary single mothers in the community because these return migrated children could become symbols of their mothers' failure. Consistent with existing discussions, our research results indicate that female marriage migrants and their home families were exposed to the risk of local prejudice, including a negative image of marriage migrants regarding involvement in certain types of service industries (see, for example, Tosakul 2010: 194–5). Therefore, community members could harbour ill feelings toward the children of marriage migrants. For instance, one interviewee reported the following typical narrative by members of the communities:

> There are many half-Japanese children in our village, but my nephew is quite a lucky one because his mother regularly receives a remittance from his Japanese father. The father even comes to see the son once a year. But, you know, there are many miserable half-Japanese children in this area who are just discarded by the fathers. We never know if the mothers really "married" their fathers or not. They may just have engaged in some kind of shameful occupation over there.

It was observed in the field research that as soon as such children returned to their mothers' home villages, they were often met with social pressure to bring economic rewards to their families. If they were unable to provide enough rewards to meet their families' expectations, they were sometimes regarded as burdens. In some cases, the relatives' attitudes toward the children were harsh, as shown by the comments of a resident in a home village of several marriage migrants.

> You know why half-Japanese children are so miserable? First, they are abandoned by their fathers. Then, when their father's abandonment becomes clear, their mothers leave. The mothers run away to the cities, saying they will find good jobs there and send remittances to their children. But how can such village women earn good money in the cities? Sometimes, these mothers get boyfriends over there and

just remake their own lives. Then what happens to the half-Japanese children at home? Without any remittance, such children are just a burden on the family. You can imagine how the children are treated.

Studies on marriage migrants from northeastern Thailand report that relatives measure the success or failure of the women's decision to migrate based on the amount of money those women send home, and the expected amount is extremely high (Ratanaolan-Mix 2005: 17). If marriage migrants fulfil these expectations, they and their relatives can save face by following the agrarian value of sharing their resources with their families. In this way, marriage migrants can gain respect and higher social status when they visit their homes (Angeles and Sunanta 2009: 550; Ratanaolan-Mix 2005: 18; Sunanta 2008: 19). This situation is analogous to that of the return migrant children in northern Thai villages. However, the interviewed Japanese-Thai children in northern Thailand seem to face more pressure than the half-Western children in northeast Thailand described in previous studies. This is because Japanese-Thai children are accepted only when they can prove that they are rich, unlike Western-looking children who may acquire advantages simply because of their appearance (Esara 2009: 411; Tosakul 2010: 185). In Thailand, light-coloured skin is regarded as an "advantage", and Europe and America are regarded as symbols of social prestige (Ruenkaew 1999: 6). However, for Japanese-Thai children, achieving the "reputation of being a mixed child" is difficult to attain without financial support. In short, among the second generation of marriage migrants surveyed the social geography of power was power-less without economic assurance.

Conclusion

The most important finding from our investigation of return migrated Japanese-Thai children in northern Thailand is that the gendered geography of power motivating the marriage migration of the analyzed cases faded in the long term. For the offspring of these marriage migrants—children born as a result of trans-border intimacy who return migrated from Japan to the northern Thai border villages—the superiority of being a half-Japanese child quickly vanished in the absence of financial support. First, for children raised in rural areas of Thailand, having Thai nationality was a much bigger advantage in their daily lives than Japanese nationality. Second, living in Japan as a marriage migrant did not necessarily allow the mother to gain the ability to improve her financial situation on her return home. The upgrading of one's economic status in one's home village occurred only when children received remittances from their foreign fathers. In numerous cases, the expectation of receiving remittances became an illusion when the intimacy ended, which tended to occur even before marriage migrants' return home to Thailand. In fact, it was often the reason for the mothers' return home. Third, for the children of these marriages who could not enjoy economic advantages as "*rich* Japanese children", their social status in their home communities tended to be low, reflecting the persistent negative image of marriage migrants in the community.

This study may represent a first attempt to offer insight into the variability of the geographies of power underlying marriage migration. However, one important aspect of this issue, which we could not include in this chapter, was the migration of children who were products of their parents' previous marriages. As some studies indicate, marriage migration also induces the cross-border migration of children from parents' previous marriages (Angeles and Sunanta 2009: 573; Williams 2010: 215), although only a few studies have examined this issue. During our field research, we witnessed the cross-border migration of children from marriage migrants' pre-migration marriages. Further research on this form of child migration should be pursued to understand marriage migration schemas over time.

Additionally, we encountered several return migrant mixed-ethnic children who, after several years, were recalled from their mothers' homes in northern Thailand to Japan to secure their mothers' visa status. The children were needed to prove that the mothers fulfilled the requirement of being a guardian of children with Japanese nationality. In some cases, parents believed that the migration promised a better life for their children. In other cases, the parents allowed the children to migrate solely to fulfil the parents' own needs. Further research on such children who frequently migrate across borders would be useful.

Acknowledgements

The author expresses sincere thanks to all of the questionnaire respondents and interviewees—the mothers and relatives of Japanese-Thai children and the children themselves. This chapter, which is dedicated to their bright future, could not have been written without their patient cooperation. This research also would not have been possible without the patient cooperation of Saphan Fan, the NGO whose staff conducted the questionnaire survey. Additionally, Ms. Bongkot Napaumporn from Thammasat University helped the author collect the information in the Thai media mentioned in this chapter. However, the author is solely responsible for any oversights in this chapter. This research was also made possible by the financial support provided by the Japan Society for the Promotion of Science (JSPS) through the Excellent Young Researcher Overseas Visit Program 2010 and Grant-in-Aid for Scientific Research (A), 2011–13, no. 232510006.

Notes

1. "Keigo pheypho yangmaimi miamai prommaha" [Keigo Reveals that His Father Does Not Have a New Wife Yet and Is Coming to Visit Him], *Khomchadluek*, 23 May 2009; "'Keigo' phoppho somcai phokodkan ramhai" [Keigo Will Meet His Father and Will have a Deep Hug with Lamentation Soon], *Khomchadluek*, 2 October 2009; "Do. Cho. 'Keigo' topen wayrun sunMo.3—fan copparinyatori capai yipun" [Mr. 'Keigo' Grew Up, Now 3rd Year in Junior High School—Dreams to Finish University and Go to Japan], *Thairat*, 6 May 2014.
2. From an interview with a Japanese embassy officer in Bangkok, 27 May 2010.
3. Ministry of Health, Labour and Welfare, *Vital Statistics of Japan, 1992–2014*.
4. Some of the 41 children surveyed were siblings; however, we counted them individually because brothers and sisters do not always share the same situation.
5. This category includes the following: 23 children with Japanese surnames and first names, 7 children with Japanese surnames and Thai first names, and 1 child with both Thai and Japanese names who uses Japanese names in daily use. First names have more versatility in Thai society.
6. This category includes the following: 5 children with Thai surnames and first names, 3 children with Thai surnames and Japanese first names, and 2 children with both Thai and Japanese names who use Thai names in daily use. First names have more versatility in Thai society.
7. This Thai phrase usually indicates a matchmaking broker. However, in the interviewee's mind, the matchmaking broker really was a "friend of a friend" as matchmaking brokers who run businesses in northern Thailand use local human networks to find recruits.
8. She was supposed to change her visa status to a "settlement visa", which does not require the confirmation of a Japanese spouse. However, for some

reason she refused to complete this process, even though this concept had been repeatedly explained to her by the author.
9. In Thailand there is no legal status of "citizen", only "national"; hence, the use of this term here.
10. According to the interviewees, the amount is not fixed.
11. Based on information provided during the interview in 2011.
12. The amended nationality code of Thailand (Nationality Act No. 4, B.E. 2551) is available at http://thailawonline.com/en/thai-laws/laws-of-thailand/384-nationality-act-no4-be-2551-or-2008.html [accessed 23 Nov. 2015].
13. According to legal provisions, ethnic minorities who do not hold any nationality cannot cross national borders. However, I met some ethnic minorities who, despite these provisions, had undergone marriage migration and who had been living abroad, pretending to be Thai nationals in the 1990s.

References

Angeles, C. Leonora and Sirijit Sunanta. 2009. "Demanding Daughter Duty: Gender, Community, Village Transformation, and Transnational Marriages in Northeast Thailand." *Critical Asian Studies* 41(4): 549–74.

Ariyabuddhiphongs, Vanchai and Kampama Nopphawan. 2009. "Intent to Marry Inter-racially: A Test of Dependence Model of Relationships among Female Sex Workers and Female Office Workers in Bangkok, Thailand." *The Social Science Journal* 46: 282–96.

Askew, Mark. 2009. "Sex and the Sacred: Sojourners and Visitors in the Making of the Southern Thai Borderland." In *Centering the Margin: Agency and Narrative in Southeast Asian Borderlands*, ed. H. Alexander and R.L. Wadley. New York: Berghahn Books, pp. 177–206.

Chantavanich, Supang et al. 2001. *The Migration of Thai Women to Germany: Causes, Living Conditions and Impacts for Thailand and Germany*. Bangkok: Asian Research Center for Migration, Institute of Asian Studies, Chulalongkorn University.

Cohen, Eric. 2001. *Thai Tourism: Hill Tribes, Islands and Open-ended Prostitution*. Bangkok: White Lotus.

———. 2003. "Transnational Marriage in Thailand: The Dynamics of Extreme Heterogamy." In *Sex and Tourism: Journeys of Romance, Love and Lust*, ed. T.G. Bauer and B. McKercher. New York: Howorth Hospitality Press.

Constable, Nicole. 2005. "A Tale of Two Marriages: International Matchmaking and Gendered Mobility." In *Cross-Border Marriages: Gender and Mobility in Transnational Asia*, ed. N. Constable. Philadelphia: University of Pennsylvania Press, pp. 166–86.

Esara, Pilapa. 2009. "Imagining the Western Husband: Thai Women's Desires for Matrimony, Status and Beauty." *Ethnos* 74(3): 403–26.

Lieberson, Stanley, and Eleanor O. Bell. 1992. "Children's First Names: An Empirical Study of Social Taste." *American Journal of Sociology* 98(3): 511–54.

Ministry of Health, Labour and Welfare, 1992–2014. *Vital Statistics of Japan.* Tokyo: Health, Labour and Welfare Statistics Association.

Ratanaolan-Mix, Prapairat. 2005. Dreaming in the Shadows of Affluence: Marriage, Migration and Thai Women in Hamburg Germany. Paper presented at the 9th International Conference on Thai Studies, Northern Illinois University, DeKalb, IL, 3–6 April 2005.

Ratanaolan-Mix, Prapairat and Nicole Piper. 2003. "Does Marriage 'Liberate' Women from Sex Work? Thai Women in Germany." In *Wife or Worker?: Asian Women and Migration*, ed. Nicole Piper and Mina Roces. Lanham: Rowman and Littlefield Publishers, pp. 53–71.

Ruenkaew, Pataya. 1999. "Marriage Migration of Thai Women to Germany." Paper presented to the 7th International Conference on Thai Studies, Amsterdam, Holland, 4–8 July 1999.

Sue, Christina A. and Edward E. Telles. 2007. "Assimilation and Gender in Naming." *American Journal of Sociology* 112(5): 1383–415.

Sunanta, Sirijit. 2008. "Love and Marriage in 'International Villages': Cross-Border Marriages between Northeastern Thai Women and Foreign Men." Paper presented at the 10th International Conference on Thai Studies, Thammasat University, Thailand, 9–11 January 2008.

Tosakul, Ratana. 2010. "Cross-border Marriages: Experiences of Village Women from Northeastern Thailand with Western Men." In *Asian Cross-border Marriage Migration*, ed. Wen-Shan Yang and Melody Chia-Wen Lu. Amsterdam: Amsterdam University Press, pp. 179–99.

Whittaker, Andrea. 2009. "Global Technologies and Transnational Reproduction in Thailand." *Asian Studies Review* 33: 319–32.

Williams, Lucy. 2010. *Global Marriage: Cross-Border Marriage Migration in Global Context.* Hampshire and New York: Palgrave Macmillan.

Yeoh, S.A. Brenda et al., eds. 2012. "Report for Children's Geographies: Inter-Asia Roundtable on Transnational Migration and Children in Asian Contexts." *Children's Geographies* 10: 123–29.

CHAPTER 6

Assimilation of the Descendants of Caucasian Muslims in Sarawak, Malaysia

Caesar Dealwis

Introduction

This chapter focuses on the language usage of the Eurasian Muslims (the descendants of European marriage migrants) in Sarawak, Malaysia to more fully understand how and why they are gradually giving up their Eurasian culture in order to assimilate into the dominant Malay culture.

Since this is a chapter in a book about marriage migration, what does a study on cultural assimilation tell us about marriage migration? Most marriage migration studies focus on the direction of migration (for example, from the global north to the global south), difficulties that marriage migrants and their children face regarding citizenship, socio-economic status in the countries to which they move and so forth. This chapter explores a "post-migration" situation where the a small group of migrants married people from their host country and whose descendants have coalesced into a distinctive small ethnic group within a multicultural mix of larger ethnic groups. As the paragraph above suggests, assimilation becomes an issue. One question that arises is why do some groups seek to assimilate into larger ethnic groups around them?

The chapter presents findings from a study conducted by the author. The major findings show that (1) older Eurasian Muslims in Sarawak see themselves as living the "European" lifestyle of their Caucasian forebears which involves an extensive use of English in the domains of home, religion and social communications, such as voicemail and greetings, but (2) younger Eurasian Muslims identify themselves as "Malay" because doing so is more advantageous to being a Malaysian citizen. As a result,

Bahasa Malayu (Malay) is the more extensively used language for most of these younger Eurasian Muslims. These findings suggest that younger Eurasian Muslims are gradually assimilating into the larger Malay community by discarding their Western-rooted identities.

Sarawak is the largest of the 14 Malaysian states. It is located on the island of Borneo and separated from peninsular Malaysia by the South China Sea. Sarawak's cultural and racial composition is more diverse than that of peninsular Malaysia. Exogamous marriages are common in Sarawak, which has 33 different ethnic groups. The state of Sarawak is home to the Iban (the majority ethnic group), Chinese, Malays, Bidayuh, Melanau and other indigenous people. Caucasians have come to Sarawak mostly from Australia, New Zealand, Europe and America. Some of these Caucasians have married local Sarawakians, which has resulted in a distinctive Eurasian community. According to Morrison (1957), the history of the Sarawak Eurasian community began long before they were ethnically classified as Eurasians by the Sarawak government in the 1920s. Before being called Eurasians, local Malays referred to this population as *Serani* (British or Australian descendants). However, a preferred practice was always to identify Eurasians by their religious affiliations, hence, the broad designations of Christian and Muslim.

The origins of the Eurasian community in Sarawak can be traced to the adventurers, soldiers, administrators and private individuals who travelled to Sarawak from the eighteenth to the twentieth century. British, and later Australians, were among the earliest Europeans to arrive and establish their presence in Sarawak. The unions that occurred between local women and British and Australian travellers resulted in their Eurasian descendants in Sarawak. Intensive contact with Europeans began in the nineteenth century when the British adventurer-cum-sailor, Sir James Brooke, assisted the Sultan of Brunei in defeating the latter's enemies in the Brunei Sultanate and was later rewarded by the sultan with a large section of Sarawak. After he had provided assistance in several more battles, Brooke's territory further expanded (St. John 1994).

In the mid-nineteenth century, James Brooke was declared Rajah of Sarawak and thus began the White Rajah administration that was continued after Brooke's death by Sir Charles Brooke, the second rajah of Sarawak, and Sir Vyneer Brooke, the third Rajah of Sarawak. The Japanese occupation of Sarawak ended the Brooke administration in 1941 (Gin 1997: 1–4). The end of the occupation in 1944 resulted in Sarawak being handed over to the British colonial government (Talib 1999:108) until it became part of Malaysia in 1963 (Talib 1999: 148). During the

Brooke administration (which lasted about 100 years) and the British colonial government (which lasted 18 years), many Caucasians came to work as Christian missionaries, soldiers and public service officers (Low 1988: xxxv; Treacher 1891/2010: 64), particularly from Britain, Ireland and Australia. A number of them, especially Caucasian men, married local Malay, Chinese and Dayak (the general term for the indigenous peoples of Sarawak and other parts of Borneo) women.

The 1950s and 1960s saw a mass emigration of Sarawak Eurasians to the United Kingdom, Australia and other Commonwealth countries following the withdrawal of British personnel from Sarawak. Michael Boult, a pensioner whose father worked for the Sarawak Shell Oil Company in Miri between 1940 and 1965, recalls that there were around 70 Eurasian families who remained in Sarawak after it became part of Malaysia on 16 September 1963. Although some of them later immigrated to Australia, New Zealand, United Kingdom and Canada, a number chose to remain in Sarawak. The Caucasian migrants became permanent residents, and the Eurasians who stayed behind filled senior positions in the civil service.

The Eurasian community continued to shrink in number as a result of assimilation through intermarriage with other ethnic groups and as a result of continued emigration. However, the community continued to attract a small number of foreign migrants. For example in the 1950s, many talented Sarawakians were sent abroad to pursue higher education under the Colombo Plan (Colombo Plan Bureau 1958: 7, 19). A number of the men came back with foreign spouses who found a new home in Sarawak. From that time until the present, some local Sarawakians have continued to marry Caucasian men and women while studying abroad and have brought them back to Sarawak. Also, Caucasians working in the oil and gas industry and in other multinational corporations in Sarawak have married locals.

The Eurasian community has traditionally occupied a high status position in Sarawak, so it is curious that Eurasians are giving up this position to integrate into Malaysian society more or less willingly, given that ethnic relations among most Malaysian citizens of different ethnic backgrounds are quite delicate and fraught with tensions. This is also of practical interest because the success of building Malaysia as a nation is seen to rest, in part, on the process of Malaysianisation (the harmonious assimilation of indigenous and migrant cultures into the dominant Malay culture). This chapter presents a study of the Eurasian Muslim's choice of self-identity to discern if/how this usage reflects the benefits of being

Malay rather than maintaining European-oriented identities as Malaysian citizens.

Theoretical Perspective on Assimilation in Sarawak

Barry defines assimilation as "a process whereby the descendants of the immigrants adopt the behavioural pattern, identity and cultural tradition and the way of life of the host community" (quote taken from David and Dealwis, 2009). Assimilation runs from being completely integrated into a dominant group to partial integration. Malaysia in general, and Sarawak in particular, illustrate the full range of the assimilation of minor ethnic groups. Complete assimilation occurs when an outsider, immigrant or subordinate group becomes indistinguishably integrated into a dominant host society because the hosted individual or minority group has accepted and internalized the values and culture of the dominant group (Swan et al. 2004).

Assimilation of a minority group is facilitated when it shares a common religion with the dominant majority group. For example, David and Dealwis (2009) have found that the Indian Muslims in Kuching want to be identified as Malays because they share the same religion. Similarly, David, Naji and David (2003), in discussing the descendants of Pakistani men and Kelantanese women in peninsular Malaysia, show that assimilation was complete for two reasons. First, they spoke the local Kelantanese dialect. Second, sharing a common religion, Islam, was seen as an important condition to complete assimilation into the larger Kelantanese community. A third example is the complete assimilation of Indian Muslims in Kuching and Pakistanis in Kelantan. Being minute ethnic communities, both had adapted and assimilated with the local Malay culture in their geographical locations (David and Dealwis 2006).

Whatever the degree of assimilation, it is a gradual but complex process marked by two features. First, assimilation is driven both by the community being assimilated and the community being entered. Second, certain groups within the community being assimilated actively pursue assimilation while other groups may passively (or actively) resist. The following studies illustrate the above features by tracing changes in minority groups' language use in Malaysia.

Nambiar (2007) points out that Muslim Malayalees in Malaysia wanted to be identified as Malays and that the process is driven by the marriages of early Malayalee traders with local Malay women, Islam as a common religion and the desire to be given the privileges that Malays enjoyed as *Bumiputra* (sons of the soil). Mohammad Subakir's (1998) study of the Javanese in Sungai Lang reveals that the Javanese wanted to be identified as Malays and were shifting from their Javanese mother tongue to Malay in the home domain.

Assimilation is not only a process reflecting the desires of a minority group to assimilate into a dominant group. It is also driven by intended and/or unintended pressure from the dominant group. This has been documented in a number of studies investigating the relationship between the dominant Malay ethnic group and minority non-Malay groups in Malaysia. Bibi Aminah and Abang Ahmad Ridzuan (1992) found that the younger generation of the *Orang Miriek* (a small ethnic group living around Miri) classified themselves as *Orang Melayu* (Malays) rather than Orang Miriek and used *Bahasa Miriek* (the Miriek language) only when speaking with elders in the home domain. Tunku Zarinah (1978) pointed out that the young Orang Miriek did not want to speak Bahasa Miriek because they were ashamed to speak in a *bahasa kuno* (primitive language), whereas Sarawak Malay was regarded as more modern. Although the Telegu minority of Sarawak are Christians and do not share a common religion with the local Malays, the second generation of this minority group have assimilated into the majority Malay.

When cultural elements of another ethnic group are incorporated into one's own culture and passed on to the next generation, assimilation becomes a significant phenomenon (Tan 1993). This raises a question not answered by this study but deserves investigation in the future: the controversial issue of the link between language and ethnicity. Some sociolinguists show that there is no extrinsic correlation between language and ethnicity. For example, Omar (1991) shows this is the case in a study on Kuala Lumpurians who have shifted to English. Other sociolinguists, such as Fishman (1989), assert that there is an extrinsic correlation between language and ethnicity. Views regarding the connection between language and ethnicity, therefore, appear to vary. While for some communities ethnic identity and language maintenance are closely connected, for others the ethnic language may not form an important part of their identity. David (1998) explains how the Sindhi language is no longer a marker of ethnic identity for the Malaysian Sindhi community. Fishman (1989) states that two factors other than language potentially contribute to the identity of a group of people. One is patrimony (cultural practises) and the other is patriarchy (birthright).

Aims of the Study

According to Lasimbang and Miller (1993), people react negatively if they feel they are being subsumed into a larger group on an unequal basis, but they may readily shed their identity for a larger group's identity if such integration is perceived as being in their best interest. The aim of this study was to determine what factors have led Eurasian Muslims in Sarawak to readily assimilate into the more dominant Malay community through practising Malay cultural norms. Using a sample of 108 Caucasian Muslims, the study was also concerned with the magnitude of change in respondents' lifestyles.

Methodology

Respondents were found through snowball sampling. The respondents were professionals, businessmen and businesswomen who were fluent in English and Malay. Interviews were conducted in the respondents' homes and business premises. The survey asked respondents to comment on the following topics: sense of having inherited a "European" lifestyle and choice of language in the domains of religion, family, social communication and marriage. Unstructured interviews were also conducted with 33 Eurasian Muslims who lived in Kuching, Sri Aman, Sibu, Bintulu, Mukah, Sarikei, Miri, Lawas and Kapit in the state of Sarawak during a period of six months, from January to June 2011. The results of this research study are presented and discussed below in terms of the following age groups: 60+, 40–59, 22–39 and 12–21.

Sense of Inheritance of a European Lifestyle

This study was concerned with whether or not respondents felt that they maintain what local people call a European lifestyle (the patterns of living passed down by family members among Eurasians in Sarawak). The findings revealed that 83.2 per cent of the respondents in the combined age groups 12–21 and 22–39 view their lifestyle as "mostly Malay" as opposed to "European". In contrast, more than half of the respondents in the older age group (63.4 per cent) live what they consider to be a European lifestyle passed down from previous generations. A central aspect of this lifestyle has traditionally been the Sarawakian Eurasians' extensive use of English following their English-speaking forebears.

Language Choice in the Home Domain

The respondents in the 60+ age cohort learned English as their first language because their parents came to Kuching from European countries as civil service officers during the Brooke era and could not speak the local languages. On the other hand, although the majority of the respondents in the 12–21 age cohort (63.4 per cent) learned English first as their mother tongue, 36.4 per cent first learned Malay as their mother tongue. According to Respondent 16, a 17-year-old male, "My father is English and mother is Malay and they wanted us to speak good English and Malay so that we could go overseas to study and work in Malaysia later."

Interview data indicated that language utility (the choice of the language best suited to realize a particular social and/or economic goal) has influenced language choice at home. Although the majority of the respondents in the 22–39 age cohort and 40–59 age cohort (92.1 per cent and 93.1 per cent, respectively) first learned English as their mother tongue, the reason given for not speaking Malay was that their parents were highly educated and preferred speaking English at home. Thus, the statistical evidence clearly shows that, while 100 per cent of the respondents in the 60+ age cohort speak only English, this percentage declines as the age cohorts become younger (74.5 per cent for the 40–59 age cohort, 63.4 per cent for the 22–39 age cohort and 45.5 per cent for the 12–21 age cohort). The remaining respondents use a mixture of Malay and English as the home language. Respondent 15, a 16-year-old female said: "My maternal grandparents who are Malays speak only Malay. We were raised by them while our parents went to work. So, definitely, we speak better Malay. However, with our parents we speak a mix of English and Malay."

Language Choice in the Religious Domain

Of respondents in the 40–59 age cohort, 87.7 per cent use English at their place of worship while the rest use Malay. As for respondents in the 22–39 age cohort, only 55.8 per cent use English at their place of worship while the rest use Malay. However, 45.5 per cent of the respondents who are in the 12–22 age cohort said that they use English at their place of worship while 54.5 per cent use Malay. Therefore, the use of Malay increases with a decline in age, providing evidence that assimilation with Malays is occurring among the younger cohort of Eurasian Muslims. The decline of English language as a language of choice is evidenced in the reading of religious books because the younger Eurasian Muslim Tamils in the 12–21 age cohort tend to use less stand-alone English (68.2 per cent) when compared with the older cohorts (100 per cent for those above age 60, 89.3 per cent for the 40–59 age cohort and 75.6 per cent for the 22–29 years age cohort).

Respondent 22, a 19-year-old male respondent said: "I prefer reading religious books written in Malay in regard to religious books because in school I was taught Islamic teachings in Malay and Arabic. I learned the prayers in Arabic." However, a number of respondents in the age cohorts of 22–39 years and 40–59 years also read religious books in Malay (41.3 per cent and 51.7 per cent, respectively). However, a higher number of the respondents in these two age groups (58.7 per cent and 48.3 per cent) still continue to read religious books in the English language. A total of 100 per cent of those 60 years and above read religious books in English only. Notably, the Caucasian Muslims in the 60+ cohort practised other faiths before converting to Islam through exogamous marriage with Muslim Malays. (See details about conversion of Malay to Islam in Sarawak area in Winzeler 1995.) Similarly, the age cohorts of 22–39 years and 40–49 years choose the English language as the medium of silent prayer to Allah, compared with 50 per cent of the respondents in the 12–21 age cohort who choose the Malay language. Respondent 9, a 14-year-old male said: "I pray in Malay and Arabic because my Allah speaks Arabic and can understand Malay. You'll feel closer to Allah when you pray in Arabic." The other 50 per cent of respondents in the 12–21 age cohort choose a code-switching pattern of more Malay with less English (13.6 per cent) and stand-alone English (36.4 per cent) when praying silently. These are respondents whose home language is English and who have no immediate relatives living with them who are Malay.

All of the respondents who are 60 years and above speak English to the mosque imams as do most (93.1 per cent) of the respondents who are 40–59 years old. However, only 3.4 per cent of the respondents in the 40–59 years age cohort speak English to the imams. Respondent 33, a 44-year-old male, said: "I mix Malay with English especially for certain common items when discussing certain matters with the imam. He's from Malaysia; he understands them because these are local terms and he has a good command of English." The majority (90.5 per cent) of the respondents in the 22–39 age cohort speak Malay to the imams while the remainder use Arabic. All of the respondents in the 12–21 age cohort speak in Malay and Arabic to the imams. Respondent 27, a 17-year-old female said: "The imam speaks good Malay and Arabic. He speaks Malay and Arabic with me so I just accommodate."

Patterns of Language Use in the Social Domain

Similar shifts in language choice appear in social settings. A number of the respondents in the 12–21 age group (45.5 per cent) report that they use more Malay with less English when sending voicemail via mobile phones. However, 36.4 per cent of the respondents in the 12–21 years age group use stand-alone English when sending voicemail via mobile phones. Only 18.2 per cent of the respondents in the 12–21 age group use stand-alone Malay when sending voicemail via mobile phones. Respondent 19, a 20-year-old male said: "I mix Malay with English more often than my parents. I realize that. Maybe because that's the style my Malay friends are using currently." As for the respondents in the 22–39 years age group, 46 per cent have chosen to use English when sending voicemail via mobile phones. Another 42.9 per cent use more English with less Malay when sending voicemail via mobile phones. The majority of the respondents in the 40–59 years age group (82.8 per cent) use English when sending voicemail via mobile phones. Respondent 36, a 53-year-old male said: "I speak more English…in fact only English because I cannot really speak good Malay." All the respondents who are 60 years and above also select English for sending voicemail via mobile phones.

The different percentages of English language use among different age cohorts indicate a shift from English (the heritage language) to Malay. The percentage of respondents in the 22–39 age cohort who choose to use stand-alone English is lower (55.6 per cent) than that of respondents in the 40–59 age group (89.7 per cent). About 28.6 per cent and 3.4 per cent of the respondents who are in the 22–39 years and 40–59 years age cohorts, respectively, said that they code-switch using more English with less Malay. Respondent 11, a 45-year-old male respondent said: "I speak English in the office because all my friends do the same and we feel very close. However, I see the younger Eurasian Muslims boys and girls mix English with Malay in school. I think they assimilated with Malay influence." Notably, 35.3 per cent and 9.5 per cent of the respondents who are in the 12–21 years and 22–39 years age cohorts, respectively, said that they speak stand-alone Malay with other Malays in school and in the workplace. Respondent 13, a 23-year-old male respondent said: "I speak Malay because the Malay people who I always talk to, although they are educated, like to speak Malay. Anyway, I feel more comfortable speaking Malay with them."

About 37.4 per cent, 47.6 per cent and 20.7 per cent, of the respondents who are in the 12–21 years, 22–39 years and 40–59 years age cohorts, respectively, said that they code-switch using more English with less Malay when speaking to other Eurasian Muslims. However, 27.3 per cent, 31.7 per cent and 60.9 per cent of the respondents who are in the 12–21 years, 22–39 years and 40–59 age cohorts, respectively, said that they use stand-alone English when speaking to other Eurasian Muslims in the mosques. All the respondents 60 years and older speak stand-alone English with other Eurasian Muslims in the mosque. Respondent 63, a 62-year-old male respondent said: "The Eurasian Muslim children currently do not speak a lot of English. I hear them mix-mix. Not my generation. We all speak English only." Approximately 45.5 per cent of the respondents in the 12–21 years age group select Malay for greeting Malays, 31.8 per cent select a mixture of Malay and English, while 18.2 per cent give greetings in English. Other trends appear in this setting for the other age groups of 22–39, 40–59 and 60+ who still use English when giving greetings. Nevertheless, 34.9 per cent of respondents in the 22–39 years age group select a mixture of Malay and English, compared to 12.7 per cent who tend to use stand-alone Malay when greeting Malays.

Selection of Marriage Partners

Interestingly, approximately 65.3 per cent of the respondents in the 22–39 age group were of the view that their marriage partners should be Malay. This is more important for the younger respondents. The younger the respondents, the more they were concerned that the life/marriage partner should from the same community (that is, Malay). Nevertheless, 34.7 per cent of respondents in the 22–39 age group reported that the ethnicity of the partner made no difference to them. On the other hand, 100 per cent of the 60+ respondents prefer to have children-in-law who are Muslims.

Marriage Migrant Descendants' Assimilation to the Malay Mainstream

The differences observed in the patterns of language choice between younger and older cohorts may not necessarily reflect a sociolinguistic change. David notes that:

...[the] difference between the age groups in their language use patterns may reflect radically different causes depending on whether these are new developments not experienced by earlier age cohorts when they were at that age (in which case genuine sociolinguistic change exists) or merely a pattern of age-related changes experienced by the previous cohorts as they went through the life cycle as different linguistic behaviour is expected of the people at different ages. (2005: 266)

Changes have occurred in the language use patterns between respondents in the 12–21 years age cohort and those in the 60+ age cohort. Examining the use of English in the home domain, the results clearly show a decline from 100 per cent of stand-alone English for the 60+ age cohort to a mixed code pattern of English and Malay for the 12–21 years age cohort. A decline exists in the use of stand-alone English in the home domain. In contrast to English, an increase in the use of Malay in the home domain is evident among the younger age cohorts. However, it might be noted that the decline in the use of English among those in the 40–59 years age cohort is less compared to the increase in the use of Malay in the home domain. The findings here suggest that all respondents who are 40 years and above are still maintaining the use of English in the home domain. The language practices of the younger cohorts in the home domain could be shaped by the use of Malay in the Malay-medium schools they attend.

Although brought up in a multiracial environment like their parents and grandparents, it may be that the younger age cohorts of 12–21 and 22–39 years have been greatly influenced by the prominence of Malay in social media, language policies and education system of Malaysia, that is, a more Malaysian sociocultural and linguistic environment, compared with the English-dominated environment in which their parents and grandparents lived under the British colonial government.

An elderly Caucasian Muslim said that the children of recent Caucasian immigrants who have married local Malays tend to be more Malay—speaking Malay and practising Muslim cultural norms, such as speaking more Malay than English at home; having other markers of Malay/Muslim identity, such as wearing the *baju kurung* (Malay traditional dress for women), *tudung* (head scarf) and *baju Melayu* (Malay traditional dress for men); and eating Malay food that is halal (not touched by pork). This respondent also pointed out that bachelors among the early immigrants married local Malay women and lived in Malay-dominated areas in the cities and in large towns, leading to the use of Malay among their children in the home domain. Because they converted after marrying local Malays and shared the Muslim religion with the Malays, the early immigrants were well accepted in the Malay community. Non-structured interviews conducted with elderly Caucasian Muslims indicated that there has always been greater affinity with the Malays from the early days of their arrival. Respondent 21, a 62-year-old respondent said:

> I am close with the local Malays. I'm staying in the Malay area in this town and join them for many religious events. We share the same religion, which is Islam. I seldom see other Caucasian Christians. My children who are considered Eurasian Muslims are closer to the Malay children than to the Caucasian Christian children.

All of the 10 Malay respondents who were randomly interviewed also felt that the Caucasian Muslims and their children who are Eurasian Muslims are Malays because they practise Islam and their children speak the Malay language and practise Malay cultural norms. Respondent 3A, a 42-year-old Malay male said:

> When I was in school, I never saw my friend Mohd. Rahim bin Firdaus as a Mat Salleh (term referring to Caucasian). I know his father was British but I consider him just like me–Malay. He speaks English and Malay just like other urban Malays and on Fridays we go to the mosque together with other Muslims from school.

Although Eurasian Muslims seem to have a real desire to be a part of the Malay community, they also recognize its economic benefits (David and Dealwis, 2008; Nambiar 2007). Being a part of the Malay community carries more economic advantages than being a part of the smaller Eurasian community. Under the national Economic Policy, which was launched in 1970, the Malays, as the indigenous community in Malaysia, are given benefits that include economic, social and educational privileges to improve their socio-economic status. The numerous exogamous marriages between Caucasians and Malays in the past decades and the conversion of Caucasians to Islam have facilitated the assimilation of the Eurasian Muslims into the larger Malay community. The Eurasian Muslim community has shifted from being a Caucasian Muslim community where only English is spoken to a Eurasian Muslim community where more Malay is spoken, and this shift has caused the weakening of ethnic boundaries. All the Eurasian Muslims interviewed stated that their national registration cards have classified them as Malays. Respondent 12 said, "When my parents (dad English, Mum Malay) made my

IC, Mum put my Race as Malay and my Religion as Islam. So, I'm Malay officially, although I'm actually a Eurasian Muslim."

What makes it easy for the Eurasian Muslims to take on a Malay identity is the fact that the definition of Malay in the Malaysian Constitution shows great flexibility. According to the Constitution, a Malay is defined as one who practises the Islamic religion, practises Malay customs and speaks the Malay language. In the native Court of Sarawak (*Mahkamah Adat Istiadaat*), a non-native is eligible to apply to be identified as a Malay if he or she professes the religion of Islam, habitually speaks the Malay language and observes or conforms to the Malay customs and culture and if his mother or father is a native of the Malay community of Sarawak (Laws of Sarawak 1977). Therefore, individuals may become Malay (David and Dealwis 2009) as long as they convert to Islam, practise Malay customs and use the Malay language.

Regarding dietary habits, the younger respondents frequently eat more Malay food compared with the older respondents. The data indicated that the younger respondents have assimilated more culturally compared with the older respondents. This finding could reflect the younger respondents' desire to maintain their Malayness despite the eventual loss of their Eurasian identity. For all these markers of assimilation, no statistically significant differences were found between male and female respondents. This implies that there were no marked gender differences in the process of assimilation as they shift slowly from a Eurasian identity for the older age group towards a Malay identity for the younger age group.

Conclusion

Based on the above cases, this study sheds light on how Eurasian Muslims in Sarawak are exchanging their Eurasian identity for that of the larger Malay group because it is in their best interest politically, economically and socially as citizens of Malaysia. Eurasian Muslims whose ancestors came from Christian countries are experiencing assimilation just as other minority communities in Sarawak are. Whereas older Eurasian Muslims maintain their ancestral language in peer interaction, younger Eurasian Muslims have moved towards Malay. The aforementioned identity shift from Eurasian to Malay suggests that for the descendants of European marriage migrants in Sarawak, being Eurasian is rather unstable, multiple, fluctuating and fragmented, whereas being Malay is much more stable as national discourses heavily influence their daily experience.

References

Bibi Aminah Abdul Ghani and Abang Ahmad Ridzuan. 1992. "Language Shift among the Orang Miriek of Miri Sarawak." In *Shifting Patterns of Language Use in Borneo (Borneo Research Council Proceedings Series, 3)*, ed. Peter W. Martin. Williamsburg, VA: Borneo Research Council, pp. 121–46.

Colombo Plan Bureau. 1958. *The Colombo Plan: Facts and Figures*. Colombo: Colombo Plan Bureau.

David, M.K., 1998. "Language Shift, Cultural Maintenance and Ethnic Identity: A Study of Minority Community: The Sindhis of Malaysia." *International Journal of the Sociology of Language* 130: 67–76.

David, M.K. 2005. "The Network Theory and Language Maintenance: A Study of Three Communities in Peninsular Malaysia." In *Creating Outsiders: Endangered Languages, Migration and Marginalisation*, ed. Nigel Crawhall and Nicholas Ostler. Bath: Foundation for Endangered Languages, pp. 153–57.

David, M.K. and Caesar Dealwis. 2006. "Close and Dense Networks: Do They Lead to Maintenance of the Ethnic Language? Focus on the Telegu Community in Kuching, Sarawak." *Migracijske Etnicke Teme* [Migration and Ethnic Themes] 22(4): 343–61.

⸻. 2008. "Why Shift? Focus on Sabah and Sarawak," *Contemporary Linguistics* 66(2): 261–76.

⸻. 2009. "Evolving Identity: A Study of Indian Muslims in Kuching." *Language In India* 2: 36–42.

David, M.K., Ibtisam M.H. Naji, Sheena Kaur David. 2003. "Language Maintenance or Language Shift among the Punjabi Sikh Community in Malaysia?" *International Journal of the Sociology of Language* 165: 0161-0001.

Dealwis, Caesar. 2011. "In Search of an Identity: Children of Indian Immigrants—Bidayuh in Mixed Marriages." Paper presented at International Conference on Dynamics of Marriage or Divorce-Related Migration in Asia. Tokyo University of Foreign Relations, Tokyo, 26 Nov. 2011.

Fishman, Joshua A. 1989. *Language and Ethnicity in Minority Sociolinguistic Perspective*. Clevedon, England: Multilingual Matters.

Gin, Ooi Keat. 1997. *Of Free Trade and Native Interests: The Brookes and the Economic Development of Sarawak, 1841–1941*. Kuala Lumpur: Oxford University Press.

Laws of Sarawak. 1977. *Majlis Adat Istiadat Sarawak Ordinance: 1977*. Kuching: Sarawak Printing Press.

Lasimbang, Rita and Carolyn P. Miller. 1993. "Language Labeling and Other Factors Affecting Perception of Ethnic Identity in Sabah." In *Language and Oral Traditions in Borneo: Borneo Research Council Proceedings 2*, ed. James T. Collins. Williamsburg, VA: Borneo Research Council, pp. 115–39.

Low, Hugh. 1988. *Sarawak: Notes during a Residence in That Country with H.H. The Rajah Brooke*. Singapore: Oxford University Press.

Mohammad Subakir Mohd Yasin. 1998. *Language Allegiance and Language Shift.* Bandar Baru Bangi: *Universiti Kebangsaan Malaysia* (UKM), Faculty of Language Studies.
Morrison, Hedda. 1957. *Sarawak.* London: Macgibbon and Kee.
Nambiar, Mohana Kumari. 2007. "Language Shift in the Malayalee Community: A Study of Intra Group Variations." PhD diss., University of Malaya.
Omar, Asmah. 1991. *The Linguistics Scenery in Malaysia.* Kuala Lumpur: Dewan Bahasa dan Pustaka.
Treacher, W.H. 1891/2010. *British Borneo-Sketches of Brunei, Sarawak, Labuan, and North Borneo.* Open Library. https://openlibrary.org.
St. John, Spenser. 1994. *The Life of Sir James Brooke Raja of Sarawak: From His Personal Papers and Correspondence.* Kuala Lumpur: Oxford University Press.
Swan, Joan et al. 2004. *A Dictionary of Sociolinguistics.* Edinburgh: Edinburgh University Press.
Talib, S. Naimah. 1999. *Administrators and Their Service: The Sarawak Administrative Service under the Brooke Rajahs and British Colonial Rule.* New York: Oxford University Press.
Tan Chee-Beng. 1993. *Chinese Peranakan Heritage in Malaysia and Singapore.* Kuala Lumpur: Fajar Bakti.
Tunku, Zainah Tunku Ibrahim. 1978. "Malay Ethnicity in Sarawak: The Case of the Orang Miri." MA thesis, Malaysia Science University, Penang.
Winzeler, Robert L. 1995. *Latah in Southeast Asia: The History and Ethnography of a Culture-bound Syndrome.* New York: Cambridge University Press.

PART III

Marriage Migrants as Multi-marginalized Diaspora

CHAPTER 7

Lives in Limbo: Unsuccessful Marriages in Sino-Vietnamese Borderlands

Caroline Grillot

Introduction

In 1991, Vietnam and China reopened their borders. Since then, economic development based on international trade in their border cities has caused a considerable increase in migration to the border areas. The reopening of these border areas led to an influx of people, which recomposed the social landscape and led to an increase in phenomena such as human smuggling, prostitution and cross-border marriage.[1] A significant number of Vietnamese women are involved in these activities. Although these activities are not new, they have become more visible and have attracted increased attention since the reform era, highlighting the crucial social changes that have occurred in both countries. Social changes are particularly noticeable in the realm of conjugality.

In this chapter I demonstrate how the position of subalterns or stigmatized individuals—on whom this research focuses—leads them to adopt non-conventional marriage patterns as a tactic of the marginalized. This point illustrates how, in the words of Susan Bibler Coutin, "borders between existence and nonexistence nonetheless remain fuzzy and permeable" (2003: 186). Indeed, the main findings of this study emphasize that a subtle stigmatization of mixed couples occurs in their hosting communities. This stigmatization results either from the marriages themselves or from the participants' initial social positions that caused some individuals to be excluded from conventional marriage markets in their countries (Grillot 2010). As a result, both Chinese men and Vietnamese women who become involved in cross-border marriages find themselves in challenging positions that often weaken the sustainability of their relationships. It is important to note that some informants, particularly the women, did not willingly enter into marriages with their Chinese partners. In addition, they did not wish to raise children with their partners. During fieldwork interviews, these informants had decided to either accept their marriages or leave them. The following analysis draws upon conversations with numerous members of the mixed communities living in the Sino-Vietnamese borderlands and narratives of more than 50 mixed couples collected between 2006 and 2010 during extensive ethnographic fieldwork.[2] Fieldwork was conducted in two pairs of border cities: Hekou and Lào Cai in the western borderlands (Yunnan) and Dongxing and Móng Cái in the eastern borderlands (Guangxi) as well as in several surrounding villages (Figure 7.1). My subjects, recruited through snowball sampling methodology, were mainly Vietnamese women and Chinese men between 20 and 60 years old who were previously or currently involved in cross-border marriages, as well as some of their acquaintances.

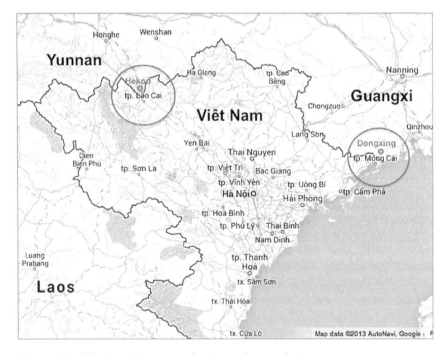

Figure 7.1 The Sino-Vietnamese border and research sites
Source: Grillot (based on a Google map).

This study analyses the phenomenon of cross-border relationships using the perspectives of the actors and individuals involved in them. It questions a large body of existing academic literature on human trafficking or mail order brides in which Vietnamese women occupy a rather privileged position among researched target groups. In this field, Sino-Vietnamese cross-border marriages are often seen as the consequences of demographic imbalance and economic dichotomy (Bélanger, Hong and Duong 2007), hence poverty. These viewpoints built upon both fieldwork data collected in borderlands and extensive research conducted on the specific cases of Sino-Vietnamese marriages in Taiwan and Singapore, and South Korean-Vietnamese marriages in Korea. Although they occur in different surroundings, mainland marriages were often perceived as a local ersatz, and/or associated with cases of human trafficking. Therefore, although qualitative studies on either the actual human trade phenomenon at the border (Action Aid International Vietnam 2005; Child Exploitation and Online Protection Centre 2011; Linh 2005; Molland 2010; Wang 2005), including marriage by deception (Anh 2003; Sun and Li 2006), or local romance and pragmatic relationships (Cham 2014; Chan 2013; Luo and Long 2008; Zhou 2002) were published by scholars and activists during the 2000s, few have effectively explored the impact of historical background, cultural compatibility, personal strategy and the communities' role in these specific alliances.

To contribute to this existing literature, when confronted with local narratives, I have positioned my work within two other fields of scholarship. First, based on the literature on international migration for marriage in Asia (Constable 2003, 2009; Jacka 2006; Jones and Shen 2008), my research provides an alternative approach by underlining the specific circumstances of mainland border societies and how ambiguous relationships between local communities often interfere with personal marital choices. The data that I gathered do not presume or discuss the general understanding of cross-border marriages as a result of economic migration through a well-organized network and a personal strategy. Instead, my research emphasizes the combination of multiple factors that might have led to a romance or a pragmatic temporary alliance. Hence, this study finds more relevance within the fields of kinship, understood as "an active process of *becoming* that is always situated within wider, historical-political, economic and sociocultural relations—in other words, a metamorphosis" (Brandtstädter and Santos 2009: 10; italics added). Because recent upheavals, which have changed Chinese and Vietnamese societies and their engagement with modernity, are also a source of kinship transformations (Bélanger and Barbieri 2009; Yan 2003), my research engages scholarship on social and identity construction in this region, notably within the framework of migration.

Second, I situate this study on cross-border marriages in the field of liminality/marginality versus normality, both in a concrete and symbolic sense. I explore how borderlands represent a liminal space that transgresses rules and provides a social space for marginal groups. In this chapter, I focus on how couples involved in mixed marriages cope with their uneven situation regarding the law and their delicate relationship with the communities where they live. To assess how families negotiate their social positions, I built upon the innovative concept of "spaces of nonexistence", which Coutin (2003) defines as spaces of invisibility, exclusion, repression, exploitation and violence (be it physical or psychological). This concept, which the author applied to the situation of illegal Central American migrants entering and then living in the United States is relevant to explaining the liminal state of many Sino-Vietnamese families in the social spaces of borderlands because Vietnamese women and their Chinese husbands generally live a "normal life", albeit an illegal one.

A Question of Destiny? "The Rice is Already Cooked" (*Sheng Mi Zhu Cheng Mi Fan*)

How do the informants themselves articulate the so-called "normal life"? Almost all the Vietnamese women interviewed in this study generally portrayed their lives and the lives of other Vietnamese women using one particular term: *khó* (*xingku* in Chinese). This Vietnamese term can be translated to mean "harsh/bitter/difficult". From the informants' perspective, this single term defines the essence of Vietnamese women's lives in general. The word usually occurred in the introductions or conclusions of their narratives and was often accompanied by a sigh or a smile. Some of these women were coerced or deceived into leaving their countries and hometowns, but they remained where they landed because they made pragmatic choices. In contrast, other women chose to leave their homes because they hoped to have new experiences. They were then forced by circumstances to remain in their new locations. The process involved in building a life out of a given socio-economic ground once again blurs the dichotomy between the active and the passive (or trafficked) migrant. I refer to the choice that emerges from these interstices as a "choice by default".

Destiny versus Tactic: Improvising an Alliance

The Vietnamese women informants expressed a strong consensus when they articulated their inner perspectives on their own lives. This consensus emerged repeatedly during most of the interviews: "This is my destiny" (*zhe shi wo de ming*). The women used this saying to describe unfortunate events. When they spoke of fortunate encounters with lovers or husbands, the expression was transformed into "This is predestined affinity" (*zhe shi yuanfen*). These narratives were offered without suggesting that destiny provided a universal explanation for an individual's plight or that destiny served as an "excuse" for all social behaviours. However, the responses underscored the complex interplay that occurs between perspectives emerging from different cultures. My informants' explanations of their own and others' trajectories revealed no evidence that a clear delineation existed between a Vietnamese and a Chinese definition of "destiny/fate" (*ming*). It could be clearly distinguished when the informants perceived "destiny" as a philosophical concept or when they used the popular definition of this type of signifier. Nevertheless, Vietnamese informants invoked this explanation more frequently than Chinese informants. If we assume that Chinese philosophy and Buddhism have defined East Asian culture, particularly Vietnamese culture, then this definition of destiny or fate should convey similar meanings for both Chinese and Vietnamese speakers. With respect to the region under examination and among individuals whose regular migrations expose them to additional external and uncontrollable life disturbances, the belief in destiny articulates the vicissitudes of these individuals' lives and expresses the consequences of risk-taking behaviours in particular.

Because they have lived on the fringes of society, and because of and despite the plights inflicted on them by destiny, some women have found ways to resist these forces and chalk out new paths. The perception of destiny as the only relevant framework cannot explain why some women have accepted their predicaments and others have challenged them. As I learned from several women whose life stories I recorded, some life sequences can indeed be attributed to destiny. Others, however, can be understood as tactical moves that are quite at odds with the supposed passivity of these women. Thus, an individual's ability to exploit certain situations allows that individual to maintain some control over the course of his/her existence, though the extent of these exploits could be limited. Borderland residents believed that the decision of many Vietnamese women to settle in Chinese communities resulted from their implementation of migration strategies, by any available means (including their bodies and/or their working skills). However, empirical data has demonstrated that in most situations, the women's decisions to arrive, stay and depart from China and their decisions to marry Chinese men were spontaneous decisions rather than carefully planned arrangements. Nevertheless, most of these women become pregnant rather quickly once they become involved in relationships in China. They conceived children as a method to help settle their personal lives. Thus, their new lives are indeed the results of their destiny, but they are also sources of worry.

The Child Issue: "Asking for a Child" versus Yearning for an Heir

When the Chinese borderland residents I interviewed discuss the issue of Sino-Vietnamese marriages, the question of children often emerges as a sensitive topic. Indeed, an affair between a man and a woman that ends because one or the other cheats does not exert a significant impact on society. In general, the affair does not offend community sentiment. It is solely a private matter, although it might become a topic of discussion and gossip. However, the family has more interactions with society than the couple. The connections created by the family affect and include more individuals. Due to the One-Child Policy, the child has become an object of extreme care and concern in contemporary China, more than ever before in modern history. The precious only child of each family, also called the "little emperor" for he/she generally receives extreme care and attention from his family, has also become the object of tremendous expectations with respect to his/her future responsibilities towards his/her family. Chinese families expect children to support their parents during old age. Bachelors yearn for wives who can produce heirs. When a bride enters a family, her reproductive functions receive considerable scrutiny. Thus, another significant issue emerges when the centre of the family—the Chinese son—becomes the object of negotiations and blackmail between his parents. It is not surprising that some Chinese men seek fertile women and future mothers from the available Vietnamese women because they are relatively isolated from their Vietnamese family; hence, they are more vulnerable to pressure from their in-laws. The marriages contracted with the mothers of their children could be grounded in affection and hopes for stable conjugal lives. However, these men request that their children remain in China when their mothers make return visits to Vietnam. These requests may reflect the husbands' anxieties about the security and well-being of their children, but the precautions may also result from stories and rumours many men have heard about women who flee with their offspring, vanish, leaving their Chinese husbands in despair.

These stories gain some credence because of tales told about single Vietnamese women and the "ask for a child" (*xin con* in Vietnamese) phenomenon among single women in Vietnam. Rather than viewing Vietnamese women through the lens of the reproductive dimension of femininity, we can instead examine the emotional lives of lonely women and their intimate yearnings for maternity. Indeed, regardless of socially normative behaviours, some Vietnamese women who have been excluded from the marriage/remarriage market have found ways to satisfy their need for company, affection, love and support. They become single mothers who operate outside the normative structure of the family. They may find lovers and become pregnant, or they may ask men whose various attributes they appreciate to inseminate them. They might even go to hospitals to receive anonymous insemination (Phinney 2005). The donors may or may not be aware of the consequences (they could be single or already married). These mothers-to-be clearly hope to raise their children singlehandedly. They also hope to fill the vacuum in their lives by properly becoming women. Although they may not be perceived symbolically as respectable women in the eyes of their community, they do achieve that status from their own perspectives. Thus, they reject male involvement in their lives, challenge social norms related to family structure and act according to their will without heeding society's rules.

Vietnamese women who live near Chinese borderlands and become aware of the availability of potential fathers for their children in China could begin to contemplate this option. Although no available empirical data confirms the impact of the "asking for a child" phenomenon in China, several elements corroborate the occurrence of the practice. First, the Marriage Law in Vietnam supports single women. It guarantees legal status to children born out of wedlock, which is not the case under the Chinese Marriage Law. According to the Chinese law, recognition and registration are contingent on the parents' payment of fines. Further, comments by some Vietnamese women who were interviewed revealed that maternity was clearly more important than conjugal life. They stated that if their relationships with their current Chinese husbands were jeopardized, they would not hesitate to return to Vietnam with their children. Some Chinese men who reside in the borderlands have blamed their former Vietnamese wives for disappearing with their children. From the perspective of these Chinese husbands, these Vietnamese mothers "stole their children". They did not ask permission, which hurt the Chinese men. In these cases, not only their feelings but also their pride and masculinity were hurt. In addition, their families and communities also experience pain. Such stories by men who were allegedly deceived and deprived of their children and heirs contribute to the general suspicion about Vietnamese women among Chinese people.

As a result, a variety of anxious and conflicting perspectives have developed toward children born out of unregistered and, thus, vulnerable marriages. Consequently, parents often negotiate their positions. Questions related to a child's registration in a parent's *hukou* (household registration book), schooling, provision of care by in-laws and language learning become elements that ease and orient an individual's social existence. They also transform into parental strategies that could later be misused. Data suggests that parents demonstrate a clear tendency to register their children on the fathers' hukou if the families possess the means to pay the fines and/or if the child is a boy. A father can exert greater control over the choices related to his son, such as selecting a school and health services. However, the registration of the child on the mothers' Vietnamese hukou is more common when the child is a girl; if fathers already have Chinese (non-divorced) families, that is, when the fathers' relationships with the Vietnamese partner is bigamous; or if the fathers have already produced the maximum legal number of children allowed.

In that case, the responsibility for the child remains with the mother. The father is excluded from any official role. The decisions made at this stage of a relationship reveal a great deal about gender imbalance as well as the prospects that both spouses may imagine for their future. Therefore, mixed couples face complex positions when they address their responsibilities as parents. These situations also reveal the levels of trust that exist between the couples and the importance of family pressure on the couples to secure their children's future, whether the child lives in China or Vietnam. Then, mixed children become symbolic figures who are used by parents to articulate their prospects for the future and as methods to cope with social nonexistence (Luo and Long 2007, 2008). However, these children could also remain in vulnerable positions within their societies because they must regularly adapt to parental choices based on changes in the relationship between the couple.

Recognition: The Condition that Leads to Sustainability

As mentioned earlier, the existence of children as "natural" outcomes of marital alliances reopens the debate over the legal legitimacy of Sino-Vietnamese couples who, for the most part, encounter difficulties when they attempt to register their relationships. Indeed, even if many of the couples tend to avoid compliance with the formal administrative procedures for registering their marriages while they are childless, the occurrence of pregnancies and the birth of children generally compels these couples to find ways to secure the current and future status of their families, whether they live in Vietnam or China. However, whether their marriages result from arranged unions or spontaneous love affairs, Sino-Vietnamese couples encounter many difficulties that may prevent them from sustaining their relationships over the long term.

Space of Nonexistence

According to recent research conducted on international marriage migration in Asia, government policies do not fully encourage the trend of international marriages. Although these marriages might help ease demographic and social pressures that create marriage squeeze in rural areas and a general drop in the birth rate, such as in South Korea and Taiwan, the flexibility and clarity of government policies regarding marriage for migrants is less evident, particularly for the acquisition of citizenship (Kim 2010). Here, Chinese authorities face a dilemma. Chinese authorities attempt to control and regulate migration, deter registration and scrutinize reproduction. Although many cross-border marriages are non-registered, officials tend to tolerate these marriages because they believe it may serve the interests of local traders, or solve demographic imbalance on the marriage market in rural areas, that is, the lack of marriageable women. This tolerance may increase when officials in charge of policy implementation are also members of the scrutinized community. Such officials may feel sympathetic towards families in despair. These situations frequently occur in rural settings where officials are more likely to reside where they work and maintain personal connections with local communities. However, because many levels of government and various offices are involved in controlling illegal populations and their activities in Chinese borderlands, the situation becomes more complex. For instance, a village leader might be more open-minded about the presence of illegal Vietnamese wives than a county-level officer from family planning who needs to meet high-level requirements for fertility rates and birth quotas or an immigration officer responsible for preventing underground migration and trade.

Meanwhile, at the societal level, a certain amount of official tolerance can create resentment among community members who conform to normative patterns of family structure and need to cope with reproductive restrictions. Therefore, despite apparent integration into the community, Sino-Vietnamese couples who fail to comply with the law enter into a space referred to as the "space of nonexistence" (Coutin 2003). To assess the methods used by such families to negotiate their social positions, we can further examine this innovative concept from migration studies used to describe spaces of invisibility, exclusion, repression, exploitation and violence. This concept can be used to explain the liminal state of many Sino-Vietnamese families who reside in the social spaces of the borderlands. Ultimately, Vietnamese women and their Chinese husbands live "normal lives", albeit illegal ones. However, the idea of nonexistence also indicates that, in many cases, nonexistence is also a social status regardless of whether or not the families possess legal recognition. The concept of nonexistence presents the idea that groups of people can be excluded from public life and recognition because of their questionable legal status, even when their lives are similar to those of others in their community. The line between registered unions and common-law marriages may not be overtly embodied; it may remain blurry in practice. Similarly, attempts to classify those circumstances that reflect the most genuine, intimate engagement between two partners in the case of marriage, alliance, cohabitation, prostitution or partnership can somehow seem meaningless when all individuals occupy a common liminal ground. The ambiguous content conveyed by these terms reflects how the notion of legality, as a living reality, has lost most of its significance in the borderlands.

Manipulating the Interstices of the Law

We need to avoid the portrayal of stigmatized people as passive and helpless victims of an imposed burden. Rather, we must consider the variety of methods that these individuals use to articulate their existence and plight and to negotiate their social positions. We must observe how they exercise their agency during various acts of resistance. For instance, migrant Vietnamese women use several tactics when they confront

Chinese authorities. They return to Vietnam to comply with the requirements of the Chinese law, and often return to China within a few hours and resume their daily lives. Several Chinese residents interviewed in Hekou and Dongxing explained how Vietnamese people with illegal status cross the border and return to their native land when political tensions impose more severe enforcement of border controls than usual. They then wait for the situation to return to "normal". Thus, their own "normality" is affected by this non-existent position.

Some Chinese scholars have labelled Vietnamese women in China the "women of no nationality" (Li, Luo and Long 2006). These women do not expect China to grant them residential rights. Nor can they rely on asylum policies because China does not provide legal recognition for refugee status. Rather, China considers them illegal economic migrants. Therefore, whether they choose to migrate or remain in China, they are unable to claim residential rights. They risk deportation back to Vietnam. However, Vietnamese women in China rarely complain or seek help. They understand the political regime that operates in their host country and realize that they cannot protest. As a result, they do not resist Chinese immigration policy. They remain in the shadows of the borderlands and attempt to remain inconspicuous. In the case of Sino-Vietnamese cross-border marriages, families face serious problems. They must consider the difficulties of marriage registration, access to Chinese citizenship, permanent residential rights, children's identities, citizenship and the right to education.

However, from the public and official perspective, although these marriages appear to result from Chinese economic reforms, the opening of the borders and the increase in friendlier policies towards neighbouring countries, they are seen as disadvantageous to China rather than the migrants involved. The problematic status of these couples, particularly the status of certain Vietnamese women in China who have been labelled victims of trafficking or illegal migrants, represents a threat to the Chinese nation-state and the management of Chinese society. This argument is common in the media and academic literature in China. In an article that clearly aims to provide policy makers with a clear picture of cross-border marriages to improve their ability to resolve the issues, two Chinese scholars summarize this widespread viewpoint:

> Some Vietnamese borderlanders enter [China] with opium, heroin and other drugs inflows into China, whereas others are involved in firearms and ammunition trafficking and smuggling, resulting in an

increase of cross-border criminal activities. In addition, some Vietnamese women called "flying pigeons",[3] cause the emergence of many single-parent families, or empty nesters, and child rearing and education are increasingly becoming a social problem in Chinese border areas. (…) [Sino-Vietnamese cross-border marriages are] not conducive to border community management. Because Vietnamese women who marry Chinese men do not hold Chinese nationality and residence, offices that manage national security, family planning and other aspects encounter considerable difficulties. (Luo and Long 2007: 18; translated from Chinese by the author)

The contrasting Chinese categorizations of "illegal migrants" (*feifa yimin*), "trafficked people" (*guaimai renkou*) or "flying pigeons" (*fei gezi*) have become stereotypical figures within the social landscapes of the borderlands. However, if we consider that the majority of cross-border marriages are non-registered, that is, they are rather vulnerable and non-recognized unions, we can relate their positions to those of liminal individuals. The participants of these marriages are situated between the positions of being single and being a spouse. They possess a status that generates comments, suspicion and worry among local people. These marriages also trigger scrutiny and, at times, intervention from Chinese and Vietnamese authorities. Because they create an abnormality within the realms of migration, conjugality and social welfare, these marriages threaten normality. They conceptually disturb the notions of sacredness associated with marriage by changing its practices. Thus, they affect social morality at a local level. Vietnamese women could steal Chinese money, or steal the Chinese husbands of other women. They may provide alluring spaces where Chinese men can satisfy their needs, and so on. They also produce children who become burdens to Chinese society because their status is associated with that of "black children" (*hei haizi*), or non-existent children (Greenhalgh 2003). They also create inequality and generate animosity among members of the community. In short, these couples threaten social stability.

Cross-border families have little opportunity to leave this liminal state. Over the long term, existence in these liminal spaces generates the development of social fringes, that is, people who are legally "non-existent" for an indefinite period. Because they live in vulnerable conditions, these individuals may adopt tactics to respond to changing environments that could potentially jeopardize their already insecure positions. On a metaphorical level, a liminal person is "invisible". Translated into the context of the borderlands, this means that such couples and families are, in general, neither legally nor socially recognized. Hence, these marriages are not labelled or classified under the category of "marriage". However, the obstacles they encounter at various levels as they attempt to become "properly married" are so serious that most individuals are unable to find their way out of the allegedly temporary state of liminality. Many of the men and women in these marriages initially sought social recognition by finding mates.

They transformed themselves from bachelors, single people, divorcées, ex-convicts, ex-prostitutes, elderly people or any other sort of social outcast position to the status of a normative "married person". However, in so doing, they may actually have entered other realms of marginality. This marginal status may be due to the continuing social stigmatization attached to mixed marriages. It may also directly relate to their administrative status, which deprives them of the advantages of citizenship. Because they are caught between "before-lives" from which they hope to emancipate themselves and "after-lives" that can only be partially achieved with respect to social position, these couples discover that they are in non-existent positions. They remain in liminal spaces that create conditions necessary for resistance. If problems arise, they can leave, cross the border, return to their hometowns, become visible in their own spaces, reconnect with their "before-lives" or indefinitely remain on the fringes of either society.

Some families manage to circumvent legal requirements related to family planning, marriage and birth registration. However, during interviews, many informants noted that it had become very difficult to achieve this without sufficient financial support. For example, it had become particularly difficult to buy property. According to them, a few years ago, an individual could easily purchase a hukou from the location where the individual wanted to establish residency status.[4] Now, however, the law had changed and this option was no longer possible. Currently, when most people hope to change their hukou from their native location to a new place of residence (in the context of permanent migration), they try to select property that will allow them to obtain a new hukou, which eases many of the formalities linked to family. For example, it allows people from borderland spaces to arrange marriage registrations more easily when they do not possess the financial means to travel across China to secure a stamp or an appointment with an official. As Jiang, one Chinese informant who is officially married to his Vietnamese wife, stated, "Registering a marriage is also a responsibility towards spouses' parents. It is an expression of filial piety. It relieves both families of worries. It is a way to respect them." However, in Hekou or Dongxing, many men who reside with Vietnamese partners are recent migrants who do not necessarily intend to spend their lives in Hekou. They do not want to move their hukou to Hekou because their hometowns may provide easier access to other living necessities.

They have no desire to lose these benefits for the sake of marriage registration. Consequently, many couples remain unregistered. Here, as mentioned earlier, authorities play very delicate roles and are often in awkward moral positions when they must address these relationships once they have become established. With respect to village life and cross-border marriages, authorities adopt compassionate and compromising attitudes towards mixed couples. In some villages, local officers may simply register the presence of Vietnamese wives, but they may not provide permanent residence cards or counselling on international marriage procedures. Therefore, in some villages, legal authorities vacillate between two possible behaviours. They can either denounce the illegal status of the Vietnamese women and ruin the lives and hopes of local families, or they can tolerate the women's existence, disregard central regulations and adopt flexible attitudes that allow mixed couples and families to remain united. This may occur under various conditions negotiated between the parties including include the payment of bribes, maintaining low profiles in the community and close surveillance. However, local administrators are perfectly aware of the concerns of their fellow community members who may be relatives, schoolmates, friends or acquaintances. These dilemmas occur within a complex web of social networks in which the individual who represents the law and other authorities must choose between the rejection of central regulations or rejection of his/her own network of social connections. It is an awkward position to negotiate that leads to various compromises, complicity and an uneven status quo for mixed families.

In sum, to avoid inviting the Chinese state into their private lives, some couples have explored a variety of methods to manipulate the interstices of laws and regulations and obtain or maintain their marital status including false IDs, phony marriage certificates, foreign hukou registrations and adoption. On the Vietnamese side, legal arrangements could be even more difficult to make. Ultimately, Vietnamese women who are unable to return to Vietnam regularly to update their administrative status may face increased marginalization. Because they cannot obtain marriage certificates, they will be unable to obtain regular residence cards in China. In addition, they also lose their legal rights in Vietnam. Some women who leave their communities fail to notify the government of their temporary absences. When they return to Vietnam, they may find that their names have been erased from the permanent registration books. If they manage to return home, these women face difficulties when they begin the registration process to regain their rights as Vietnamese citizens. This position jeopardizes their mere existence as (any type of) citizens and, thus, deprives them of citizenship rights in any location. This situation leaves them in a state of profound vulnerability and leads them to enhance their survival skills. The attempts of these women to discover a social existence in spaces of legal nonexistence are one of the most difficult challenges that they face.

Emotional Limbo: A Consequence of Nonexistence

Close examination of several cases of cross-border marriage in these borderlands leads us to admit that despite the personal efforts of these individuals to integrate into communities and regardless of the extent of their success in these endeavours, the problem of their social nonexistence remains. This problematic status adds to the precariousness of cross-border marriages that might otherwise be considered a method on which individuals can rely to sublimate various personal frustrations.

Ostracism That Prevails Over Integration Attempts

Some Vietnamese women manage to gain the respect they deserve by adopting firm positions when confronted with gossip and stories that disclose their identities during social conversations. However, even in the case of voluntary unions and despite appearances, the integration of Vietnamese women into Chinese society by marriage will remain limited as long as negative representations about cross-border marriages are circulated locally.[5] The narratives of several informants articulate a sense of disillusionment that lurks behind satisfied faces. However, these individuals also share a common reality. They understand that the range of alternative options is narrow. They are convinced that, at the very least, they escaped or avoided potentially worse scenarios in Vietnam. Women's choices to live, study and work in China with Chinese men must accommodate impossible returns. They are left with uncertain and limited possibilities to integrate into their host society.

Separation

The problem of authority over children creates emotional dilemmas for many mixed couples. For these couples, the prospect of a separation becomes an even more complicated problem than it would be for other divorced parents. For example, the lack of legal parental recognition for even one of the parents prevents a legal agreement on shared custody. In general, if the child is a boy who has been registered on his father's hukou, then the Chinese father will tend to exert his power over the child's mother. When a couple agrees to separate, a space may exist for informal negotiation over the custody of the children. However, if a Vietnamese woman desires an escape from an unbearable life with her Chinese husband and fails to take her children along, then this might lead to a complete loss of the child's custody for the mother. Generally, because they lack conjugal or strong community support, many Vietnamese women ultimately return to Vietnam in final attempts to rebuild their lives. These attempts result in nothing but sorrow. Some women manage to find other Chinese partners so that they can remain geographically close to their children. However, few possess sufficient power to take stands against Chinese families who often remain strongly committed to protecting their heirs. Therefore, those Vietnamese women who fail to find satisfaction in their marriages in China must leave their children if they wish to and are able to return to Vietnam. Their alternative is to accept their plight in China. In both cases, they remain relatively helpless and lack support both in China and in Vietnam. They have little support at either the institutional or the local level.

Indeed, the stigma attached to returnees from China remains strong in Vietnam. Although some women suffer from their experiences, they rarely receive compassionate acceptance when they return home, even from their families. The luckiest manage to remarry in Vietnam into understanding families. However, they often marry people who are socially less established than they are, that is, they marry men who belong to the lowest ranks in the social hierarchy. Others remain alone and single. They are prepared to live unsupported lives. Many of these women eventually return to China in final attempts to find suitable partners. However, such choices may result in various potentially negative experiences. Some of my informants changed partners several times. Others had been cheated on or accused of cheating by their partners. These women generally lived in very modest circumstances. They were distressed and psychologically affected by their marginalization. They relied on a limited network of Vietnamese acquaintances to maintain their survival in China. These women lived in an emotional limbo created by the absence of efficient support from their communities. They may have been denied support because of stigma and stereotypes. This denial could also have resulted from the attitudes of local governments that continue to see these women as illegal migrants. Thus, these women may often be forced to live far away from their children. They may also be forced to enter into realms of illicit activities such as smuggling or prostitution, which only serves to deepen their liminality.

The Rented Womb: Anecdotal Exploitation of Nonexistence at the Intimate Level

Some Vietnamese women are placed in difficult positions when they remain in Sino-Vietnamese borderlands. They may attract abuse from local individuals. These forms of abuse may extend far beyond forced marriage or prostitution to the commodification of their bodies. There are plenty of rumours in the borderlands about surrogate mothers. Although surrogacy is still legally banned, it is a widespread phenomenon in Mainland China for Chinese people. According to some informants, the circumstances in the borderlands may increase the number of women in need of financial support who are willing to serve as surrogates for prospective families who hope to sire children. These women will be more willing to comply with cheap arrangements and poor conditions for pregnancy compared to women from other situations. Families that require surrogate mothers may search within the pool of illegal migrants that includes abandoned Vietnamese wives. It is difficult to define whether these widespread scenarios should be labelled as adoption, child trafficking, surrogacy or simply personal arrangements. However, they can definitely be discussed as examples of the potential consequences of emotional limbo experienced by Vietnamese women once they leave unsuccessful relationships in Vietnam or China.

My purpose here is to highlight a specific form of abuse that occurs within the situation of marginality that could entrap some Vietnamese women. The cases of surrogacy illustrate the extent of the commodification of the women who make themselves available to "womb purchasers".[6] They also offer insight into the candidates' motivations that extend beyond the financial benefits they might gain. Although I interpreted this from second-hand stories that lacked details and subtleties, some women clearly stated that they had offered their wombs in exchange for relationships. Money alone was not the motivation. Then, we must ask: how true are these surrogacy stories? What really happens when Chinese men buy wives to bear and raise their children? What occurs when a Vietnamese woman asks a Chinese man for a child (whether she discloses her purpose) and then flees with the baby? How does the economy address the emotional and security needs of these men and women who may believe that children are strategies they can use to create families or structures, albeit unstable structures, upon which they can rely? What is the role of moral values in these situations?

Conclusion: Making an Escape or Sinking into Marginality?

Regardless of whether or not Vietnamese women who engage in cross-border marriages with Chinese men entered willingly into these relationships, most continue to live illegally in China. When they are unable to register their marriages, they become partners, mistresses, mothers or domestic workers. Many possess neither rights nor possible claims for protection or support. During the last 20 years, the number of mixed couples has increased. This increase is associated with demographic crisis, economic cooperation and social changes that have created an open space for interaction between two societies. However, despite increasing visibility of this segment of the population within local communities, the media and public discourse, the lack of authentic information or guidance provided to them causes many mixed couples to live on the fringes of their societies. When Vietnamese women fail to adjust to a normative model of conjugality, their situation worsens. They find it very challenging at that stage of their adult lives to reintegrate into either Chinese or Vietnamese society. In this study, I have discussed the ways in which personal projects increase individual impulses to cross social and physical borders and challenge predetermined social positions. I also endeavoured to outline how the idea of social identity lies beyond the articulation of a wide range of intimate yearnings and resistance manifested in the form of actions. Normativity is at play in the dynamics of these cross-border alliances because every individual has the right to seek out his or her own wellbeing, regardless of his or her previous life experiences. The core question is not located in national identity or its meanings, despite social representations of mixed couples that limit their possibilities of open existence within the community and in the eyes of the state.

Indeed, marriage across borders is not aimed at conveyance or adoption of Chinese or Vietnamese identity. It does not concern the embodiment of the archetype of an imagined and idealized conjugal figure. Rather, it may simply concern the yearning to be part of a couple, to become part of a normative structure and to join a conventional pattern of family in societies that are strongly structured by the entity of marriage, that is, marriage is a milestone in life. However, when these individuals fail to successfully navigate the passage between singlehood and marriage, they remain marginalized and "non-existent", which is barely a sustainable position. Therefore, for these Vietnamese women and Chinese men, the social identity that marriage provides (specifically, the image of "spouse") allows them to interact with the rest of the society and, hopefully, to gain social recognition, that is, to exist as members of the society than as outcasts. Ultimately, this depends on the form that each couple actually adopts, displays or performs. The state of marginality, particularly when embedded in a physical space of liminality, results from the creation of a "site" that is governed by different rules. This site allows the transgression of rules that results in an absence of limits on people's actions and exerts an impact on life flexibility. However, this position remains at odds with sought-after normality. From this perspective, we can deem cross-border marriages a possible method for overcoming socially disadvantaged positions. Alternatively, we can view cross-border marriages as uneven and exposed pathways that cause individuals to sink further into non-existent positions on the fringes of society. For a migrating Vietnamese woman, this status can signify a switch from a position as an outcast in Vietnam to a position as a subaltern in China.

Notes

1. No accurate data currently exist on the extension of the Sino-Vietnamese cross-border phenomenon discussed in this chapter. Many of these marriages are not documented according to marriage policies in Vietnam and China. Although the presence of Vietnamese migrants living in common-law marriages with Chinese citizens might be registered at the local level, they do not officially exist. Reports by media and international organizations occasionally mention quantitative data, but most are questionable because they are based on operations rescuing "trafficked women". In addition, the official data based on properly registered marriages were unavailable to me when I was conducting the fieldwork. Therefore, it is difficult to accurately depict a phenomenon that is mostly invisible in official statistics

and that has spread throughout China for the last 25 years on the basis of historical human exchanges that have always included marriages. I chose to analyze the nature rather than the scale of this phenomenon.
2. This study is based on a chapter of my doctoral thesis, "The Fringes of Conjugality: On Fantasies, Tactics, and Representations of Sino-Vietnamese Encounters in Borderlands", which focuses on Sino-Vietnamese cross-border marriages (Macquarie University, Australia, 2012; Vrije Universiteit Amsterdam, The Netherlands, 2013).
3. Original emphasis.
4. I was unable to obtain consistent, reliable official information about this policy. I was also unable to discover the methods of implementation used in migration locations such as border towns.
5. This negative figure contrasts with that of the trafficking victim: some Vietnamese women are blamed for marrying Chinese men, even providing them with heirs, and or and for disappearing soon after with their husbands' savings and sometimes children.
6. Author's emphasis.

References

Action Aid International Vietnam. 2005. *The Trafficking of Vietnamese Women and Children*.

Anh, Dang Nguyen. 2003. "Cross-Border Migration and Sexuality in Vietnam: Reality and Policy Responses." In *Living on the Edges: Cross-Border Mobility and Sexual Exploitation in the Greater Southeast Asia Sub-Region*, ed. Muhadjir Darwin, Anna-Marie Wattie and Susi Eja Yuarsi. Yogyakarta: Gadjah Mada University, Center for Population and Policy Studies, pp. 47–96.

Bélanger, Danièle and Magali Barbieri. 2009. *Reconfiguring Families in Contemporary Vietnam*. Stanford, CA: Stanford University Press.

Bélanger, Danièle, Khuat Thu Hong and Le Bach Duong. 2007. "Transnational Migration, Marriage and Trafficking at the China-Vietnam Border." In *Watering the Neighbour's Garden: The Growing Demographic Female Deficit in Asia*, ed. Isabelle Attané and Christophe Z. Guilmoto. Paris: Committee for International Cooperation in National Research in Demography, pp. 393–425.

Brandtstädter, Susanne and Gonçalo D. Santos. 2009. *Chinese Kinship: Contemporary Anthropological Perspectives*. London: Routledge.

Cham, Nguyen Thi Phuong. 2014. "Cross-Border Brides: Vietnamese Wives, Chinese Husbands in a Border-Area Fishing Village." *Cross-Currents: East Asian History and Culture Review* 11: 92–117.

Chan, Yuk-Wah. 2013. *Vietnamese-Chinese Relationship at the Borderlands. Trade, Tourism and Cultural Politics*. London: Routledge.

Child Exploitation and Online Protection Centre. 2011. *The Trafficking of Women and Children from Vietnam.*
Constable, Nicole. 2003. *Romance on a Global Stage: Pen Pals, Virtual Ethnography, and "Mail-Order" Marriages.* Berkeley: University of California Press.
———. 2009. "The Commodification of Intimacy: Marriage, Sex, and Reproductive Labor." *Annual Review of Anthropology* 38(1): 49–64.
Coutin, Susan Bibler. 2003. "Borderlands, Illegality and the Space of Nonexistence." In *Globalization under Construction: Governmentalities, Law, and Identity*, ed. Richard Perry and Bill Maurer. Minneapolis, MN: University of Minnesota Press, pp. 171–202.
Jones, Gavin and Hsiu-hua Shen. 2008. "International Marriage in East and Southeast Asia: Trends and Research Emphases." *Citizenship Studies* 12(1): 9–25.
Greenhalgh, Susan. 2003. "Planned Births, Unplanned Persons: 'Population' in the Making of Chinese Modernity." *American Ethnologist* 30(2): 196–215.
Grillot, Caroline. 2010. *Volées, Envolées, Convolées. Vendues, en Fuite ou Re-socialisées: Les "Fiancées" Vietnamiennes en Chine* [Stolen, Vanished, Wedded …Sold, Runaway or Re-socialized: the Vietnamese "Brides" in China]. Paris: Connaissances et Savoirs.
Jacka, Tamara. 2006. *Rural Women in Urban China: Gender, Migration, and Social Change.* Armonk, NY: M.E. Sharpe.
Kim, Minjeong. 2010. "Gender and International Marriage Migration." *Sociology Compass* 4(9): 718–31.
Li, Juan, Luo Liuning and Long Yao. 2006. "Renleixue shi ye zhong de 'Wu guoji nüren.' Yi Guangxi Daxin xian A cun wei li" [Women of 'No Nationality' in the Perspective of Anthropology. Taking A Village of Daxin County in Guangxi as an Example]. *Journal of Baise University* 20(1): 7–14.
Linh, Hoang Thi To. 2005. *Cross-border trafficking in Quang-Ninh province, Vietnam.* Retrieved from the Asia Pacific Migration Research Network Website: http://apmrn.anu.edu.au/regional_members/vietnam.html [accessed 10 Nov. 2015].
Luo, Liuning and Long Yao. 2007. "Zhong Yue bianjing kuaguo hunyin de liubian jiqi sikao" [Pondering on Changes of Transnational Marriages of Sino-Vietnamese Border]. *Journal of Baise University* 20(1): 1521.
———. 2008. "Zhongguo–Dongmeng jiagou xia Xinan bianjing kuaguo hunyin zinü de shehuihua" [Socialization of Children from Transnational Marriage in South-west China Frontier]. *Journal of South-Central University for Nationalities (Humanities and Social Sciences)* 28(1): 33–7.
Molland, Sverre. 2010. "'The Perfect Business': Human Trafficking and Lao-Thai Cross-Border Migration." *Development and Change* 41(5): 831–55.
Phinney, Harriet M. 2005. "Asking for a Child: The Refashioning of Reproductive Space in Post-War Northern Vietnam." *The Asia Pacific Journal of Anthropology* 6(3): 215–30.

Sun, Xiaoying and Li Bihua. 2006. "Guanyu fandui kuaguo guaimai Yuenan funü ertong de diaocha baogao" [On the Investigation to the Illegal Cross-border Marriage of Trafficking Vietnamese Women as Wives]. *Around Southeast Asia* 12: 28–39.

Wang, Yi. 2005. *Trafficking in Women and Children from Vietnam to China: Legal Framework and Government Responses*. Québec: Oxfam Québec. Available at http://www.humantrafficking.org/uploads/publications/oxfam_antitrafficking_program_in_vietnam.pdf [accessed 10 Nov. 2015].

Yan, Yunxiang. 2003. *Private Life under Socialism: Love, Intimacy, and Family Change in a Chinese Village, 1949–1999*. Stanford, CA: Stanford University Press.

Zhou, Jianxin. 2002. *Zhong Yue Zhong Lao Kuaguo Minzu jiqi Zuqun Guanxi Yanjiu* [Sino-Vietnam and Sino-Laos Cross-Border Ethnic Groups and Ethnic Relationship]. Beijing: Minzu Chubanshe.

CHAPTER 8

Lives of Mixed Vietnamese-Korean Children in Vietnam

Hien Anh Le

Introduction

This chapter focuses on children whose future is at risk because they are in the "borderlands" between Vietnam and Korea. The children are stateless for all intents and purposes because they have Vietnamese mothers who escaped[1] from their Korean husbands for various reasons and who secretly brought their children back to Vietnam without their husbands' permission. However, these mothers refuse to give up their children's Korean nationality for Vietnamese nationality because they believe that maintaining the nationality of an advanced country, that is Korea, will benefit their children. In reality, being stateless has seriously disadvantaged these children and jeopardized their future.

An increasing number of Vietnamese women are marrying Korean men. In fact, Vietnam has surpassed China as the country with the most cross-border marriages with Korea. However, a significant number of these marriages end in official and unofficial divorces. In official divorces, Vietnamese women must leave their children, particularly their sons, in Korea with their husbands although the women themselves can continue to work in Korea. However, because these women have little formal education, they have difficulty accessing the legal system in Korea. Without support from lawyers or counsellors coupled with a lack of financial resources, the mothers lose the child custody battle for their children. In unofficial divorces, however, the women can return to Vietnam with their children, or they can send their children to Vietnam while they remain in Korea. In the former case, these divorced women may remarry or obtain new jobs, and consequently leave their children in the care of their parents, a responsibility the grandparents can often ill afford.

Consequently, the children suffer the psychological and economic consequences of the divorce. Furthermore, their relocation to Vietnam induces a loss of social status and cultural identity. By maintaining their Korean nationality, these children also encounter problems due to government policies of both countries, particularly as regards their formal education. Whether or not these children can adapt to their new environment in Vietnam is a primary concern. These problems can have a lasting effect on a generation of Vietnamese-Korean migrant children. They deserve to be recognized so that coordinated government policies from both countries can be implemented.

This study focuses on the children of Vietnamese and Korean couples who have been unofficially divorced, particularly children who are Korean citizens living in Hau Giang Province, which is located in southern part of Vietnam. This province was chosen as the area of study because it has the second highest number of women who legally marry Taiwanese and Korean men.

The Study

To obtain the data for this study, survey questionnaires were administered. Additionally, interviews were conducted with 30 return-migrated Vietnamese women, 2 grandparents and 10 provincial officials in charge of cross-border marriages or heads of hamlets, some of whom were high-ranking officials in the province. Discussions with government authorities in Hau Giang were also conducted to provide a complete picture of the current situation of these divorced women and their children, particularly these children's structural isolation, that is, their separation from their fathers or, in some cases, from their mothers, and its impact on their growth and development.

Cross-border Marriages between Vietnamese Women and Korean Men

Statistics show that the number of marriages between Vietnamese women and Korean men has risen recently. According to the Korean Justice Department, from 2000 to 2006 the number of marriages between Vietnamese and Koreans was 100,000. The Korea National Statistical Office also noted that from the years 2003 to 2008, this number rose dramatically to 122,522. In a meeting with the Vietnamese Youth Delegation to Seoul on 16 April 2012, the Vietnamese Envoy in Korea, Nguyen Manh Dong, announced that in 2012, the number of Vietnamese marrying Koreans had reached 45,000. Additionally, Lim (2012) noted that in marriages between Korean men and Asian women, the number of Vietnamese women surpassed the number of women from other Southeast Asian countries, such as the Philippines, Cambodia and Thailand. Finally, Lee Sang Lim from the Korean Institute of Studies noted that 7,636 Vietnamese women married Korean men in 2011, surpassing the Chinese men in this regard, with 7,549 (cited in Tran 2012a).

It is interesting to note that there is a significant difference between the number of marriages registered in Korea and Vietnam. There are two ways of obtaining legal documents for marriages between Vietnamese women and Korean men. The first way is by registration of the marriage in Vietnam. In this registration process, both partners must be present, interviewed and approved by local Vietnamese authorities. In the second way, the Korean groom can simply register the marriage in Korea; his Vietnamese bride does not need to be present. Documentation that the groom is single is all that is required. The Vietnamese bride can then report the registration to the local Vietnamese authorities. The second method is much less time consuming and therefore is more popular.

Most of the Vietnamese women referred to in the above statistics hail from rural areas, particularly those in South Vietnam, where the standard of living is very low. Social researchers Kim and Shin (2007) note that 85 per cent of Vietnamese wives in Korea come from Southwest Vietnam. Marriage registration statistics for Hau Giang Province show that the number of Vietnamese women from this province tend to marry Koreans much more than men from other countries, particularly in cases where the couples register their marriage in Korea and the Vietnamese government merely notarizes the marriages. However, this may be due to the fact that Vietnamese women who intend to marry Korean men go to Hau Giang Province as the visa interview process there is relatively easier.

Figure 8.1 shows that the number of Vietnamese-Korean marriages has decreased slightly in recent years. However, based on my interview with officials from the Justice Department in charge of interviewing cross-border marriage couples in Hau Giang Province on 14 October 2012, it appears that the decline was caused by a shortage of single

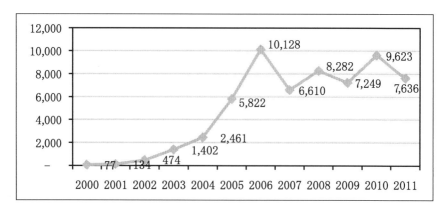

Figure 8.1 Number of Vietnamese-Korean marriages
Source: Department of Justice in Hau Giang Province, 2012.

women in the province. Thus, the decline in the number of marriages shown in Figure 8.1 could be misleading.

Why Vietnamese Women Marry Korean Men

Tran (2009) notes that the poverty in Vietnam, the women's low education level and the similarity of cultural backgrounds between Vietnam and Korea are the three main reasons why Vietnamese women marry Korean men, even though they know very little about these men and their future living conditions. Tran (2009) estimated that 77.7 per cent of his 1,483 Vietnamese respondents who married Korean men were economically motivated. They viewed the marriage as an opportunity to have a better life, look for a job and earn more money to support their parents.

My discussions with both return-migrated Vietnamese women and government officials revealed that the women had limited exposure to foreign cultures. The women's understanding of Korea was based on Korean television dramas, which often paint a very rosy picture of life in that country. Therefore, these women imagined that marriage to a Korean man would be an opportunity to pursue a better life. Further, as dutiful Vietnamese children, they hoped that, once in Korea, they could help support their parents in Vietnam financially by sending money which they would earn or that their husbands would give them. (Unlike those who marry Taiwanese men, Vietnamese women who marry Korean men are allowed to work.)

A Justice Department official I spoke to reported that there are efforts to dissuade the women from marrying Korean men, especially when the future husbands are much older than the women. The officials try to persuade the Vietnamese women to reconsider the marriage during their interviews with them. They show the women newspaper articles and videos showing the reality of many unhappy Vietnamese-Korean marriages and even invite women who have escaped from their Korean husbands to talk with the interviewees. However, the women cannot be persuaded. They would say, "My parents already have miserable lives. If I can go to Korea, even being treated badly there cannot be worse than my life in Vietnam. In addition, maybe I can earn some money to support my parents." Alternatively, they would say, "When watching TV, I find that living in Korea cannot be more miserable than living in Vietnam. Just consider this marriage a chance for me to travel to Korea. If I am unhappy, I will go back to Vietnam." Given these circumstances, it is indeed understandable why these young women seek better lives by marrying Korean men.

While Vietnam is located in Southeast Asia and Korea is in the northeast, both countries are influenced by Confucianism. Therefore, many similarities exist between the two cultures. For instance, both countries adhere strongly to the traditional values of respect for the elderly and harmony among family members. The majority of Korean men looking for Vietnamese women are farmers who are low-income employees in the cities or elderly or divorced men who cannot marry Korean women. They look for wives who can take care of their parents and help them with farming. Therefore, Vietnamese women in rural areas are good candidates. The majority of these women are very faithful to their husbands; they are hard workers and are excellent at taking care of their families. Women from the south have also gained the reputation of being gentle, easy-going and attractive. These strong virtues lead Korean men to believe that their Vietnamese spouses will be good wives and obedient daughters-in-law.

Cross-border Divorces between Vietnamese Women and Korean Men

Korean Statistics show that the divorce rate between Korean men and foreign wives is increasing. In 2007, the total number of divorce cases was 8,828, up by 40.6 per cent from the previous year. Further, data from "Emergency Call Operation-1366", an emergency call service operated for foreign female victims, show that the number of women requesting divorce consultants was 13,277; of these calls, 42.94 per cent were from Vietnamese wives of Korean men.

The Reality of Vietnamese Women's Lives in Korea after Marriage

Kim and Shin (2007) state that in Korea many foreign brides and their children suffer from social exclusion. Moreover, they are confronted with linguistic and cultural barriers. Discussions and interviews with the return-migrated Vietnamese women revealed these obstacles to adapting to life in Korea.

First, many Vietnamese women face a language barrier. An estimated 90 per cent of Vietnamese immigrant brides cannot speak the Korean language before going to Korea. A respondent in this study described the impact of being unable to communicate as follows:

> Life in Korea was not as beautiful as I had expected. My husband lived in a remote area where I could see only mountains around me. My husband went to work, so I had to stay at home with my parents-in-law. My mother-in-law would ask me to do many things without having a rest and she talked a lot. Because I could not speak Korean much, I could not understand what she said. Having no friends and not being able to communicate in Vietnamese made me feel as if I were suffocating.

Because of their language deficiency, not all Vietnamese women could adapt to Korean society in general and to their husbands' families in particular. The Korean government's policies help to support the foreign women's effort to integrate into Korean society and offer them many opportunities to obtain employment.[2] The Korean government asks many departments to implement policies that support multicultural families by offering them a number of benefits (Ly 2012). Nevertheless, their language deficiency causes 40.3 per cent of women to miss out on these opportunities (Tran 2012a: 96). In Korea, a mother's role is primarily to take care of her family and take charge of her children's schooling. However, the Vietnamese women's inability to communicate in Korean hinders the Vietnamese wife from functioning efficiently. Her language deficiency causes misunderstandings not only between her and her husband but also between her and her mother-in-law. This deficiency also limits the women's communication with the outside community, particularly in regard to her children's schooling.

According to the returned women who were interviewed, to mitigate the women's language deficiency problem the Korean government has established many centres that support multicultural families. These centres offer various services. They offer Korean language classes and computer classes; they provide information about the traditional Korean culture; and they offer counselling services. As previously mentioned, most Vietnamese women who marry Korean men hail from the countryside and only have an elementary school education; thus, their education level is very low. Given their background, it is very difficult for these Vietnamese women to overcome the language barrier. According to data from Gyeongbuk province in Korea, the Korean language proficiency of 71.5 per cent out of 3,469 foreign wives of Korean men falls in the middle to low levels. This is particularly true of Vietnamese wives (Tran 2012b). It is therefore not surprising that the lack of proficiency in the Korean language is regarded as a cause of the increase in divorces between Korean men and their foreign wives, which rose from 1,744 in 2002 to 8,671 in 2007, 11,255 in 2008, and 11,692 in 2009 (Kim and Shin 2007).

Second, the influence of Confucianism is much weaker in Vietnam than in Korea. This cultural difference sometimes creates difficulties for Vietnamese marriage migrants, as typified by the following narrative from one of the respondents.

> I was not allowed to eat meals at the same time as my husband. I had to serve him and his family first, and then my mother-in-law and I could eat later. In Vietnam, I did not have to do that. My parents and I always had a very comfortable relationship. So, my husband's family's behaviour humiliated me.

Following Confucian principles, Korean people, particularly those with large extended families living in rural areas, place great importance on the strict hierarchy in the family. They believe that this is the foundation for a successful society. As Nguyen (2012) notes, relationships between parents and children, husbands and wives, and older and younger brothers are based on absolute submission in a traditional Korean family. Further, Korean men in rural areas tend to be more authoritarian than men in urban areas. They are very conservative and traditional in their view of their wives' roles: to care for the family and serve their parents-in-law. The men's role is to earn money while the women's role is to take care of the family, including the children. Daughters-in-law must serve their parents-in-law under a condition known as called *sijipsari* (three years of being blind, deaf and mute).

Despite being similarly influenced by Confucian ideology, among the Vietnamese the relationship among family members is much more equitable and comfortable. The family hierarchical authoritarianism still dominates, although the influence of Confucianism in this regard is weaker in the south. Additionally, the relationship between daughters-in-law and mothers-in-law is less severe in the south than in the north.

The cultural differences described above aggravate the linguistically-generated conflict between Vietnamese wives and their Korean family members.

Finally, prejudice toward marriage migrants from Southeast Asia makes it difficult for Vietnamese women to adapt to life in Korea. Although the multi-cultural family concept is no longer a novel one, some Korean people still have a negative view of cross-border marriages. This prejudice prevents foreigners, particularly women from developing countries, from integrating into Korean society. This applies not only to the women but also to their children, who can easily become isolated and bullied at school and in society. This situation is aggravated by the fact that their mothers cannot protect them because of their own language deficiency and lack of a social network.

In-depth interviews with eight women respondents who escaped from their husband's family and returned to Vietnam revealed the above reasons for the difficulty in adapting to life in Korea. The limited language ability and its accompanying problems, the differences in culture and prejudice convinced the Vietnamese women that life in Korea was not as happy as they had expected it to be.

Returning Migrant Children

Having suffered the difficulties of adapting to Korean life, a considerable number of Vietnamese women began to bring their children back to Vietnam. Further interviews with officials in charge of justice at the city, village and hamlet levels and with the police department in Hau Giang Province revealed that there was no official record of the number of divorced women returning to Vietnam. This was because these women are not legally required to register their marital status with the authorities when returning to their hometowns. It is only when they want to remarry or for other reasons, like obtaining official certification when seeking employment or admission into hospital, that they must report their status to the officials. Nevertheless, according to the interviewed officials, the number of divorced women had increased recently, particularly among women divorcing husbands from Korea. Although no official statistics exist for the 74 villages in Hau Giang Province, Justice Department officials estimated that four to five women in each village have divorced their Korean husbands.

After returning to their hometown, most of the divorced women who are still young (in their thirties) go to the city to look for jobs or to remarry. When they do so, they leave their children with their parents. Although these children are not resented by their grandparents, caring for them is a financial burden. Interviewed grandparents described their situation as follows:

> My grandchild is not isolated from my neighbours. We, people in the southern rural areas, do not hold severe prejudice against those who marry foreigners. A lot of girls in our neighbourhood married Taiwanese or Koreans. People just think that my daughter is unlucky so she had to come back. My neighbours like my grandchild because he can speak Korean.
>
> I'm very poor. I earn my living as a farmer. When my daughter got married to a Korean, I thought that she could have a better life and that she could send some money for me, as other surrounding girls do to their parents. However, now she has come back with her child. I can't help take care of my grandchild so her mother can go to Ho Chi Minh City to work.
>
> My daughter was not as lucky as the other girls in my hamlet, so she had to return to Vietnam with her child. My wife and I are old. We just have small business like fishing and selling. Our live is not easy. Now, we have to take care of our grandchild, so our life has become more difficult.

Problems confronting the returned migrant children in Vietnam are related to their legal status, which in Vietnam impacts on their education. Vietnamese law specifies that only children with Vietnamese birth certificates, that is, Vietnamese citizens, can be admitted to public schools. Having been born in Korea, these return migrated children had Korean citizenship. They did not have a Vietnamese birth certificate. Besides, because their parents' divorce was not officially approved by Korean authorities, when these children arrived in Vietnam, they had to maintain their Korean nationality. (Some children were able to get a Vietnamese birth certificate either because their mothers had a good relationship with the authorities, or there was a mistake and the authorities inadvertently issued the children a birth certificate.) Consequently, the children lost all rights accorded to Vietnamese citizens, including the right to officially attend school and access social welfare. Sometimes, when a family had a good relationship with the school or when the village officials were sympathetic, the grandparents could send the children to school. However, they were only allowed to study unofficially up to the third or fourth grade. This is because in Vietnam when children get to the fifth grade, they are required to take the elementary graduation examination and obtain a diploma. The following accounts by some respondents depict this situation.

> My niece is in kindergarten. Now, she can study there because I know some people there. They are sympathetic towards my niece's case, so my niece is allowed to study there. Next year, my niece will enter elementary school. I don't know how I can apply for her schooling. I heard that in order to enter a government school, my niece needs Vietnamese citizenship. However, now she has Korean nationality. I don't want to give up her Korean nationality. Maybe in the future, if she wants to go to Korea, she will have no problem.
>
> My son is now in grade 4. Because of my close relationship with the official of that school, I could send my son there. I don't know how he can continue his studying when he enters Year 6. He doesn't have a birth certificate as a Vietnamese citizen. If I change my son's nationality to Vietnamese, I have to think it over carefully because I want him to go to Korea in the future. It will be better for him because he still has relatives there.

The returned migrant children's grandparents and mothers have difficulties sending them to a government school because they do not have Vietnamese citizenship; however, they still hesitate to change the children's citizenship because of their hope that in the future their children will have the opportunity to return to Korea and live there. Expensive private schools or international schools are out of reach for these low-income single mothers. If we assume that in one village, there are four to five returned migrant children who will remain uneducated because of the situation described above, in the entire province, there will be hundreds of these uneducated children.

Conclusion

This study has demonstrated that the future of a large number of children in the "borderlands" of Vietnam and Korea is at risk. Born in Korea, these returning migrant children maintain their Korean nationality, although this status does not benefit them in the remote rural villages in Vietnam to which they have returned. The children live in these economically disadvantaged rural areas, where they cannot enjoy the civil rights accorded to all Vietnamese citizens, because their mothers refuse to give up their children's Korean nationality. Consequently, such returning migrant children suffer from de facto statelessness, caught between the advanced country that they can reach only in their imagination and the real country where they reside.

In some cases, dual citizenship for these children is strongly recommended, along with the proper support of both governments. These measures can reduce these children's isolation from society, help to promote the stability of their identities and reconstruct their lives.

Notes

1. I use the word "escape" because the women left Korea with their children and returned to Vietnam without their husband's permission. Their strategy was to plan ahead, pick the children up from school and go to the airport directly for a flight back to Vietnam.
2. It is estimated that 84 per cent of foreign women from Southeast Asian countries hope to work in Korea after marrying Korean men (Tran 2012a: 95).

References

Kim, Soon-yang and Shin Yeong-gyun, 2007. "Multicultural Families in Korean Rural Farming Communities: Social Exclusion and Policy Response." Paper presented at the Fourth Annual East Asian Social Policy Research Network International Conference, Tokyo, Japan on 20–21 October 2007.

Lim, Choi Ho. 2012. "Reasons for the Increase of Korean Men-Vietnamese Girls Marriages." Paper submitted to a lecture in the Asian-Korea Center in Korea on 25 October 2012.

Ly, Xuan Chung. 2012. "Tìm hiểu các biện pháp hỗ trợ gia đình đa văn hoá ở Hàn Quốc" [Survey on measures to support multi-cultural families in Korea]. Tạp chí Hàn Quốc [Magazine on Korea] 1: 46–57.

Nguyen, Van Tiep. 2012. "Gia đình Hàn, Việt-những yếu tố tương đồng và dị biệt" [Korean-Vietnamese Families: Similarities and Differences]. Paper presented at "Quan hệ Việt Nam-Han Quốc từ quá khứ, hiện tại đến tương lai" [The Vietnam-Korea Relationship: From the Past, Present to Future], International Conference organized by the University of Social Sciences and

Humanities, Ho Chi Minh City and Korean Studies Association of Southeast Asia (Kosasa) in Vietnam 2012.

Tran, Ngoc Them. 2009. "Tập huấn về Hàn Quốc học dành cho lãnh đạo địa phương Việt Nam." Lecture given at Training on Korean Studies for the local authorities in Vietnam held in Can Tho Province on 14–17 April 2009.

Tran, Huu Yen Loan. 2012a. "*Minh In Cheol* Plan for Exploding the Labor Resource from Married Foreign Women Migrants for Urbanized Center in Gwang-ju". In *Proceedings of International Conference on the Occasion of the 20th Anniversary of the Establishment of the Diplomatic Relationship between Korea and Vietnam* published by Chosun University, Gwang-ju, Korea on 21 August 2012.

———. 2012b. "The Study of Features of Vietnamese International Marriages." Paper presented at the International Conference on the Occasion of the 20th Anniversary of the Establishment of the Diplomatic Relationship between Vietnam and Korea held in Gwang-ju, Korea on 21 August 2012.

Websites

http://en.wikipedia.org/wiki/Multicultural_Family_Support_Center_in_South_Korea

http://vnexpress.net/gl/doi-song/cau-chuyen-cuoc_song/2012/04/co-dau-viet-trong-van-phong-ching-phu-han-quoc/

http://www.top10best.net/2012/03/01/top-10-countries-with-the-highest-divorce-ratio/

CHAPTER 9

Born to Be Stateless, Being Stateless: Transnational Marriage, Migration and the Registration of Stateless People in Japan

Lara, Chen Tien-shi

Introduction

Statelessness is generally understood as resulting from conflicting nationality laws between one's country of origin and country of residence, and sometimes from incoherent administrative procedures (Okuda 2003; Ōta, Taniai and Yōfu 1995; Sakamoto 2008). If the existence of stateless people has attracted little or no attention (Manly and van Waas 2014: 3–10), the connection between statelessness and transnational marriage (couples with different citizenships) has received even less attention. This chapter presents three cases from Japan that demonstrate three ways in which the state relegates individuals in transnational marriages to statelessness in which the lack of citizenship causes individuals' lives to become insecure in all their aspects. The first case examines the circumstances that led to the decision of a transnational couple (a stateless Rohingya husband and his Indonesian wife) to have the husband enter Japan under false pretences to work in order to better their family's life; the second case traces the difficulties of a transnational couple, one of whom is stateless and the other is a Japanese citizen, trying to legally register their marriage so that they can live in Japan and the third case illustrates how children born in Japan to transnational couples can become stateless. These cases and others like them deserve close examination to better understand and to think about how the Japanese state can respond to statelessness in ways that are both just and humane.

The chapter is divided into six sections. Section 1 defines statelessness. Section 2 outlines the Japanese government's criteria for determining the citizenship of people born in Japan and the government's procedures for determining the citizenship of foreigners entering Japan. Sections 3 to 5 each present one case described above and point out the inability of the government's policies and procedures to resolve these cases. Section 6, the conclusion, argues that by making people stateless (albeit unintentionally) the Japanese state denies stateless people their human rights to contract a legally recognized marriage, to legally register children as one's own and to earn a living for oneself and one's family. However, before effective state policies and procedures can be formulated, it is important to raise awareness of the issue of statelessness and to carefully discuss its relationship to transnational marriage, migration and registration.[1]

Stateless People in Japan

International law provides us with the definition of a stateless person as one "who is not considered as a national by any State under the operation of its law" (United Nations High Commissioner for Refugees 1954). There are an estimated 10 million stateless people around the world (United Nations High Commissioner for Refugees 2014).[2]

In Japan, it is difficult to obtain reliable statistics of stateless people (*mukokusekisha*) for two reasons: Japanese law does not provide a clear definition of statelessness, and the Japanese government does not have an adequate system in place for identifying and dealing with stateless people living in Japan (Abe 2010; Odagawa 2013). Nevertheless, data gathered by the Japan Immigration Association and statistics reported by the Ministry of Justice reveal certain trends (see Figure 9.1).

There was a sharp upswing in the number of recorded stateless people in Japan from 1992 to 1997. Thereafter, there was a gradual decrease of recorded stateless people from 1997 to 2013. The sudden drop in stateless people from 1,100 people in 2011 to 649 people in 2012 reflects a change in the registration system for foreigners in Japan and the way stateless people are counted rather than an actual decrease in their numbers.[3] These numbers rise when you add the number of unregistered children (see the case of Anna below).

Putting aside the problems of accurately determining the number of stateless people in Japan, it can be argued that the Japanese government's

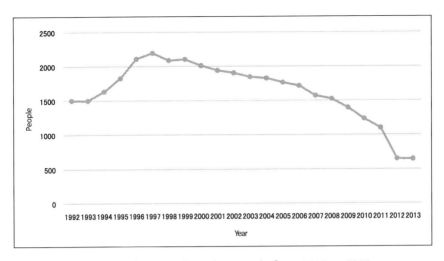

Figure 9.1 Number of registered stateless people from 1992 to 2013
Source: Japan Immigration Association, 1992–2013.

policies and procedures adequately control the numbers of stateless people in Japan. If stateless persons try to enter Japan, Japanese immigration officials will stop them unless they apply as refugees, in which case they are granted temporary residency while their cases are assessed. Even if we consider the loophole illustrated by the first case below,[4] the problem seems negligible. However, there is another, equally important problem. The first case points to the fact that statelessness is the result of political and legal inconsistencies between nation states, inadequate administration and insufficient information relating to marriages and births (Sakamoto 2008). These causes of statelessness need to be addressed. Hence, statelessness is a problem of a nation's ability and willingness to balance legal justice, social justice and humane treatment for all who live within its borders. Globalization and the attendant movement of people throughout the world have made it increasingly important for all societies to understand the connections between statelessness, the individual, the family and issues of human rights.

Stateless Migrants Entering Japan: Mr. Tin

Mr. Tin is a Rohingya male who was born around 1970 in western Myanmar's Rakhine state (formerly Arakan). He states "I was born in Myanmar; however, because I am a Rohingya, I did not have the freedom to find a job, receive higher education or move."[5] The Rohingya are an ethnic minority that is being discriminated against by the Myanmar government. They are treated as illegal immigrants. In recent years, scores of the Rohingya have been killed and wounded in the state of Rakhine. The Rohingya people have been fleeing Myanmar as refugees and their situation has received international attention in the media.

Why have Mr. Tin and his compatriots been forced to flee Myanmar? The short answer is that the government of Myanmar does not recognize the Rohingya as citizens although they once were. There are many debates regarding whether the people, currently called "Rohingya", are indeed indigenous to the western area of Myanmar, which they regard as their homeland (Ba 1960). However, it is clear that the Rakhine, one of the indigenous peoples of Myanmar, ruled the Kingdom of Arakan from 1430 to 1785. It encompassed the area near the border between Myanmar and Bangladesh in what is now south-eastern Bangladesh between Cox Bazaar and Chittagong. The Kingdom of Arakan became part of Burma, which later became a British colony. The name "Arakan" is a general term that refers not only to the Rakhine but also to 7 to 13 smaller ethnic groups. In 1948, Myanmar gained independence from British rule. However, the border between Myanmar and Bangladesh (at that time, East Pakistan) was not defined until 1966, when the Nave River became the border. Until the border was set in 1966, the Bangladeshi, Rakhine and Rohingya peoples were able to freely move between the two countries.

Rakhine (Arakan) is estimated to have a population of 30 million people. Myanmar's parliamentary government (1948–62) recognized the Rohingya as citizens and issued them government identification cards and official documents. However, in 1962, after the Myanmar coup d'état that led to forming a socialist military regime under the politician and military commander, Ne Win, the Rohingya began to lose their citizenship. When a new citizenship law was passed in 1982, Myanmar citizens were classified as Citizens, Second-class Citizens and Naturalized Citizens. After an arbitrary application of this law, the Rohingya found themselves unable to fit into any of the three categories, thus making them stateless (Uda 2010). From 1978 to 1991, the Rohingya were subjected to forced labour, the seizing of their assets, rape, obstruction of education and commercial activities through restrictions on their movements and other oppressive restrictions by the Myanmar military government. As a result, between 200,000 and 300,000 Rohingya have fled to Bangladesh, and the numbers continue to rise.

Born in Rakhine and of Rohingya descent, Mr. Tin experienced forced labour as a teenager and lived in fear and anxiety. As a Rohingya, he was prevented from studying at a university in Yangon, where the universities were located. Such restrictions led Mr. Tin to obtain a forged identification card showing that he was a citizen of Myanmar. In 1990, he was accepted to a university, but the universities were closed for a long period of time due to the political chaos in the country. Mr. Tin participated in democratic movements with other Rohingya youth in Rakhine and came under police surveillance. To escape from this chaotic situation and to have a new chance at bettering his life, Mr. Tin fled his home in 1996 by taking a 35-minute boat ride from Arakan to Bangladesh. "At that time, the people of Bangladesh would help people into the country for just two days' worth of pay. The border management was very lax, no identification was necessary", states Mr. Tin. Through a network of Rohingya, Mr. Tin prepared to go to Malaysia. Because he was stateless, he had to obtain a passport to go to Malaysia. He was able to buy a poor quality forged passport for JPY10,000 (two to three months' worth of wages in Malaysia).

In 1996, Mr. Tin arrived in Malaysia where he planned to study at a university. Despite the poor quality of his false passport and because of the lax border controls, Mr. Tin was able to enter the country. However, because the passport was false, he was prohibited from enrolling in a university, so instead he started working at places like Internet cafes and factories. Although the practice of Islam was looked down upon in Myanmar, this was not the case in Malaysia where Islam is an official religion, and Mr. Tin enjoyed the freedom to practise his religion.

While in Malaysia, Mr. Tin started to date an Indonesian woman from the factory where they both worked. Both were of the Islamic faith and immigrants to Malaysia. Because they were also separated from their families, they were able to find many things they shared in common, and they decided to live together. Mr. Tin told his girlfriend that he was a stateless Rohingya. While living with her, he was arrested many times because he did not have a proper visa in his false passport. His girlfriend suggested, "If you go to Indonesia and get an identification card, this problem would be solved." With this suggestion in mind, they went to Indonesia in 1999 and bought a birth certificate for Mr. Tin. At that time, a person could buy a birth certificate for an average of two to three months' worth of pay in Indonesia. After living in Indonesia for six months, Mr. Tin was able to get an Indonesian ID and passport. He then married his girlfriend.

The couple then moved back to Malaysia, and with his new ID, Indonesian nationality and the money he had been saving, Mr. Tin started an import-export business selling clothes as well as an Internet café. His business was running well and making a good profit. However, as a foreigner with a thriving business in Malaysia, he was forced to pay high taxes. In a few years, Indonesia's economy began to grow, and Mr. Tin, who was disgruntled with Malaysia's high tax rates, was again urged by his wife to "move back to Indonesia and start a business there". Mr. Tin agreed, and they moved to Indonesia.

After moving to Indonesia and living with his wife's family, Mr. Tin started an Internet café and arcade parlour. Business was very good; however, his difficult relationship with his mother-in-law and brother-in-law became a serious problem. His mother-in-law claimed ownership of his business because she was disappointed that her daughter had not married the Indonesian man she wished her daughter to marry. This led his mother-in-law to dislike him even before his return to Indonesia. A short time later, his brother-in-law claimed that assets from the business were his. When Mr. Tin refused to give these to his brother-in-law, the brother-in-law started to threaten to tell the police that his identification was forged and to demand money every few days. Mr. Tin paid his brother-in-law many times to maintain his silence, but he found that the situation unbearable, so he planned to move abroad. After much research, he decided to go to a country that would possibly take him in as a refugee.

Mr. Tin consulted with an overseas travel broker based in Malaysia who suggested Japan. It is a developed country and has ratified the Convention Relating to the Status of Refugees. At that time, with an Indonesian passport, one could get a tourist visa in a short period of time. As a result, Mr. Tin entered Japan on a 14-day tourist visa in 2006. Helped by a Rohingya democratic movement support group, he was able to find a place to stay. Before his visa expired, he applied for refugee status in Japan. When turning in his application, Mr. Tin revealed that he was actually a Rohingya from Myanmar, which made it clear that the Indonesian passport he had used to enter Japan was forged. This revelation was subsequently used as a basis for rejecting his application for refugee status. However, with a group of Rohingya in Japan, Mr. Tin filed a class-action lawsuit against the Japanese government; this case has yet to be resolved.

Currently, Mr. Tin is on provisional release status but he is not a legal resident of Japan. This means that he cannot work and that his movements are also restricted. He must pay for any medical treatment he receives. Worst of all, his Indonesian passport has been invalidated, preventing him from going back to Indonesia. Mr. Tin has three children who ask, "Why doesn't daddy come home?" They also ask in worry, "Is he not our real daddy?" Mr. Tin's wife is very understanding about his situation, but his mother-in-law threatens to have her daughter and Mr. Tin divorced if he cannot return to Indonesia. Mr. Tin calls his wife and children by videophone every day.

Mr. Tin says, "Living a life while not being able to see your wife and family is painful. I am really grateful toward my wife who is taking care of our three children while I am away." Mr. Tin's wife and children always carry a portable computer and Wi-Fi with them (just like Mr. Tin). Although they are always connected through the Internet, they have been living as a "virtual family" for years. However, Mr. Tin's legal status leaves him trapped in Japan, and his wife and children's financial and legal situation does not allow them to migrate to Japan. Being stateless, Mr. Tin and his family are experiencing an uncertain life marked by constant discrimination, denial of education, disruption of married life and other situations that condemn stateless people to a marginal existence.

Nationality, Transnational Marriage and Statelessness

Individual belonging and individual human rights are closely intertwined in the workings of the state. Nationality provides the legal connection between the individual and the nation state. Having or not having a nationality is fundamental to identifying one's legal status, which affects not only schooling, employment, marriage and child care but also various individual rights and responsibilities. As we shall see below, transnational marriages in which one person is stateless present three related but distinct situations that are not well understood but challenge the Japanese state to find ways of equitably integrating stateless persons who live in its midst.

Most people in Japan assume that if a Japanese national wishes to marry a non-Japanese national, legally registering the marriage and obtaining a spousal visa that grants residency to the non-Japanese partner will be a straightforward matter. This is the case if the non-Japanese national has attestable citizenship in another country. However, it is virtually impossible to register a marriage legally so that a couple can live in Japan with residency rights extended to the non-Japanese partner if this person is stateless. Understanding why stateless people cannot easily marry in Japan begins by putting the notion of nationality in its socio-political context.

Generally, nationality is a "certification that an individual is a member of a specific nation state" or has "a legal connection that binds an individual to a specific country" (Egawa et al. 1989). In short, being a national of a modern sovereign nation ties an individual politically and legally to a nation and determines an individual's status as a member of the state. For an individual, the state is the foundation upon which nationality is based and from which numerous forms of social services and benefits as well as diplomatic protection in foreign territories are derived. Through their nationality, individuals are recognized as members of a specific country and provided with membership in a specific collective (Endo 2010; Hiraga 1950; Torpey 2000).

In Japan, the family registration system (*koseki*) is described as "an authentic record of a person's kinship ties from birth until death that establishes a person as a Japanese national (*nihon kokumin*). It is the sole system for authenticating Japanese nationality."[6] For the Japanese, the koseki is the primary register that records and authenticates the legal status of one's nationality. It also establishes the household unit (a married couple and their unmarried children)[7] as a nuclear family. The principle of "same name, same koseki" (*dōitsu shi dōitsu koseki*) guarantees that everyone in the same koseki has the same family name. Recorded in the one koseki are the original domicile (*honseki*) of that koseki and the head of the family (*hittosha*). If a legal spouse is a foreign national, the marriage does not appear on the koseki; instead, it is recorded in the reference column (*mibun jikōran*). If a would-be spouse is stateless, a marriage cannot be entered into the *mibun jikōran* because the stateless person's identity has not been authenticated by another state.

Stateless Spouses in Japan

This second case illustrates how difficult it is for transnational couples, one of whom is stateless and the other is a Japanese citizen, to secure the legal documentation from the stateless person's country of origin. If stateless persons cannot establish their nationality, they cannot satisfy Japanese legal requirements to legally register their marriage in Japan and to acquire nationality there.

Mr. Tanaka is an engineer in his late twenties. He works for a Japanese company, and his hobby is to travel abroad with his friends on vacation. He became acquainted with a local young woman of the same age, Ms. Yok, when he frequently travelled to Thailand. He got along well with Ms. Yok, and they did not find it difficult to break through the language barrier. They often went out for dinner and spent their holidays together whenever he visited Thailand. When they were separated, they frequently kept in touch over the Internet. After a short acquaintance, they thought about getting married. Mr. Tanaka decided to marry Ms. Yok when they found that she was pregnant.

As Mr. Tanaka made preparations to register their marriage, Ms. Yok informed him that she is stateless. However, Mr. Tanaka did not really understand the meaning of statelessness, so Ms. Yok and he visited the government office of the community where she lived as well as the Japanese consulate in Bangkok to register their marriage. Because Ms. Yok did not have any identification such as a birth certificate, they could not submit their notification of marriage. Mr. Tanaka did not know what he should do, so he decided to ask a lawyer in Bangkok to address this issue. The lawyer discovered that Ms. Yok's birth had not been registered. An old woman, whom Ms. Yok called grandmother, had raised her. The woman explained that she frequently babysat for the villagers in her community and that one day Ms. Yok's mother left her saying that she would be back soon, but she never returned. The lawyer started to look for Ms. Yok's parents to provide proof of her birth, but he did not have enough information and months passed. Before long, Mr. Tanaka and Ms. Yok's baby was born. Because Ms. Yok did not have any identification, her nationality could not be identified. As a result, it was impossible for the couple to obtain a notice of their baby's birth in Thailand. Mr. Tanaka wanted to register their child in Japan. However, the documents from Thailand were insufficient, so he could not complete the necessary procedures to be legally recognized as the child's father. As a result, their baby also became stateless.

Eventually, with the cooperation of support groups, Ms. Yok was officially registered by the Japanese authorities. However, because her birthdate was unclear, the Thai authorities registered Ms. Yok as a stateless person. After that, Mr. Tanaka and Ms. Yok finally registered their marriage officially and were recognized as a married couple by both the Thai government and the Japanese consulate. As a result, Mr. Tanaka could acknowledge the baby as their daughter, and he was able to obtain a visa to take Ms. Yok and the baby to Japan. After three years of pursuing their case, their children—the couple has had a second child— have obtained Japanese citizenship. However, Ms. Yok has obtained only a spouse visa in which she is recognized as a "stateless person", meaning that Ms. Yok is only allowed a residential status; she still does not have any state identifying her nationality. This case demonstrates how difficult it is for stateless people to obtain a more secure legal status (nationality) through cross-border marriage.

Stateless Children Born in Japan

Most people in Japan make a second assumption: if a child is born in Japan to a transnational couple and one parent is Japanese, the child is automatically a Japanese citizen. This is the case if the parents have duly registered the child's birth. It is not the case if the parents have not. Failure to register a birth can lead a child to become stateless. Indeed, children below the age of 14 consistently make up a large group of stateless people.

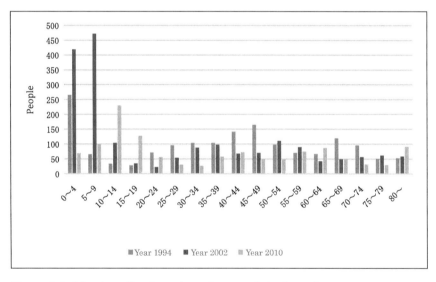

Figure 9.2 Number of registered stateless people in Japan by age
Source: Japan Immigration Association, 1995, 2003, 2011.

For example, if we compare the recorded stateless people by age for the years 1994, 2002 and 2010 (Figure 9.2) with the total number of recorded stateless people, we find that in 1994, there were 366 children below the age of 14 (22.4 per cent of all recorded stateless people in Japan). In 2002, there were 996 children (52.3 per cent of all recorded stateless people in Japan). In 2010, there were 399 children (32.3 per cent of all recorded stateless people in Japan for 2010). This situation arises from a complex set of circumstances.

The close tie between nationality and the koseki has consequences for unmarried transnational couples and their children. For these couples, the relationship does not give non-Japanese partners the right to residence in Japan unless they hold visas allowing them to stay in Japan independently of their relationship with their partners. This requirement has unintentionally contributed to some children becoming stateless when they are born to unmarried transnational couples in which the man is a Japanese citizen and the woman is a migrant worker from East or Southeast Asia, particularly migrant women workers from the Philippines. This problem surfaced after Filipinas, as well as women from other countries in East and Southeast Asia, came to work in Japan amidst a bubble economy and a tight labour market in the 1980s. Many Filipinas worked as singers, dancers or hostesses in nightclubs. In the course of their work, some became intimate with Japanese men but remained unmarried. Some couples had children known as Japanese-Filipino Children or JFCs (Chen 2011; Okuda 1996; Tateda 2012). There are many reasons why these couples did not marry. For instance, I know couples that could not marry because one or both of them were already married. I also know a case in which a foreign woman could not complete the legal document necessary for marriage because her Japanese was poor, so she entrusted the completion of the legal processes to her partner. As is often the case, however, he did not complete the legal procedures and, in effect, faked their marriage. These relationships often broke up, and as business conditions grew steadily worse after the collapse of the bubble economy, it became more difficult for foreigners to find jobs in Japan. Some female migrant workers could no longer obtain a certification of employment, but they stayed in Japan illegally after their visa expired, often to raise their children in Japan. However, these children had become stateless because of the close tie between nationality and the koseki.

While there are clear guidelines and procedures for determining the nationality of children born in Japan and whose births have been duly registered by their parents, there is no way to identify children whose births are not registered until the authorities accidentally discover these children. The children of an unmarried transnational couple can become stateless if the Japanese parent does not register the child's birth or if the non-Japanese parent does not register the child's birth with her embassy. The failure to register a child's birth often results from the fact that most transnational relationships between unmarried Japanese men and migrant women workers do not continue for long. The men move on, and migrant worker mothers either abandon their children or continue to stay in Japan, even after their work visas have expired, and care for their children. Either way, these children are not named in their father's family register nor registered in their mother's embassy. Thus, they become stateless (Chen 2010).

The Case of a Stateless Child: Anna

Anna, a JFC, was born in Japan in the late 1990s; she still lives in Japan. She has never met her father, who she has been told is Japanese. She was raised by her mother who migrated to Japan from the Philippines in the early 1990s. Anna has lived in Japan her entire life and has never travelled to another prefecture or another city. While attending the local public high school, her teacher announced that they were planning to go to New Zealand for a school excursion and asked all students to prepare their passports. Anna went home and asked her mother to get a passport for her, but her mother was unwilling to do so because she wanted to avoid all contact with government officials, lest they discover she was illegally staying in Japan. At first, Anna did not understand the reason, but finally Anna and her teacher realized that she was unregistered and had no nationality.[8]

Under the new residency management system that started in 2012, people without resident status are more strictly regulated than the old system. Previously, even though they did not have resident status, some people were issued alien registration cards by their municipal government if they registered. However, under the new residency management system, it is more likely that a person without resident status can no longer be issued a registration card nor can they use government services, such as the maternity health record book and birth registration. It is feared that in the future, an even greater number of children born of parents without resident status will not be named on the family register and become stateless like Anna.

Anna and her teacher tried hard to get her a passport so she could join the school excursion. To get the passport, they had to register Anna's birth for her to receive resident status and to clarify what nationality Anna may have had. However, this process alone takes a few months. They had to submit many documents, such as her mother's nationality certification, birth registration and Anna's birth document from the hospital. During the process, they found that they could not even get these documents for her mother. Because time was limited, Anna gave up joining the school excursion. Anna and her schoolteacher still tried hard to overcome her nationality issues for any future challenges that might arise.

From this case, we can see that migration and transnational marriage are intertwined. Therefore, this may cause children from such marriages to become stateless if their parents fail to complete the necessary legal procedures.

Conclusion

The cases in this chapter demonstrate how the states legally exclude stateless individuals in transnational marriages and their children from the security conferred on people with citizenship. The first case shows how stateless people in transnational marriages are deprived of opportunities to make a better life for themselves and their families. The second case shows how difficult it is for stateless adults to gain citizenship in their spouse's country based on the spouse's citizenship. The third case illustrates how children can become stateless in Japan as result of the inability and/or unwillingness of parents in a transnational relationship to secure citizenship for their children.

As the number of people who cross borders has grown rapidly, it has also become clear that many children become stateless because of conflicts involving nationality laws and because of cultural differences in the recognition of the laws and legal procedures that apply to migration. In addition, it is clear that people are made stateless by political and legal factors in some countries. In many cases, the issue of transnational marriage and statelessness is neglected because no one can find a way to resolve it. The state's failure to act sometimes results in stateless people obtaining fake identification documents to cross borders, in an attempt to improve their lives. However, this often causes more hardship for these people who have no country to be deported back to, and who are prevented from having a normal life. A better understanding of the issues of transnational marriage and statelessness is crucial in order to rethink the connections between sovereignty, human rights and identity, and to help forgotten individuals who are struggling to survive and win human rights that will support their efforts to build a secure and peaceful life for themselves and their families.

Notes

1. The author's point of view in this chapter has developed from her involvement in helping the principal individuals in the above cases (as well as other individuals in other cases) to resolve their legal problems as a part of her NGO (Stateless Network) activities. Names used in these sections are pseudonyms in order to protect the privacy of the individuals discussed.
2. UNHCR cannot provide definitive statistics on the number of stateless people around the world; however, they estimate the total to be up to 10 million, which includes 3.5 million people in the 64 countries for which there were reliable statistics. For more information, see http://www.unhcr.org/pages/49c3646c26.html.
3. The Alien Registration system was abolished and replaced by a new residency management system that was implemented in July 2012 under the amended Immigration Control and Refugee Recognition Act. The 1992–2011 statistical data are based on the Alien Registration system, and the 2012–13 data are based on the residency management system, both of which are under the Ministry of Justice.
4. If stateless people contract transnational marriages outside of Japan and manage to obtain the citizenship of their spouses through illegal means, they can obtain visas to work in Japan with temporary residency rights.
5. Interviews were conducted with Mr. Tin (alias) in June 2012 in Tatebayashi, and in October 2012 in Tokyo. Interview conducted with Mr. Tin's wife and children in February 2013 in Indonesia.
6. See the home page of the Ministry of Justice (http://www.moj.go.jp/MINJI/koseki.html).
7. Once the children marry, they create their own koseki.
8. The interview was conducted in May 2010 and again in November 2010.

References

Abe, Kohki. 2010. *Overview of Statelessness: International and Japanese Context*. Tokyo: United Nations High Commissioner for Refugees.

Ba, Tha. 1960. "Roewengyas in Arakan." *The Guardian Rangoon* 7(5).

Chapman, D. 2011. "Geographies of Self and Other: Mapping Japan through the Koseki." *The Asia-Pacific Journal* 9(29): 1–12.

Chen Tien-shi. 2010. *Wasurerareta hitobito—Nihon no 'Mukokuseki' sha* [The Forgotten People: Japan's Stateless People]. Tokyo: Akashi Shoten.

———. 2011. *Mukokuseki* [Stateless]. Tokyo: Shinchosha.

Egawa, Hidebumi, Ryōichi Yamada and Yoshirō Hayata. 1989. *Kokusekihō* [Nationality Law]. Tokyo: Yūhikaku.

Endō, Masataka. 2010. *Kindai Nihon no shokuminchi tōchi ni okeru kokuseki to koseki: Manshū, Chōsen, Taiwan* [Nationality and Family Registration within

Modern Japan's Colonial Territories: Manchuria, Korea and Taiwan]. Tokyo: Akashi Shoten.
Hiraga, Kenta. 1950. *Kokusekihō* [Nationality Law], Vol. 1. Tokyo: Teikokuhanreihōki shuppan.
Japan Immigration Association, 1999, 2003, 2005, 2011, 2012. *Statistics on the Foreigners Registered in Japan*. Tokyo: Japan Immigration Association.
Manly, Mark and Laura van Waas. 2014. "The State of Statelessness Research." *Tilburg Law Review* 19(1–2): 3–10.
Ministry of Justice home page. Available at http://www.moj.go.jp/MINJI/koseki.html. [accessed 14 June 2013].
Odagawa, Ayane. 2013. "Kokuseki Mukokuseki nintei no genjyo to Kadai" [The Current Situations and Challenges of Determinations on Nationality or Nationality-less]. *Migration Policy Review* 5: 22–33.
Okuda, Yasuhiro.1996. *Kazoku to Kokuseki: Kokusaika no susumu naka de* [Family and Nationality: Reflecting the Progress of Globalization]. Tokyo: Yuhikaku.
———. 2003. *Kazoku to kokuseki–Kokusaika no susumu naka de* [Family and Nationality: Within Internationalization]. Tokyo: Yūhikaku Sensho.
Ōta, Toshiko, Kayoko Taniai and Yōfu Tomomi. 1995. *Koseki, Kokuseki to kodomo no jinken* [Children's Rights, Family Registration and Nationality]. Tokyo: Akashi Shoten.
Sakamoto, Yōko. 2008. *Iwanami bukkuretto No. 742 hō ni hikerareru kodomotachi* [Iwanami Booklet: The Children Rejected by Article 742]. Tokyo: Iwanami Shoten.
Tateda, Akiko. 2012. "Kettousyugi to Oyako Kankei: Saikousaihanketsu wo sozai ni shite" [*Jus Sanguinis* and Family Relations: From Supreme Court Decision in Japan]. In *Ekkyō to aidentifikeeshon—kokuseki, pasupooto, ID kaado* [Crossing Borders and Identification: Nationality, Passport, ID Card], ed. Chen Tien-shi, et al. Tokyo: Shinyōsha, pp. 43–68.
Torpey, John. 2000. *The Invention of the Passport: Surveillance, Citizenship and the State*. Cambridge: Cambridge University Press.
Uda Yuzho, 2010. "Biruma seibu: Rohingya mondai no haikei to genjitsu" [Western Burma: the Background and Reality of Rohingya Issue]. *Kokusai jinken hiroba No. 90*. Tokyo: Asian Pacific Human Rights Information Center.
United Nations. 1995. *A Study of Statelessness*. New York: United Nations High Commissioner for Refugees.
United Nations High Commissioner for Refugees. 1954. *Convention Relating to the Status of Stateless Persons*. Available at www.unhcr.org/3bbb25729.html [accessed on 30 Nov. 2015].
———. 2014. *Stateless People Figures*. Available at http://www.unhcr.org/pages/49c3646c26.html [accessed on 31 Oct. 2014].

CHAPTER 10

Legal Problems of Marriage between Irregular Workers from Myanmar and Thai Nationals in Thailand

Chatchai Chetsumon

Introduction

To marry and establish a family is a fundamental, natural human right with no restrictions in terms of race, religion or nationality. From this point of view, cross-border marriages between people from different countries are similarly unrestricted. However, marriage is not the wedding ceremony in legal terms, that is, a social celebration for the bride and groom. Marriages and families are not legally recognized unless couples complete the legal formalities required by the civil authorities that register their marriage.

This chapter illustrates how cross-border marriages are legalised or rejected in Thailand when couples, one of which is an irregular worker from Myanmar and the other is a Thai national, apply to register their marriages legally in an effort to normalize their lives. In particular, this chapter will do the following:

- set this situation in its wider socio-economic context—the migration of ethnic minorities from Myanmar into Thailand seeking a more secure life;
- illustrate in two case studies how officials' refusals to register marriages deprive both Thai nationals and irregular Myanmar workers of the fundamental right to marry each other and establish a family;
- suggest that officials' refusal to register marriages contracted by Thai nationals and irregular Myanmar workers stems from (1) equating

illegal migrant workers with illegal persons and (2) justifying their decisions on administrative directives rather than legislated laws; and
- point out that the Thai legal system obligates registrars to correctly understand and apply Thailand's marriage laws.

The Context: Thailand and Cross-border Workers

Thailand has a large number of cross-border workers from the neighbouring countries of Cambodia, Lao PDR and Myanmar. Table 10.1 shows the number of legal workers in Thailand broken down by type of work visa.

Table 10.1 Legal status of migrant workers in Thailand

Type of Migrant	Number
Permanent workers*	983
General workers*	101,507
Nationality Verification (NV) workers from Cambodia*, Lao PDR and Myanmar*	966,902
Imported workers*	225,361
Incentive investment workers†	36,888
Minorities‡	23,617
Total (January 2015)	1,355,258

Notes: *Workers brought into Thailand under Article 9 of the Foreign Employment Act of 2008.
†Workers brought into Thailand under Article 12 of the Foreign Employment Act of 2008.
‡Workers brought into Thailand under Article 13 of the Foreign Employment Act of 2008.

Source: Ministry of Labour, Department of Employment, Office of Foreign Workers Administration.

A large number of these migrant workers cross the border from Myanmar into Thailand in search of a safer and better life. This number has greatly increased since the mid-1980s because of the fighting between the Myanmar army and ethnic groups in the border areas of Kachin, Shan, Kayah, Kayin, Mon and Tanintharyi. Myanmar does not recognize most of these ethnic groups as its citizens. As a result, they are stateless and not permitted to avail of benefits accorded to Myanmar citizens by their government. Many of these people arrive in Thailand as undocumented persons, but most slip into the country as illegal workers looking for employment in the border provinces and later in other provinces, especially the Bangkok area, where they seek better paying work. Because of their illegal status in Thailand, these migrants can only get dirty, difficult and dangerous (3D) work (Wickramasekera 2002: 3). They are not treated well and they usually achieve only a minimum standard of living.

To resolve the problem of illegal migrant workers, Thailand has concluded three Memoranda of Understanding (MOUs) with Laos PDR (2002), Cambodia (2003) and Myanmar (2003) to legalize the status of the illegal migrant workers from these three neighbouring countries (International Organization for Migration 2009). These workers have to have their nationality verified and obtain a temporary passport issued by their country of origin to stay in Thailand and apply for temporary work legally. The Working of Alien Act of 2008 allows Nationality Verification (NV) workers to work in fisheries, fish processing, construction, agriculture, animal rearing, restaurants and domestic labour. The Thai government has extended the duration of temporary work visas several times because Thailand lacks unskilled agricultural and industrial workers. Additionally, NV workers can renew their work visas.

However, most migrant workers cannot verify their nationality and legalize their status. They are "irregular migrant workers", that is, people who (1) have not been granted permission to enter, live or seek employment by the state in whose territory they are present or (2) have not fulfilled the conditions under which they have entered, reside or are employed (Wickramasekera 2002: 22). When irregular migrant workers meet and cohabit with Thai nationals, some of them desire to legalise their unions in Thailand. This is when they begin to face obstacles as described in the case studies below.

Cross-marriage between Thai Nationals and Irregular Myanmar Workers

The following cases provide a sense of the social cost to Thai nationals and irregular Myanmar migrant workers when officials refuse to register their marriages as legally recognised unions.

Case 1: Ms. Ken and Mr. Wan (Pseudonym)

Ms. Ken was born on 8 February 1986, in Shan State, Myanmar, but her birth was not registered anywhere. Her parents are of Tai (Shan) ethnicity. Her father disappeared during the armed conflict between the

Burmese government and Shan State fighters and other anti-government ethnic groups in Myanmar. In 1994, her mother decided to escape from Shan State. Without any personal documents, Ms. Ken and her mother crossed the border into the Khun Yuam District of Mae Hongson Province in northern Thailand. They first worked and lived in a rice field in Khun Yuam District. After a couple of months, they left the rice field and went to Chiang Mai Province because her mother was offered work in a restaurant. While her mother was working in the restaurant, they were arrested by the immigration authorities and spent a day in jail. Then, her mother was offered work as a housemaid in Lampang Province, which she took. While Ms. Ken's mother worked as a housemaid, Ms. Ken began working temporarily in a ceramics factory. A month later, she began working as a nanny.

Ms. Ken's mother decided to apply for NV worker status, which would legalise her presence in Thailand with limited rights to reside there and work at types of job specified under the NV scheme, despite her initial illegal entry. Both mother and daughter were given 13-digit identification numbers and had their status recorded in the Profile Registration of Aliens with Leniency for Temporary Residence in the Kingdom of Thailand as Special Cases (Tor Ror 38/1). Ms. Ken was also allowed to stay in Thailand temporarily as the child of an NV worker.

Ms. Ken applied for an NV visa later. To do so, she had to personally verify her nationality as a Myanmar citizen. Myanmar rejected her application for nationality verification because she did not have documents showing she had been born in Myanmar. This resulted in her being registered in the Thai Profile (Tor Ror 38/1) as an irregular migrant worker from Myanmar, which meant that she was no longer a stateless person but that she had the status of a nationality-less person with neither Thai nor Myanmar citizenship. She has never gone back to Myanmar. She speaks only Thai and does not speak a Myanmar language or dialect.

In 2003, Ms. Ken began working in a toothpick factory in Lampang, where she met Mr. Wan, a Thai national and owner of the factory. That same year they wed and began living together. A year later, they had their first child, and in 2010, they had a second one. Then they decided to marry under Thai Law and establish their family legally.

They applied to register their marriage with the local registrar in the Muang Lampang District of Lampang Province. Their first application was denied because Ms. Ken is an irregular worker. After consultation with the Bangkok Clinic, Faculty of Law, Thammasat University, they reapplied to have their marriage registered on the grounds that Thai law gives irregular workers the right to marry in Thailand. The registrar recognized her right to marry and establish a family, but he denied the couple's application because it lacked a document that showed Ms. Ken was not currently married to another person. The registrar suggested they go to court to prove that she could meet this requirement. In effect, he made Ms. Ken's right to marry depend on the decision of the court. As we shall see, the registrar's denial was based on an incorrect understanding of Thai laws concerning marriage.

Case 2: Mr. Tan (Pseudonym)

This case involves Mr. Tan, a male irregular worker in a district in Lampang Province. Mr. Tan was born in Myanmar and is approximately 50 years. He cannot remember his exact birth year. His family fled from Myanmar and entered Thailand through Mae Sod District, Tak Province when he was young. He spent his younger days in the Mae Sod District and moved to Bangkok to work in construction. He met his partner there, and they have lived together for more than 30 years without registering their marriage. They have one child. He later moved to work in Nakornsawan Province; he now lives and works in Lampang Province as a carpenter and agricultural labourer. He sometimes goes back to Myanmar to visit his relatives there. He carries only an identification card issued by Myanmar—not a passport. During the interview, Mr. Tan stated the following:

> I do not know how to exercise my right to marry and found a family legally in Thailand. I am afraid of the authorities because of my unlawful migration, illegal stay and work in Thailand. I have not applied for NV worker status under the MOU between Thailand and Myanmar to obtain a 13-digit identification number under the Profile Registration of Aliens with Leniency for Temporary Residence in the Kingdom of Thailand as Special Cases (Tor Ror 38/1). If possible, I want to marry my partner in Thailand.

A Reflection on the Case Facts

The above cases raise two questions: (1) do Thai administrative officials have the authority not to register cross-border marriages between Thai nationals and irregular Myanmar workers and (2) does this authority have a legal basis?

Irregular Workers' Right to Marry in Thailand

Not all migrant workers register as NV workers. Most of them are still irregular workers who enter, stay and work in Thailand illegally. However, their status and fundamental human rights are recognized under Thai law and international law (for example, the rights to be recognized by the state, to education, to health, to access justice, and to establish a family).

The Thai legal system reflects the basic right to marry and establish a family as well as other fundamental human rights stated in the Universal Declaration of Human Rights (United Nations 1948), the International Covenant on Civil and Political Rights (Office of the High Commissioner for Human Rights. 1976a), and the International Covenant on Economic, Social and Cultural Rights (Office of the High Commissioner for Human Rights. 1976b). When a man and a woman decide to marry and establish a family, they can be of different nationalities, religions, languages, cultures and races. The conditions to marry and establish a family do not depend on the legality of one's entry, residency or employment in Thailand. So, irregular Myanmar workers have the right to register their marriages and establish a family in Thailand. Mr. Tan's marriage (between a Thai national and a Myanmar citizen) and Ms. Ken's marriage (between a Thai national and a nationality-less person) are cross-border, international marriages, which fall under the private international law system and Thai Conflict of Law Act of 1938, which involves Thailand's private and public law.

The Basis for Refusing to Register Cross-marriages

The fact that administrative officials regularly deny applications to register marriages between Thai nationals and irregular Myanmar workers raises a second question: on what basis do officials justify their decisions? The answer lies in the administrative directives in circular briefs. For example, the Department of Administration, Ministry of Interior sent a circular brief in 2000 to the governors of every province and the Permanent Secretary of Bangkok directing them to require marriage applicants to show certificates issued by their home countries to meet Thailand's conditions for registering a marriage (Ministry of Interior 2000). However, the registrar recording the marriage of Mr. Wan and Ms. Ken did not consider the following. The registrar seems to have overlooked a 2009 directive that revised the 2000 directive. The new directive stated that only persons with nationality or citizenship in a country must produce certificates from their home countries to establish their eligibility to marry. The requirement did not apply to stateless or nationality-less persons (Minister of Interior 2009). Ms. Ken did not need to produce documents from the Myanmar authorities regarding her current marital status.

However, even if the 2009 directive had not been issued, the rejection of Ms. Ken's application would have been still based on a wrong understanding of the laws of Thailand concerning marriage.

The reason is as follows. The role of the registrar is specified by the Thai Family Registration Act of 1934, which empowers registrars to record the marriages of couples who fulfil the conditions of marriage under the laws of their respective countries in which they are citizens. When administrative directives run contrary to legislated laws, the Thai legal system requires registrars to follow legislated laws rather than administrative directives.

Because Mr. Wan (and the partner of Mr. Tan) are Thai nationals, the Thai Civil and Commercial Code, Book V Family Law of 1976 governs the conditions of their marriage. These conditions include age, health, legal status, bigamy, marriage after termination of marriage, blood relations, adoption, consent to marriage for minors, consent to marriage, marriage registration, records by the Registrar, marriage in a foreign country and special circumstances (Thai Family Law 1976: Sec. 1448 et seq.).

Because Ms. Ken does not have citizenship or nationality in any state, Thai law requires her to satisfy the conditions of marriage for international marriages specified by the Thai Conflict of Law Act of 1938 and the Thai Civil and Commercial Code of 1976. Article 19 of the Thai Conflict of Law Act of 1938 states that the laws of each party's nationality govern the conditions of marriage which they must satisfy. The Thai Conflict of Law Act of 1938 further states that if a person has no nationality, the law of his domicile will govern. If his domicile is unknown, the law of the country where he has residence will govern. Since Ms. Ken has no nationality but has domicile and residence in Thailand, the conditions of marriage that she needed to satisfy are under the Thai Civil and Commercial Code, which are similar to those under the Thai Family Law 1976: Sec. 1448 et seq. To settle the question of whether she was currently married to another person, the law required her to produce people who knew her and could attest to the fact that she was not married to another person to prove she would not be a bigamist if she married Mr. Wan. Ms. Ken and Mr. Wan were unnecessarily prevented from registering their marriage in Thailand because the registrar did not understand that the Thai Conflict of Law Act of 1938 (Art. 6, Para. 4) did not require Ms. Ken to produce documentation from Myanmar. Once Ms. Ken married Mr. Wan, she could apply for Thai nationality because she is married to a Thai national (Thai Nationality Act. 1965: Sec. 9).

In the case of Mr. Tan, because his nationality is Myanmar (based on his ID card), the conditions of his marriage in Thailand under the Thai Conflict of Law Act of 1938 are governed by Myanmar's private law (which is similar to the Thai Civil and Commercial Code) and laws of his religion (Gutter 2001; Huxley 1987, 1997; Kyaw 1994; Sen 2001). As pointed out above, the conditions to marry and establish a family do not depend on the legality of one's entry, residency or employment in Thailand. These laws make it possible for Mr. Tan to register his marriage in Thailand, despite his status as an irregular worker. If Mr. Tan and his partner marry, he can apply for naturalization as a Thai national later (Thai Nationality Act 1965: Sec 11).

Conclusion

The above-mentioned cases provide insights into how the Thai state absorbs or rejects irregular workers who try to normalize their situations through legal means. Marriage between irregular workers from Myanmar and Thai nationals is recognized by natural law. Ms. Ken and Mr. Tan are human beings and possess human dignity, rights, liberties and equality. They also have the right to marry and establish a family under natural law. Irregular migration, residence, work, nationality and statelessness do not contravene the conditions of marriage under Thai law. The legal problems with registering cross-border marriages stem from officials' lack of understanding of how to enforce the law correctly.

These problems can be solved more easily if the officials involved in registering marriage become committed to respecting the dignity and human rights of irregular workers and enforcing the laws correctly. Also essential is the development and promotion of international collaborative legal frameworks that help stateless people normalise their lives.

References

Gutter, Peter. 2001. "Law and Region in Burma." *Legal Issues on Burma Journal* 8: 1–17. Available at http://www.ibiblio.org/obl/docs/LIOB08-pgutter.law%20andreligion.htm. [accessed 26 Nov. 2015].

Huxley, Andrew. 1987. "Burma: It Works, But Is It Law?" *Journal of Family Law* 23: 23–34.

———. 1997. "The Importance of the Dhammathats in Burmese Law and Culture." *Journal of Myanmar Studies* 1: 1–17.

International Organization for Migration. 2009. "Procedures for Nationality Verification of Myanmar/Burma Nationals in Thailand." *Migrant Information Note # 2*. Available at http://www.burmalibrary.org/docs08/IOM-Migrant_Info_Note_No2(en).pdf. [accessed 26 Nov. 2015].

Kyaw, Aye. 1994. "Religion and Family Law in Burma." In *Tradition and Modernity in Myanmar: International Conference Held in Berlin from May 7 to 9, 1993*, ed. Uta Gärtner and Jens Lorenz. Berlin: Asien–Afrika–Studien, Band 3/2, Fakultätsinstitut für Asien: und Afrikawissenschaften der Humboldt–Universität zu Berlin, pp. 237–86. Available at https://books.google.co.th/books?id=z3ksqJOnY7sC&pg=PA237&lpg=PA237&dq=Religion+and+Family+Law+in+Burma,+in+Tradition+and+Modernity&source=bl&ots=VjxAA6hETY&sig=RciWGd-zskNDlP8ZmxH0cQJ0uTw&hl=th&sa=X&ved=0ahUKEwic1PzzhqbJAhXoHKYKHTxoA8gQ6AEIGjAA#v=onepage&q=Religion%20and%20Family%20Law%20in%20Burma%2C%20in%20Tradition%20and%20Modernity&f=false [accessed 26 Nov. 2015].

Memorandum of Understanding between the Royal Thai Government and the Government of Lao PDR on Labour Cooperation. 18 October 2002. Available at http://www.humantrafficking.org/uploads/govt_laws/MOU_Lao_Thai_on_Labor_Cooperation.pdf. [accessed 26 Nov. 2015].

Memorandum of Understanding between the Government of the Kingdom of Thailand and the Government of the Kingdom of Cambodia on Cooperation in the Employment of Workers. 31 May 2003. Available at http://www.ilo.org/dyn/natlex/docs/ELECTRONIC/93356/109100/F-1475198314/INT93356%20Eng.pdf. [accessed 26 Nov. 2015].

Memorandum of Understanding between the Government of the Kingdom of Thailand and the Government of the Union of Myanmar on Cooperation in the Employment of Workers. 21 June 2003. Available at http://www.ilo.org/wcmsp5/groups/public/---, asia/---ro-bangkok/documents/genericdocument/wcms_160933.pdf. [in Thai] [accessed 26 Nov. 2015].

Ministry of Interior, Department of Administration. Circular Brief No. Mor Tor 0310.2/Wor 1170. 31 May 2000. Available at http://www.tobethai.org/download-law.pdf, pp. 2–3 [accessed 26 Nov. 2015].

———. Circular Brief No Mor Tor 0309.3/Wor 14753. 22 December 2009. Available at http://www.tobethai.org/download-law.pdf. p. 5 [accessed 26 Nov. 2015].

Ministry of Labour, Department of Employment, Office of Foreign Workers Administration. Available at http://wp.doe.go.th/wp/images/statistic/labor/58/se0158.pdf. [accessed 14 Feb. 2015].

Office of the High Commissioner for Human Rights. 1976a. *International Covenant on Civil, and Political Rights, art. 23.* Available at http://www.ohchr.org/en/professionalinterest/pages/ccpr.aspx. [accessed 26 Nov. 2015].

———. 1976b. *International Covenant on Economic, Social and Cultural Rights, art. 10.* Available at http://www.ohchr.org/EN/ProfessionalInterest/Pages/CESCR.aspx. [accessed 26 Nov. 2015].

Sen, B.K. 2001. "Woman and Law in Myanmar." *Legal Issues on Burma Journal*, 9. Available at http://www.burmalibrary.org/docs/LIOB09-women_and_law_in_burma.htm. [accessed 26 Nov. 2015].

Thai Family Registration Act of 1934. Available at http://web.krisdika.go.th/data/law/law2/%A801/%A801-20-9999-update.pdf [in Thai] [accessed 26 Nov. 2015].

Thai Civil and Commercial Code, Book V Family Law of 1976, sec. 1448–60. Available at http://thailaws.com/law/t_laws/TCCC-book5.pdf. [accessed 26 Nov. 2015].

Thai Conflict of Law Act of 1938. Available at http://thailaws.com/law/t_laws/tlaw0063.pdf. [accessed 26 Nov. 2015].

Thai Nationality Act of 1965. Available at http://thailaws.com/law/t_laws/tlaw0474.pdf. [accessed 26 Nov. 2015].

United Nations. 1948. *Universal Declaration of Human Rights, art. 16 (1).* Available at http://www.ohchr.org/EN/UDHR/Documents/UDHR_Translations/eng.pdf. [accessed 26 Nov. 2015.]

Wickramasekera, Piyasiri. 2002. "Asian Labour Migration: Issues and Challenges in an Era of Globalization, International Migration." *International Migration Paper 57.* Geneva: International Labour Office, International Migration Programme.

Working of Alien Act. 2008. Available at wp.doe.go.th/wp/images/law/4/aliens/pdf. [accessed 26 Nov. 2015].

CONTRIBUTORS

Sari K. Ishii is an associate professor of sociology in the Department of Social Sciences at Toyo Eiwa University, Japan. Her main research topic is social change of ethnic minorities from northern Thailand with a focus on their participation in the global economy, especially migration and tourism. Recently, her research has focused on migrants between northern Thailand and Japan, with particular focus on trans-border migration of marginalized people.

Masako Kudo is professor of Cultural Anthropology at Kyoto Women's University, Japan. She has conducted research on Japanese women married to Pakistani Muslim migrants in Japan and abroad. More recently she has carried out research in the United Kingdom, where she studied the changing socio-economic status and identity issues of British women with a Pakistani background.

Chie Sakai is an associate professor of international sociology at the Department of Sociology, Kansai University, Japan. Her research interest is changes in gender relations and the family in the global era.

Linda A. Lumayag is a senior lecturer at the Department of Southeast Asian Studies in Faculty of Arts and Social Sciences at the University of Malaya. Her research interests focus on transnational migration, marriage migration, childhood studies and stateless children. In addition to her teaching and research, she coordinates the co-curricular courses of the university. She is also a volunteer/consultant for a local church-affiliated non-governmental organization in Kuala Lumpur, which serves migrant communities, especially migrants from the Philippines.

Ikuya Tokoro is a professor of cultural anthropology at the Research Institute for Languages and Cultures of Asia and Africa (ILCAA) at the Tokyo University of Foreign Studies, Japan. He obtained his Ph.D. in anthropology from the University of Tokyo. His main research field is the

Southeast Asian maritime world, especially the Philippines and Malaysia. His major research topics are border crossing and migration, Islam in Southeast Asia, power and colonialism in the Philippines and shamanism.

Caesar Dealwis is a senior lecturer of sociolinguistics at the University of Technology MARA Sarawak, Malaysia. His research interests include language choice, maintenance and transformation among the minority groups in Borneo.

Caroline Grillot is a research fellow in the "Traders, Markets, and the State in Vietnam" Research Group of the Department of Resilience and Transformation in Eurasia at the Max Planck Institute for Social Anthropology, Germany. She spent more than ten years in China, most notably at Shandong University (1994–95) and Sichuan University (1998–2000). She also assisted UNESCO (Beijing 2003) in the Human and Social Sciences sector, and translated several Chinese novels into French (Bleu de Chine). Her research focuses on social marginalities in China and Southeast Asia. She received her Ph.D. in social anthropology for research on the topic of cross-border marriages in the Sino-Vietnamese borderlands from Macquarie University in Sydney, Australia, in 2012, and Vrije Universiteit in Amsterdam, The Netherlands, in 2013.

Hien Anh Le is a professor of Korean culture in the Faculty of Korean Studies at Ho Chi Minh City University of Social Sciences and Humanities, Vietnam National University. Her research interests include current social issues in Korea and Vietnam.

Lara, Chen Tien-shi is an associate professor at the School of International Liberal Studies, Waseda University, Japan. Her research interests focus on diaspora and statelessness. She received the Asian Pacific Research Award for her dissertation, "The Networks and Identities of Overseas Chinese Entrepreneurs", in 2002.

Chatchai Chetsumon is a lecturer in the Faculty of Law at Thammasat University, Thailand. His main research interests lie in the area of legal aid for people involved in cases concerning public international law, private international law and human rights law.

INDEX

assimilation, 135, 138, 147

bargaining power, 37
borderland, 154, 156, 161–2, 164, 169

child, 158–9, 169
  Japanese-Thai children (JTC), 119, 124, 130
  mixed-ethnic children, 123, 131
  multicultural children, 68
  return migrant children, 126–8
Chinese green card, 54
citizenship, 73, 96–7, 99, 161, 163, 165, 167, 193, 199, 205, 208, *see* legal rights
  dual citizenship, 185
  full citizenship, 16
conversion, 32
cross-border marriage, 44–5, 96, 105, 108, 116, *see* marriage
cross-border migration, 131, *see* migration
cultural identity, 176, *see* identity

diaspora, 2–3, 14, 16, *see* migration
  multi-marginalized diaspora, 2
  transnational diaspora, 14
dominant group, 139
dual citizenship, 185, *see* citizenship

English language education, 35
ethnic identity, 139, *see* identity
ethnic minority, 127
Eurasian Muslim, 135, 147

false marriage, 107, 109, *see* marriage
family law, 208
female migrant, 119, 124, 127, *see* migrant
Filipina migrant, 115, *see* migrant
Filipino woman, 93–5, 97
Filipino-Japanese couple, 112
foreign domestic worker (FDW), 81
foreign worker, 85
full citizenship, 16, *see* citizenship

gender division of household roles, 57
geography of power, 9, 10, 123, 130
global hypergamy, 44, 97
global marriage-scape, 1, 6, 9, *see* marriage
globalization, 43

hierarchical authoritarianism, 182
human trafficking, 105–6, 115

identification card, 190–1
identity, 140, 147
  cultural identity, 176
  ethnic identity, 139
  multi-affiliated identity, 4, 15

international marriage, 74–5, 78, 105, 115, *see* marriage
international school, 64
irregular (migrant) worker, 204, 207, 209
isolation, 176

Japanese school, 60
Japanese woman, 27
Japanese-Thai children (JTC), 119, 124, 130, *see* child

konkyu houjin (impoverished Japanese marriage-migration man), 106, 112, 115

language choice, 141, 143–4
legal rights, 85, 97, *see* citizenship
  rights to marry, 202, 207, 209
legal status, 203
liminal space, 156, 164–5
linguistic and cultural barrier, 180

marginalization, 166, 168
marriage
  cross-border marriage, 44–5, 96, 105, 108, 116
  false marriage, 107, 109
  global marriage-scape, 1, 6, 9
  international marriage, 74–5, 78, 105, 115
  transnational marriage, 193, 199
migrant, 135
  female migrant, 119, 124, 127
  Filipina migrant, 115
  migrant worker, 203–5, 207
  Pakistani labour migrant, 27
migration, 153, 161–2, 164
  cross-border marriage migration, 45

cross-border migration, 131
diaspora, 2–3, 14, 16
marriage migration, 12, 44, 50, 75, 81, 98, 135
migratory trajectories, 6–7, 16
mixed-ethnic children, 123, 131, *see* child
multi-affiliated identity, 4, 15, *see* identity
multicultural children, 68, *see* child
multi-marginalized diaspora, 2, *see* diaspora
multiracial environment, 145
Muslim, 28

nationality, 118, 124–5, 130, 187, 193–4, 197, 199, 204, 208
  nationality verification, 204–5
  nationality-less, 205, 207–8, *see* stateless
nationality verification, 204–5, *see* nationality
nationality-less, 205, 207–8, *see* nationality, stateless
NV worker, 204, 207

Pakistani labour migrant, 27, *see* migrant
primary language, 62

remittance, 34
residential visa, 127, *see* visa
return migrant children, 126–8, *see* child
rights to marry, 202, 207, 209, *see* legal rights
Rohingya, 189–90

Sino-Vietnamese couple/Sino-Vietnamese marriage, 155, 158, 161–2

social exclusion, 180
social status, 176
stateless, 124, 175, 187, 189, 199, 203, 205, 208–9, *see* nationality-less

transnational diaspora, 14, *see* diaspora
transnational family, 28
transnational marriage, 193, 199, *see* marriage
true Islam, 32

unmarried transnational couple, 197

Vietnamese woman, 153, 155–6, 159
visa, 29
    residential visa, 52, 127
    work visa, 54

work opportunity, 92
work visa, 54, *see* visa

KYOTO CSEAS SERIES ON ASIAN STUDIES
Center for Southeast Asian Studies, Kyoto University

The Economic Transition in Myanmar after 1988: Market Economy versus State Control, edited by Koichi Fujita, Fumiharu Mieno, and Ikuko Okamoto, 2009

Populism in Asia, edited by Kosuke Mizuno and Pasuk Phongpaichit, 2009

Traveling Nation-Makers: Transnational Flows and Movements in the Making of Modern Southeast Asia, edited by Caroline S. Hau and Kasian Tejapira, 2011

China and the Shaping of Indonesia, 1949–1965, by Hong Liu, 2011

Questioning Modernity in Indonesia and Malaysia, edited by Wendy Mee and Joel S. Kahn, 2012

Industrialization with a Weak State: Thailand's Development in Historical Perspective, by Somboon Siriprachai, edited by Kaoru Sugihara, Pasuk Phongpaichit, and Chris Baker, 2012

Popular Culture Co-productions and Collaborations in East and Southeast Asia, edited by Nissim Otmazgin and Eyal Ben-Ari, 2012

Strong Soldiers, Failed Revolution: The State and Military in Burma, 1962–88, by Yoshihiro Nakanishi, 2013

Organising Under the Revolution: Unions and the State in Java, 1945–48, by Jafar Suryomenggolo, 2013

Living with Risk: Precarity & Bangkok's Urban Poor, by Tamaki Endo, 2014

Migration Revolution: Philippine Nationhood and Class Relations in a Globalized Age, by Filomeno V. Aguilar Jr., 2014

The Chinese Question: Ethnicity, Nation, and Region in and Beyond the Philippines, by Caroline S. Hau, 2014

Identity and Pleasure: The Politics of Indonesian Screen Culture, by Ariel Heryanto, 2014

Indonesian Women and Local Politics: Islam, Gender and Networks in Post-Suharto Indonesia, by Kurniawati Hastuti Dewi, 2015

Catastrophe and Regeneration in Indonesia's Peatlands: Ecology, Economy and Society, edited by Kosuke Mizuno, Motoko S. Fujita & Shuichi Kawai, 2016